Tayos Gold

Tayos Gold
The Archives of Atlantis

Stan Hall

© Stanley Hall 2006
ISBN 1-931882-67-3
For more information on the author, see: www.goldlibrary.com

Production: D-sine
Cover design: Eileen Hall
Author photograph: Cathleen Hall

Photographs and illustrations courtesy of Tayos project participants Virgilio Aviles, Ceturis, Arthur Champion, John Frankland, Peter Holden, Philip Maxwell, John Whalley, JohnWright, Alexander Hirtz, Michel Merlyn and Stan Hall.

Every effort to trace the copyright owners of drawings and photographs in this publication was made. For further information, please contact the publishers.

Adventures Unlimited Press
One Adventure Place
Kempton, Illinois 60946-0074 USA
Tel. (815) 253 6390
Fax (815) 253 5300
www.adventuresunlimitedpress.com

Contents

To my children and the triumph of sincerity over sensationalism

Author Declaration

Regarding the Tayos treasure story, it came to pass that, in the year 1946, the man known to descendants of the ill-fated Huamboya nation as 'Blanquito Pelado' told Petronio Jaramillo A. who, in 1965, told Alfredo Moebius, who told Andres Fernandez-Salvador Z., who told Juan Moricz, who told Erich von Daniken, who wrote 'Gold of the Gods', which was read by Stan Hall who, after 30 years of historical investigation and analysis, fixed its dangerous and treacherous geographical location at:

77°47'34" West 1° 56'00" South

Introduction

'We shall save it, because there is no longer a sight of the Book of Counsel ... There was once the manuscript of it, and it was written long ago ... Great was its account and its description of when there was finished the birth of all heaven and earth.'

Maya Book of the Popul Vuh, 47-64, 71-72

El Dorado!... Atlantis!... Inca Gold!... Irresistible legends of treasure and wonders that for centuries have lured the imaginations and fortunes of kings and adventurers across oceans and continents only for their cries of 'Eureka!' to fade away in soon-abandoned dreams.

Lost lands and treasures elude the unprepared... those explorers, adventurers and prospectors... secretive, sensitive, imaginative, distrustful, persistent, egoistic dreamers... drawn, not by greed, but by an impulse to join in Creation's revelations, the first revelation being that more fortunes are lost in the seeking than ever made in the finding.

What force generates the desire for danger and excitement rushing through their veins, without which the indolent and envious would have so little to scorn? What genetic trigger, what beckoning star, draws them like lemmings to risk life and limb pursuing treacherous and unreachable goals? Neither tears nor chains can hold them, or any threatening storm change the set of their sails. They perish alone and forgotten, footprints and bones exposed on some foreign shore or jungle trail, beckoning brother adventurers to take that last aching step towards treasure beyond their wildest dreams. Ah! Dreams!... *that* word again!

In your wildest imagination you will never believe this story! Here we rediscover the above-mentioned legends in a single geographic location, sleeping a beautiful silence in the green sea and sacred valleys of an Andean-Amazonian wonderland, where unguarded euphoria is rapidly replaced by brutal lessons in self-knowledge. Those bravehearts who choose to follow the Tayos footprints and bones will advance only as far as the respect they show for those who have blazed the trail, in return for which the genuine few are destined for a life-changing adventure, not from the celluloid world of an Indiana Jones or James Bond, but from real experiences of real investigators in real situations. Here, reality reaches beyond dreams!

Tayos Cave spectacular

We journey further back in time later but begin in the period July to September 1969 when a brilliant hungarian-argentinian investigator, Juan Moricz (b. Janos Moricz Opos), announced his discovery in the eastern Cordilleras of Ecuador of a vast subterranean world containing a 'metal library' and other treasures deposited by a civilization lost to history.

Three years passed before writer Erich von Daniken met with Moricz in Guayaquil then globalised the story in *Gold of the Gods*, controversially inferring he had been taken to the treasure cave. The sensational first pages obscure important mention on page 53 that sources had informed him Moricz was *not* the original discoverer. Who cared? Readers preferred the dream to the reality!

So, who was this mysterious predecessor? We will name him soon!

I read the book in 1974 and, following a 16-hour meeting in Guayaquil with Moricz in April 1975, began organizing for July 1977 - later changed to July 1976 - a major scientific expedition to the Tayos caves

---

717502 TELRAY G
3394 GRANDH ED

3394 GRANDH ED
TLX 392
NOV 4/82

ATT: MR. STANLEY HALL

YR TELEX 3/4TH RECVD. AREA WITH PROVED MINERALIZATION EXTENDS
THREE TO FOUR KILOMETRES. AS PER OPINIONS GEOLOGISTS GOLD POTENTIAL
IS ENORMOUS. NO ACCURATE EVALUATION POSSIBLE UNTIL INVADERS ARE
DRIVEN OFF PROPERTY. ROUGH CALCULATIONS BASED ON SIGHT OF EXISTING
TUNNELS SHOW POTENTIAL SUPERIOR TO TEN THOUSAND MILLION DOLLARS U.S.
BASED ON FOURHUNDRED PER OUNCE.
FROM CAMPSITE YU KNOW TO FIRST SCARN AS CROW FLIES DISTANCE IS
SEVEN KMS AND FROM THEREON SEVENTEEN KMS. EASY TO BUILD ROAD.
WE DESIRE TO CARRY OUT QUICKLY WORK USING HELICOPTERS, DRILLS,
AND OTHER EQUIPMENT TO PROVE RESERVES.
POLITICAL SITUATION FAVOURABLE. CONSIDER THAT YR PRESENCE TOGETHER
WITH GEOLOGIST/ENGINEER ONLY PRATICAL AND CONVENIENT MEANS OF
PROGRESSING.

REGARDS
JUAN MORICZ

3394 GRANDH ED
717502 TELRAY G
VIA ITT NOV 04 1982 2005

Moricz Mining Proposal

in the province of Morona-Santiago, on the basis that if no treasure were found at least science would benefit!

A Military Junta was in power in 1976 when the British-Ecuadorian Tayos Expedition, consisting of more than a hundred military and scientists from a dozen institutions, with astronaut professor Neil Armstrong as Honorary President and participant, arrived at the entrance to the Tayos underworld. Within four weeks, almost unnoticed by the world media, a treasure trove of scientific results was realised, practically untouched by a Moricz - von Daniken controversy that had precluded *any* official search for the 'Moricz' treasure!

When this multidisciplinary expedition ended the scientists recommended the Tayos region be designated a National Conservation Area. Later, at a lecture in the British Council in Quito, one scientist declared that '*enough specimens had been collected to keep all the specialised laboratories of the world occupied for 100 years.*' Some felt they had participated in the 'expedition of the century', where scientific integrity had survived a hurricane of controversy.

§§§

I was in London in October 1982 when Moricz requested I inform British mining companies about his gold concessions in southeast Ecuador – to him, *the true El Dorado*! He sent by special courier an ore sample that assayed at 364 gms/tonne, and an estimated valuation of gold reserves in his Nambija hardrock concession of 10 *billion* U.S. dollars. Ultimately, a consortium was formed comprising Placer Mining Company of Canada, San Francisco Mining Corporation of the U.S.A., and Burnett and Hallamshire of Britain to develop 60,000 hectares of the Nambija hardrock and Yacuambi river alluvial deposits near Cumbaratza, in Morona-Santiago.

Other major concessions were promised to follow in due course. Unfortunately, news of the negotiations was prematurely disclosed to the media and, overnight, the number of illegal invaders increased from hundreds to thousands. In a single moment of *eurekaphoria* Moricz's hopes of financing his historical work vanished.

Ecuador has little tradition in mining and less in formulating laws that protect investors. In an ensuing legal battle Nambija was appropriated by a consortium consisting of a Canadian-Ecuadorian mining consultancy, the Ecuadorian Institute of Mining and, ultimately, DINE, the commercial division of the Army. The battle for Nambija was to continue for decades, the only beneficiaries being the many artesanal invaders who, with families to feed, preferred the sounds of picks and shovels to arguments. Illegal mining at Nambija has produced hundreds of tonnes of 22-carat gold as well as a deadly discharge into the Amazon basin of tonnes of mercury used in the amalgamation and extraction processes.

'At least they are doing my exploration work!' Moricz smiled ruefully. 'The one thing that eventually works in Ecuador is the Law. I will get Nambija back!' His prophetic statement was finally ratified by a High Court judgment in 2005, fifteen years after his death.

In January 1983, from a hail of rocks thrown at 'intruders' – that is, geologists from Moricz's hydra-headed consortium – 56 random samples assayed an average of 31.4 gms/tonne. (To place this in perspective, the dream discovery of any major mining company is mineralisation of 3 to 4 grammes/tonne with minimum reserves of one million troy ounces.)

Moricz's dreams of wealth, discovery and fame died from a lethal cocktail of gold fever and inexperience. Despite his boast of even better prospects in his 10-concession portfolio of 2000 square kilometres stretching from Nambija southwards to the rich Quinara and Yanganza deposits near Vilcabamba, he was never to recover from the Nambija debacle.

Given these legends and dreams of gold as background we move on to Moricz's most important objective - the subterranean archives and treasure he claimed would dramatically change ideas on the origins of Humanity and civilization!

After the 1976 Tayos expedition gathering enough information to pinpoint what might be the world's most valuable treasure involved me in decades of investigation, occasionally sparked by intuition. The result will inevitably generate criticism of why I did not report findings earlier. Surely with my experience as mentor and architect of the Tayos expedition plus 20 years contact with Ecuadorian authorities and key protagonists early disclosure should have been my first duty?

Fate decreed otherwise! Apart from the Nambija setback there were five principal reasons for the delay:

First, time needed to gather enough historical knowledge to assess whether Moricz *or some earlier protagonist* was telling the truth about the treasure.

13

Second, time to investigate *how* a vast metal library might exist on a continent where no vestige of an ancient script had ever been found.

Third, whether or not I had a right to unilaterally decide the discovery should be: a) disclosed to the authorities against the wishes of the person I had come to accept was the real discoverer: and b) developed as a World Heritage project.

Fourth, time to develop an historical *and* mytho-historical model that might conceivably accommodate the alleged discovery.

Fifth, the constant need to protect individuals and their families, as well as national and world patrimony.

There is a time for everything. Projects possess inherent factors that cannot be rushed, peppered with setbacks. Upheavals in government, speculation and paranoia surrounding the Moricz-von Daniken debacle, time needed for reassessments, plus four years processing World Heritage status, add up to a long time in Ecuadorian politics, with committees frequently producing decisions and opinions of little consequence days or weeks later. My experience concurred with my discoverer friend and bade us tread carefully! Here was a sensational dis-

Tayos Cathedral: Moricz Expedition 1969

covery made in quite the wrong place, with no room for error, no precedent, an ever-present cloud of danger, and demanding standards free from any expectation of reward.

My contribution - structuring the planning, organizing, timing and momentum of the 1976 scientific expedition - had produced hard lessons, and could never have taken place had a civilian government been in power. Whatever might be said of military dictatorships, inherent traditions of military honour and logistic efficiency favour large expeditions of a multidisciplinary nature. Later, in the 1990s, the frustrations of mobilising a 'metal library project' happened to occur when civilian governments were in office, contrasting markedly with the 1976 experience. It proved impossible to find a way through the problems that confronted us and I can predict no change that would benefit the situation in the forseeable future. One reason is that key elements of Ecuadorian society have little interest in pre-colonial history.

After the deaths in the 1990s of the two key protagonists involved in the library enigma I decided to proceed alone on the basis that a discovery of such magnitude must sooner or later generate global interest and World Heritage protection. Doing something was better than doing nothing!

By late 1992 I was becoming convinced about which of the protagonists' accounts seemed the more reliable, considering both personalities, their volunteered information, individual interests, knowledge and actions, outside and inside the central question of the 'metal library.'

Moricz, whom I had known since 1975, died from respiratory heart failure on the 27th of February 1991, shortly before his 69th birthday due March 19th, his dreams of wealth and fame, his library - *and his claims regarding an Andean-Magyar origin of global civilization* - gone forever! Somewhere in Buenos Aires is his real treasure and legacy, consisting of one of the most valuable private libraries on ancient history anywhere in the world. (Note: Retired argentinian businessman, Guillermo Aguirre, who contacted me for some information on the 1976 expedition, is preparing a biography of Dr. Julio Goyen Aguado (d.1999), an Argentine caving expert and student of Basque history, for many years a close acquaintance of Moricz and whom Aguirre believes was favoured with a visit to the treasure cave in1968.)

In 1998, with the two key protagonists now gone, how would it ever be possible for the metal library to see the light of day?

In September 1993 I had initiated project *Tayu Waa*, seeking World Heritage status for the provinces of Morona-Santiago and Zamora-Chinchipe, later to include the Province of Loretta in north-eastern Peru – all traditional Shuar-Achuar-Aguaruna territory. The plan stemmed from the 1976 Tayos expedition recommendations, impelled by the intrusive activities of oil, gas and forestry companies into the region. This ambitious project initially made spectacular advances but faltered in January 1995 when five Peruvian warplanes crossed the Cordillera del Condor and bombed the Santiago military base near the 'Cave of the Tayos.'

In an attempt to save Tayu Waa – by then endorsed by the Shuar-Achuar Federation, key Ecuadorian scientific, cultural, military and religious institutions, UNESCO and UICN, the Ministry of Agriculture, with indicative support from the European Union – I proposed a *Tayu Waa Peace Park* to resolve the border dispute, based on the success of 24 similar border parks in Europe. Instead, there followed three years of political upheaval during which three successive Ecuadorian Presidents were charged with corruption, one being jailed, the others fleeing abroad. My God! Another one has just skedaddled (mid-August 2005). *Carambas!*

Then came the final blow! In 1997 a letter soliciting European aid was lying on the desk of the Sub-Secretary of the National Development Agency, CONADE, awaiting signature to process eleven million euros for *Tayu Waa* feasibility studies over a five-year period. Political upheaval frustrated the signing, followed by an unrelated scandal in Brussels that catalysed the notorious block resignation of European Commissioners. Tayu Waa died like a beautiful princess awaiting a kiss-of-life from a prince who never came.

Why I spent so much time and energy on the Tayos expedition, Tayu Waa and Treasure projects may stretch reader imagination. It was in October 1991, seven months after Moricz died, that I teamed up with the man I came to accept was the original source of the metal library story. The treasure, he assured me, was NOT located in the province of Morona Santiago as claimed by Moricz; nor anywhere near the Cave of the 'Tayos', meaning 'birds', in the Rio Coangos area… but in a distant location he called the Caves of the 'Tayu', meaning, and short for, [the Empire of] 'Tayhuantinsuyu'! Neither Juan Moricz nor Erich von Daniken nor anyone else, he insisted, knew anything about the Tayu treasure that had not originated from *him*. His name was Petronio Jaramillo A.!

In the period October 1991 to February 1997, six years of political mayhem, Petronio and I worked on the *Tayu Waa* and *Metal Library* projects, particularly a planned 'expedition of occupation' by Ecuadorian and UNESCO authorities. A brave endeavour!

Were the reader to ask me now whether I believe Juan Moricz had found the treasure I would have to answer NO! And whether I believe the treasure exists, the answer would be YES! In addition, do I think Erich von Daniken was right to publish Moricz's story? We ...ell! The way he did it, NO! But was he right to publish it globally; today I would have to say YES!

We have a combined detective and adventure story - *but what a story!*

The Treasure Project

Quito being a capital city hosting foreign embassies and agencies made an ideal international office. We presented the Ministry of Foreign Relations and leading embassies with a proposal for an Ambassadors' Committee to supervise the treasure project. Members of the Committee would be counselled by a Scientific Committee responsible for physical occupation of the treasure and preparation of a feasibility study, patronised by the Ecuadorian State and UNESCO and chaired by a renowned figure - our suggestion being astronaut professor Neil Armstrong. By the time both Committees were functioning World Heritage status for Tayu Waa and the treasure areas would be in transit, endorsed by relevant national and international organisms.

Parallel with the seesaw frustrations of three presidential terms in the 1990s, in recognition of my 1976 Expedition and related Tayu Waa projects, I was made an 'Honorary Brother' of the Shuar Federation and nominated for an Ecuadorian 'Blue Planet' Award. I also collaborated on the translation of Pedro Durini's groundbreaking books, *Ecuador Universal* and *Ecuador Monumental*, dealing with the architectural and monumental works of the Swiss-Italian Durini family in Central and South America during the 19th century, which played a key role in propelling Quito to World Heritage status. These diversions offered a temporary and welcome return to the interdisciplinary world of building and architecture that inspired my interest in history as a battle between builders and destroyers.

The search for the truth about the Caves of the Tayos and the

17

Empire of the Tayu was never an easy task. I survived hepatitis in Guayaquil living on sardine biscuits and mineral water, slept in remote jibarias (Shuar dwellings), trekked weary kilometres through jungle and bone-shaking electrical storms, more than once facing physical danger.

Since the 1976 expedition I had been accused of removing treasure from the Tayos Caves of the Rio Coangos, of being 'the first martyr to science-fiction', of working for the British Secret Service *and* Freemasonry (is there a difference?), even of 'usurping' the work of Moricz. In effect, I left few pages of the little-known history of Tayhuantinsuyu unturned, careful to distinguish between the ruling Huancas (Incas) of Cuzco and the Caras of Quito, a vital distinction between the southern and northern regions seldom acknowledged by historians. When revered Quiteñian collector Dr. Antonio Carrillo Bucheli died in 1998 I

	Priest King Titles of the Atl Antis	Priest King Titles of the Old World	Corresponding Old World Civilization	Meaning of Titles in both the Old & New Worlds
1	Apu	Abu	Amorite	High Chief
2	Ah Kin	Akhen	Egyptian/Turco	Sun King
3	Amuru	Amuru	Amu/Amuru	Serpent King
4	Chiri-Apache	Shri/Apakh	Akkadian	Great Chief
5	Hatun	Atun/Atum	Egyptian	Great Father
6	Capa	Capa	Mongol-Tartar	Sun Captain
7	Shiri/Shyri	Czar/Sir/Sri/Shri	Syrian	Serpent King
8	Duchicela	Dux/Duke	Sumerian	Baptismal Lord
9	Hati/Ati	Khatti/Catti/Hatti	Khatti/Catti/Hatti	Noble Lord
10	Inca/Huanca	Huno	Mongol-Tartar	First Lord
11	Inti	Indi	Indostani	Sun King
12	Caraguru	Cara/Guru/Kuru	Syrio-Egyptian	Serpent King
13	Canari/Chanca	Khan/King	Eskitu-Canaanite	Serpent King
14	Kitu	Kitu	Akkad-Eskitu	Sun King
15	Maya/Ayar	Magi-Ayar	Indo-Magyar	Serpent Priest
16	Mallku	Mallku	Syrian	Serpent King
17	Manco	Mango	Mongol-Tartar	Lawgiver
18	Nahual	Nakhal	Indo-Nagpur	Serpent Prist
19	Nahuatl	Nahuatl	Mongol	Serpent One
20	Ona/Hunu	Oanes	Elamite	First Lord
21	Puruhao	Pharoah	Egyptian	Fire Lord
22	Pirhua	Pyr/Peer	Persian-Hurrian	Fire Lord
23	Shuara/Suara	Suaraj	Indostani	Sun King
24	Uru Nina	Uru Nina	Assyrian	Fire Lord

Corresponding priest-king titles of Atl Antis and the Old World

tried, as promised him, to rescue as much of his huge collection of artifacts as possible. Some 'non-archaeological' pieces were sold by the family but thanks to a benefactor in Scotland most of the collection is now on a 25-year loan to the Universidad San Francisco de Quito for purposes of creating a Museum and digital educational programme, focussing on the formative cultures of the Americas recognised to have developed on the coast of Ecuador at the end of the last Ice Age, c. 8000 BC.

I lived constantly with reservations about Moricz's claim to have discovered the metal library treasure, although sympathetic to his theory of American-Magyar prehistory and post-diluvial diffusion of American peoples, accepting this worthy of serious investigation.

Supportive friends told me more than once, as had Moricz, 'The best story is in you!' Yet I was afraid when the time came to mention part of the Tayu treasure that outshone the metal library even they must conclude I was just another deluded adventurer.

My calculated location for the treasure had to be disclosed because there was simply nobody better informed to assess it and because the number of investigators resurrecting ghosts and speculations was increasing daily. I owed it to Juan Moricz and Petronio Jaramillo who had trusted me, to my family, and to those who had supported me through difficult times. This story might have been written earlier and with adequate funding perhaps advanced more rapidly, but it would have been premature, lacking a plausible historical scenario, certain to lead to confusion, argument, and abandonment.

Alas, there can be no happy ending, rather the inevitable criticism of how I might have managed the project better. But let the criticism be constructive, and only from those with historical knowledge and experience of Ecuadorian affairs: certain not only could they have done it better but to have guaranteed the time, effort and willingness to suffer its inherent agonies and frustrations. These are the criteria that determine who might cast the first stone!

My role was investigation, discretion, patience, argument, trust, advice frequently rejected, finally focussed on a *disclosure* impelled by the deaths of personalities who had failed to work together yet both of whom I considered my friends. None of us was perfect and however much readers might wish somebody else had written this story … well … its truth and sincerity is here for them to consider alongside that of others.

Disclosure

In a letter of 17th January 2005 I advised the Ecuadorian Ambassador in London of my *calculated* location of the Tayu treasure and the launch of my website www.goldlibrary.com The following week I informed the Ecuadorian press and an article was published by 'El Universo' www.eluniverso.com on 13th March. These were actions taken to responsibly transfer information to the State of Ecuador and to safeguard the families of Petronio and myself.

Juan Moricz: Magyar Extraordinary!

1

Imagine listening to the following before deciding to plan a credible scientific expedition into unexplored Amazon territory:

'Humanity has inhabited the billions of galaxies for billions of years and has visited the Earth many times in the past. Proof lies in a metal library hidden below the Andes in Ecuador, inscribed in the mother language of Mankind – Magyar! … the language of Atlantis!

'Here, on the equator, in the Kingdom of Kitus, the true navel of global civilization, from which the city of Quito gets its name, lies the answer to the lost history of Mankind. Here, at the headwaters of the Solimoes, the old Amazon river, were built the holy cities of the Sun, the original 'uru-tzol-limas', also preserved in names

Juan Moricz & Stan Hall 1975

like Limassol, and the old name for Jerusalem - Urusalim!

'*From these ancient cities, destroyed within the last 100,000 years by interplanetary cataclysms, the surviving peoples of Atlantis - the Cara Maya, Cañari, Eskitus, Sumirs, Hunos and others - crossed the Atlantic and Pacific oceans, within the highway of the Sun between the Tropics of Cancer and Capricorn, to re-establish civilization in the valleys of the Yangtse, the Indus, the Tigris and Euphrates, the Nile, the Danube - and also the headwaters of the Amazon.*

'*The prehistory of South America is hardly known but, soon, with the revelations of the metal library, the world's religions and ideologies will be shaken to their foundations. Present concepts about the origins of civilization will change dramatically. Never again will nation war against nation, nor any individual dare to bear an evil thought against his neighbour.*'

§§§

These are not the thoughts of a madman but of an outstanding investigator of prehistory? Scholar, linguist, philosopher, explorer, Magyar extraordinary - *Juan Moricz!*

Moricz believed that prehistory lacks global vision; that the so-called New World of the Americas, after the Deluge, was the Mother Continent of civilization - and that its culture was ancient Magyar! European cultures, he affirmed, appeared suddenly, ready-made, without the indispensable logic of previous evolutionary development. They were transported from the Americas where evolutionary antecedents are simple to identify. Groups in various parts of the world survived the Deluge but those on the crests of the Andes were primarily responsible for the post-diluvian dispersion of knowledge and culture. Around 7500 BC they arrived in Lower Mesopotamia in boats of balsa wood found only in South America. In Ecuador today, place names like Shumir, Zumir (Sumeria), Shammar, Mosul, and an infinity of others found mainly in the province of Azuay, identify this region of South America as the mother country of the earliest Sumerians, whose ancient language is also derived from Magyar.

He held that the Magyars of the Carpathian Mountains of Europe were of American origin. Leaving the Andes they brought across the Atlantic Ocean idiomatic elements of the Magyar language and an accummulation of legends, traditions and beliefs. Today, in Ecuador – as in other parts of the American Continent - indigenous peoples like the Cayapo, Jibaro-Shuar, Tchachi-Colorado, Saraguru, Salasaka, and others, speak versions of the American-Magyar tongue. Place-names and dialects of Ecuador that have vanished through acculturalisation, or been eliminated by force, like the Cañari of Azuay, are numerous. The similarity between Magyar and Sumerian tongues cannot be attributed to coincidence. Apart from philological similarities there are ethnographic, religious, artistic and folkloric connections. At the end of the 8th Century AD a Magyar people called the Karas, 'royal Scythians', emigrated from India across the great eastern sea (the Sinus Magnus of Ptolemy) to their solar Motherland on the American continent. They were the same Caras who, according to late 18th Century chronicler Padre Juan de Velasco, arrived that same century in the Bay of Caraquez in the province of Manabí in Ecuador.

Too little is known of this amazing man Moricz and, because he wrote so little, that is how it will probably remain. Yet, explorers have organized expeditions of a lifetime just to experience what he lived daily. Before critics identify him as a mere adventurer here is a list of specialist investigators - apparently invisible to western scholars - who responded to an enquiry about Quechua-Magyar connections in the Andes, sent to them by the Ecuadorian Ministry of Foreign Relations at the request of Moricz. The important works of these specialists in Magyar culture and history require long overdue consideration:

Dr. Barna Kósa, Melbourne, Australia: Specialised in the cultures of Mesopotamia, Palestine and Anatolia (Turkey). Has verified and ratified the hypotheses of D. Juan Moricz with respect to cultural diffusion from America and the American origin of the Magyars. Has issued publications for half a century, including a paper concerning the discoveries of Juan Moricz.

Dr. László Rimanóczy, N.S.W., Australia: Member of Scientific Societies in Belgium. Sumerologist specialised in the cultural interchange between America and Mesopotamia. Has realised studies about the dynasties that ruled the ancient Kingdom of the Kitus (Quito). Confirms the discoveries of Juan Moricz.

Gyula Szentirmay, N.S.W., Australia: A friend of famous investigator Pataky Kálmán: scientific intermediary between Kálmán and Juan Moricz. Compiling 50 years of work concerning the American origin of the Magyars into a book.

Alexander Csoke, Schlossberg 2, Austria: Philologist specialising in the languages of the Caucasus, the Urals, Altai etc. Since the discoveries of Juan Moricz he has dedicated himself exclusively to the pre-colombian tongues of Ecuador and has confirmed Moricz's version of the American origin of the Magyars and their cultural diffusion.

Dr. Tibor Baráth, Montreal, Canada: For many years professor of History and Geography at the Sorbonne, Paris. Recognised as a foremost investigator of Sumerian and Egyptian cultures. In his book on Mesopotamia cultures he mentions the discoveries of Juan Moricz as an important clarification of prehistory.

Dr. Denes Gergely, Ontario, Canada: Eminent linguist who for many years has travelled in Central and South America investigating the origin of the Magyars. He confirmed the hypotheses of Juan Moricz, having arrived at similar conclusions after comparative studies of Magyar with the pre-colombian languages of the Republic of Colombia.

Dr. Szollosy S. Said: Germany: Investigator specialised in the cultures of Central and South America and analyser of their connections with Europe and the Near East. In a publication he has ratified the discoveries of Juan Moricz with regard to cultural diffusion from the Americas.

László Turmezei, Hutt Valley, New Zealand: Ex-member of the Hungarian Science Academy. Investigating authority on the peoples of Malaysia and Polynesia. After revising the studies of Juan Moricz he has confirmed that the discovery opens the door to a complete revision of the history of the American Continent.

Elemer Homonnay, Cleveland, Ohio, U.S.A.: Professor of History and Geography. Investigator of pre-colombian cultures and their relationship with the Magyars.

Among other notables with whom Moricz corresponded were *Dr. Gosztony* of the Sorbonne, Paris: *Dr. Alfredo Tagliabue*, Professor of History and Geography at the Universidad de la Plata, Argentina: also, *Dr. Alfredo Kolliker Freers*, historian and President of the Universidad Argentina de Ciencias Sociales, Argentina.

That many of these scholars are of Magyar background may be good and bad but reputations are not risked without justification. Collectively they know ancient Magyar history better than anyone.

§§§

In September 1969 a media report on the July expedition of Moricz into the eastern Cordilleras of the Andes rumbled like an earthquake across Central and South America. Chasing the after-shocks writer Erich von Daniken visited him in Guayaquil in 1972. In *Gold of the Gods* Von Daniken describes a visit to the metal library and other treasures, inferring he had actually been there, later claiming (after the 1976 Tayos Expedition) that he had used author's licence for dramatic effect. In fact, Moricz and Dr. Gerardo Peña Matheus had taken him on a two-day jeep trip from Guayaquil to Cuenca. He spent some hours in the Museum of the Cathedral Maria Auxiliadora with legendary Salesian priest Padre Carlos Crespi, a pioneering cinematographer and revered missionary born in Italy, whose memorial statue stands in Cuenca as a loving tribute from the populace. There was only time for Moricz to take von Daniken to a small cave entrance some thirty minutes' drive from the city.

Gold of the Gods burst upon an incredulous public in 1972-74. Stunned by what he considered a betrayal, Moricz commented, 'Von Daniken has put my work back ten years!'

On the 1st of July in 1976, a Boeing 727 of Ecuadorian Airlines touched down in Quito, heart of the ancient Kingdom of Kitus, which had once stretched from the Pacific coast to the Amazon River delta at Belen. Onto the tarmac stepped 65 British soldiers and scientists, soon to join up with an equally large group of national and international scientists and Ecuadorian military personnel. Amid a public outcry over the secrecy surrounding the operation, the well-equipped force crossed the Andes into the steaming jungles of the eastern Cordilleras, there to descend into the dark chambers of a stupendous Andean underworld.

The Tayos Expedition had arrived!

The Honorary President of the expedition was to descend a 6-inch wire ladder free- hanging 65 metres into the dark interior and explore many kilometres of these Andean Halls of Valhalla, accompanied by birds, bats, snakes, scorpions, tarantulas, and rushing underground torrents, at times up to his neck in ice-cold water. His name? *Neil Alden Armstrong, first man to step on the Moon!*

Principal objectives were to map the caves system and establish a scientific framework for long-term investigation of the area. On this particular mission there was neither intention nor hope of finding gold archives or other treasures. The entrance is located 800 metres above sea level, east of the long-disputed Cordillera del Condor, above the river Coangos, upstream of its confluence with the Santiago. The local Shuar had been aware of these spectacular caves for centuries, long before the Moricz Expedition in July 1969, which happened to coincide with the week Armstrong had stepped on the Moon.

On the 21st of July 1969 Moricz had signed a notarised document claiming legal rights over the metal library and other treasures. It is important to note the mention in this key document that his discovery was made *in the province of Morona Santiago.*

But how did this amazing story of Magyars, metal library and expeditions begin?

ORIGEN
DE LOS INDIOS
DE EL NUEVO MUNDO,
E INDIAS OCCIDENTALES,
AVERIGUADO CON DISCURSO DE OPINIONES
por el Padre Prefentado FR. GREGORIO GARCIA,
de la Orden de Predicadores.

TRATANSE EN ESTE LIBRO VARIAS COSAS, Y PUNTOS curiofos, tocantes à diverfas Ciencias, i Facultades, con que fe hace varia Hiftoria, de mucho gufto para el Ingenio i Entendimiento de Hombres agudos, i curiofos.

SEGUNDA IMPRESION.

ENMENDADA Y AñADIDA DE ALGUNAS OPINIONES, ò cofas notables, en maior prueba de lo que contiene, con Tres Tablas mui puntuales de los Capitulos, de las Materias, y Autores, que las tratan.

DIRIGIDO

AL ANGELICO DOCT. S.TO TOMAS
DE AQUINO.

CON PRIVILEGIO REAL.

Garcia Book 1729 2nd Edn.

26

The Chronicle of Father Gregorio Garcia

On a day in the late 16th Century, aboard a galleon crossing to the New World, renowned chronicler Padre Gregorio García would have gazed wistfully back at the disappearing shore of his native Spain, unaware of how his comparisons of Amerindian and Euro-Asian peoples would impel Magyar scholars to unravel the golden thread of prehistory. Even less could he have imagined the impact that his register - a copy of which (1729 2nd edition) was discovered four centuries later in a second-hand bookshop in Buenos Aires by a brilliant Hungarian investigator - would have on the quest for human origins. Was it surprising his writings were suppressed by a Holy Inquisition fresh from burning Giorgio Bruno and commencing the 30-Years War against the Protestant rebellion in Europe?

Guayaquil March 28th 1977

Stanley Hall Esq.
20 Bridge Street
Dollar Clacks. FK14 7 DE
Scotland
Great Britain.-

Dear Mr. Hall:

From our recent discussions you know that it is my intention to arrange for publication and worldwide distribution of the book " Origen de los Indios del Nuevo Mundo e Indias Occidentales" by the famous historical chronicler, Fray Gregorio García, of the " Orden de Predicadores del Convento de Santo Domingo de Baeza" who was for some years living in Ecuador in the late 16th century.

The book will be in bi lingual form, retaining the original Spanish.

It is also my intention to publish in association with the book important evidence wich will establish the authenticity of Its scholarly content.

I hereby give you my personal authorisation to arrange the contract for publication and worldwide distribution which will be subject to my final agreement by myself.

Juan Móricz

27

His *'Origin of the Indians of the New World and the West Indies'*, first published in Madrid in 1606, is a key element in our story because García objectively identified similarities in names, language and customs between peoples of the Old and New Worlds, placing emphasis on ancient Scythian (Eskitus) and Hunos (Magyar) nations.

On reading the García account Moricz was reassured about his own investigations, later acknowledging his debt to García and other Spanish chroniclers of the period, including Pedro de Cieza de Leon, Fernando Montesinos, and Padres Marco de Niza and Juan de Velasco, the last mentioned recognised as the father of Ecuadorian prehistory.

Gregorio García was for some years Director of the Apostolate of the Catholic Church in the Reino de los Quitus (Kitus), northern territory of the Inca (or Huanca-Huno-Magyar) Empire of Tayhuantinsuyu, 'Land of the Four Quarters' of *Cuntisuyu, Antisuyu, Chinchasuyu and Coyasuyu*, stretching from Chile to southern Colombia.

Ecclesiastical chroniclers have been accused of over-romanticising historical records, but why would such a learned scholar risk his life and reputation concocting a fantasy on such a scale unless convinced by the evidence?

Given the religious bigotry and censorship of the age his book was *silently neglected* and today a copy is a rare find. Fortunately, Moricz found one. Stifling a cry of 'Eureka!' he began correlating the work of García with his own and other Magyar scholars.

The story of Juan Moricz in Ecuador really begins in 1964, when he arrived with letters of introduction from prominent Argentinians addressed to Ecuadorian counterparts. In Guayaquil he teamed up with lawyer Dr. Gerardo Peña Matheus who was to become his lifetime legal adviser and associate. Invited to a meeting with historian Dr. Jorge Salvador Lara and other personalities with wide cultural interests he was asked why he had come to Ecuador. The reply stunned his audience into embarrassed disbelief:

'I have come to find a subterranean world under your country that extends from Venezuela down to Chile and Argentina.'

Unmoved by their reaction Moricz set off across the Andes, descending the eastern Cordilleras by way of the village of Limon Indanza in the province of Morona-Santiago. With provisions and hired mules his guide Perez led him deep into hostile territory. Over the following years he and Perez, a former army sergeant, became close friends. What happened on their journeys remained a mystery until, after four years of investigations, Moricz met up in Guayaquil with argentinian-born reporter Jorge Blinkhorn of *El Telegrafo* who published the most fantastic claims ever made by an explorer.

The subterranean world exists and inside its chambers I have found objects and records of great cultural and historical importance for Mankind!'

Moricz, it seemed, had completed his mission, his own personal journey to the centre of the Earth. Gathering his thoughts he turned to the task of organizing an official occupation of the discovery. Had he really found such an astounding treasure?

At that time Clauses 665 and 666 of the Civil Code stated that the value of any treasure discovered by a private party be shared equally between the discoverer and the State. Moricz, no ordinary discoverer, argued that his special discovery merited special conditions. Inevitably his proposals were rejected which led to a quagmire of frustration and distrust. The project stagnated for three years until globalised in *Gold of the Gods*.

The most significant statement in his notarised document of July 1969 is: *'I have discovered in the eastern region, in the province of Morona-Santiago, within the borders of the Republic of Ecuador, precious objects of great cultural value for Humanity... The objects discovered by me have the following characteristics which I have been able to confirm personally: One) Stone and metal objects of various sizes, shapes and colours. Two) Metal plates engraved with ideographic signs and writing, a veritable metal library which contains a chronological account of the history of Humanity, the origin of man on earth and the scientific knowledge of a vanished civilization.'*

Note the province stated is 'Morona-Santiago.' How much of his statement is true and how much might be attributed to information from another source is a subject of examination in this book.

Those who knew and understood Moricz could never imagine him wandering off into the forest on some whimsical adventure. A logical and practical individual, each step he took was backed by wide cultural knowledge and a superb intellect. In truth, one of the discoveries of South America was Moricz himself. Unfortunately, typical of pioneering investigators, he was distrustful and unrealistic in business affairs and vulnerable to the intrigues of concession invaders and government agencies. Captured in the seductive magic and mystery of Ecuador his dreams of wealth and fame were doomed.

A complex individual, he was mostly correct in his decisions and assessments yet almost impossible to deal with, perhaps because he was too idealistic and wary. His historical knowledge may have been second to none but his account of the Tayos treasure had a vital flaw, invariably overlooked by the over-awed. *Consistently he affirmed he was not the first person to discover the treasure* and that, as confirmed in his document, he had found it 'in fortuitous circumstances.'

Moricz died in February 1991 without naming this predecessor. We will identify his role later – when missing parts of the story will fall into place, revealing an even more fantastic tale!

'Understand!' Moricz said, tellingly, 'I personally have discovered nothing but I cannot afford a single error and will not be pressured. Ecuador has been the most hostile to me of all the countries in South America. I stay here because after thirty years of investigation I have found what I have been looking for and I will remain here, whatever the danger, until I am finished. Since I do not work for personal gain it would be unethical for me to expect reward or encourage sensationalism.'

Thus spoke Moricz on the day I criticised him for struggling to find his next meal whilst Erich von Daniken was laughing all the way to the bank with his story – or what I *thought* was his story! Whatever may be the claims of Moricz about a Tayos treasure his work on the origins of civilization and language justified attention *without* the need for a treasure story.

'Von Daniken is not important!' he retorted, 'The truth is I feel sorry for him! To destroy the greatest story of all time he must have had some kind of breakdown. Someday I will build a rest-home for him in the Andes where he can spend his remaining days contemplating his crime.'

I cannot always guarantee the reader the exact words of Moricz's statements but, from many years of personal acquaintance, I feel qualified to present fair and credible reports of the man and his thinking, which I am confident would be endorsed by the one person who knew him best of all and whom I consider to be the 'unsung hero' of the Moricz story - Dr.Gerardo Peña Matheus!

It is impossible to separate discussion on Moricz and the metal library from a vision of global history. Establishing some historical probability for the existence of the library is just as important as any search for it. Let us, for example, examine for a moment a similar story!

The Egyptian Tablets of the Mormon Church

2

Here we introduce the interest of senior representatives of the Church of the Latter Day Saints from 1968 onwards in the breaking story of the library, since a similarly 'invisible' metal library forms the basis of the *Book of Mormon*. From my researches I will try to establish an historical probability for the existence of the (four different sets of) brass plates of 'angel' Moroni, loaned to founder Joseph Smith on 22nd September 1827. With due apology to the Church for proceeding with the name 'Mormon' instead of 'Latter Day Saints', I hope Church historians might find the following of interest.

(Note: I never did meet with anthropologist and historian professor Paul Cheesman of Brigham Young University, who was interested in discussing my work.)

There appear to be historical connections suggesting that the original chroniclers of the brass plates were descendants of magyar-speaking egyptian-amalekites. The following might support the Book of Mormon account of the brass plates first acquired by the priest Laban.

Facsimile of characters made from the Plates of the Book of Mormon by Joseph Smith.

The Church claims that the brass plates contain the secular and sacred records of the Judahites. About 600 BC the plates were violently taken from Laban, a priest of the line of Joseph and authorized custodian, by four sons of Lehi – today revered as a Mormon prophet - who removed them to the shores of the Red Sea.

Lehi confirmed from the plates that he *and* Laban were of the priest-line of Joseph and Abraham: also, that the plates contained three important items: a) the *Pentateuch*, or five books of Moses; b) a history of the Jews down to the beginning of the reign of Zedekiah c. 600 BC; and c) the promise of a Messiah.

Before his death Lehi passed custodianship of the plates to his *youngest* son, with the egyptian-sounding name of Nephi. Nephi abridged his father's additions to the plates, adding their family history, before similarly passing custodianship on to his own son. Lehi had been a rich and rebellious prophet, scribe, and patriarch who appears c.598 BC, first year of the reign of Zedekiah following the first destruction of Jerusalem by King Nebuchadnezzar and the exile of Zedekiah's nephew King Jehoiachin to Babylon. Lehi's prophecies of doom for Jerusalem brought about his rejection by the Jewish establishment. Perhaps it was because of this he escaped the fate of Ezekiel and other priests marched into exile when Nebuchadnezzar, '… carried out thence all the treasures of the house of the Lord and the treasures of the king's house.' (Ref: II Kings 24: 8-17.)

Treasures? Thanks to Laban, perhaps not all the treasures were taken! Those removed by Nebuchadnezzar imately passed to Ezekiel and fellow priests in charge of Jewish artifacts and records in Babylon. These records, a generation earlier, had formed the basis of the 'deuteronomic monotheism' forced on the Judahites of Jerusalem in 621 BC. They were further reformed during the Babylonian captivity of seventy years. In 458 BC they were brought back from Babylon by Ezra (followed 12 years later by Nehemiah) and enforced on a weeping and wailing nation, curiously, with the help of an accompanying Persian guard of 1500 men.

Judahite priests of the Babylonian captivity, as well as local Chaldi-Babylonian and Persian priesthoods, must have encountered descendants of the ten tribes of Israel taken into exile during the earlier Assyrian invasion of 721 BC (in a manner similar to the 'mitamaes' system of the Incas of South America).

Zarathustra, born c. 627 BC, founder of a new Persian religion, was a contemporary of Ezekiel. The Zarathustrian 'god of light', Ahura Mazda, and the 'god of darkness and evil', Ahriman, are identical with the Babylonian Marduk-Jupiter and serpent Tiamat, the Hebrew Yahwe-Zedek and Levithian Serpent, the Egyptian Ptah-Isis-Atum-Re-Amon and serpent Apophis-Seth and the Greek Zeus and serpent Typhon. Here was fertile mytho-historical ground for co-operative religious and social programmes, the names and forms being tailored to the respective national interests.

An inscription on jar seals found at Debir and Beth-Shemesh in Judah reads, 'The property of Eliakim, steward of Jehoiachin', suggesting that between the 598 BC and 587 BC destructions of Jerusalem this Eliakim was left in charge of the property of King Jehoiachin during his captivity in Babylon. (Ref: The Bible as History, p.271, by Werner Keller, 1964)

There is a similarity between the names Lehi and the priestly-dynastic line of Levi, the latter being responsible for national treasures such as the Ark, the Plates of the Commandments, the Covenant, and the Tablets of the Testament. Surely this experienced Levite priesthood - serving the older *Order of Melchizedek* - would have produced a copy of their invaluable records. Also, Nebuchadnezzar could hardly have dropped in on the Judahites without warning. Both parties were aware that a nation's sacred treasures *and archives* are prime targets in seeking to subjugate a conquered people.

Did priest-custodian Laban hide the *original* plates and documents in a secret refuge known only to the Order to which 'the Josephs' Laban and Lehi belonged?

The Mormon Church has its own Order of Melchizedek, stretching back through the line of Lehi and Joseph. Founder Joseph Smith was reportedly baptised into the Order by the 'angels' Peter, James and John! There is mention in the Book of Hebrews that Jesus Christ was a member of the Order of Melchizedek.

The history of this ancient biblical Order, with its coded 'pesherism' system employed to hide the meaning of secular and sacred chronicles from the profane, calls for explanation by bible historians. Prefixing biblical names with 'the' (sometimes 'a') thus revealing hierarchical titles such as *the* Melchizedek, *the* Abiathar, *the* Rafael, *the* Sariel, *the* David, *the* Christ, *the* Joseph, *the* Miriam etc. might better explain the true meaning of these otherwise incomprehensible religious names and titles.

The Bible mentions that the Order of Melchizedek was established under Aaron, brother of Moses, during the Exodus. But, did the model for this Order originate in Egypt and its colonies? In Alma 13.15 of the Book of Mormon, we read, '…yea even our father Abraham paid tithes of one tenth part of all he possessed *to the Order of Melchizedek.*' Given that the Order existed in Egypt before Abraham's arrival, then who founded it - *and when?*

A clue could lie in the names Zedek, associated with the planet Amon-Isis-Jupiter, and Melchi, associated with the planet Ast-Archangel Michael-Venus. The title Abiathar given to members of the priesthood second in seniority was associated with Artes-Archangel, Gabriel-Mars. Thus Archangel Gabriel who *visited* Mary, wife of (the) Joseph, is here identified as a priest-angel of the Abiathar line – 'angel' meaning 'messenger' - who understood Jesus's hereditary claim to be named, collectively, *the* Joseph, *the* Christ-King, and *the* Messiah, these being hereditary titles within the Order of Melchizedek since before the Exodus!

The coming of Jesus Christ was the first time since King David that the davidic-priest and king-messiah lines had converged. However, because Jesus was not born in the month of September as traditionally ordained, the Order faced a dilemma that subsequently led to the development of Christianity.

The frequent omission of the keyword 'the' in the Bible has resulted in centuries of misunderstanding and conflict between Judahites, Christians and Moslems. Not until the global slaughter of the 20th Century did people of all religious persuasions realise the price being paid for the deliberate camouflage of historical truth. The bloody twentieth century more than any other demonstrated how ordinary people become victims of the ambitions of esoteric entities adept at doublespeak and the manipulation of awe, secrecy, and fear as weapons of mass control.

In Genesis 14:18, when Abraham returns from pursuing those kings of the north who had captured his kinsman Lot we read, 'Melchizedek, king of Salem, brought forth bread and wine: and he was priest of the Most High God.'

Neither Abraham nor Moses spoke Hebrew and it remains a mystery where the Hebrew language originated. Was it developed from an older language that was *renamed* Hebrew, derived from the names of known tribes, perhaps the *Habiru,* or *Aperu?* Was it, perhaps, Egyptian - or *Magyar?*

Only a few decades exist between Abraham's journey from the city of Ur, situated at Tell el Muqayyar (or Tell el Mugheir, both names meaning 'Hill of the Magyars'), and his grandson Joseph's amazing rise to the governorship of Egypt (Musri). *Ur* is both Sumerian and Magyar (and, I believe, Pictish) for 'Lord.' The old name for Jerusalem was Urslm, meaning Ur – City of the Sol, Zal, or Sun! Southern Egypt was at an early date called *Het Ura*, freely translatable in Magyar as 'Land of the Lord of the Seven Nations.' Northern Egypt was *On*, or *Hon*, meaning 'country' in Magyar. Urnammu was the first king of the 3rd Dynasty of Ur of the Chaldees, and Uruarti was the actual name for Mount Ararat. The Uraeus was the royal serpent symbol of the pharoahs, and Ur-Atm, Ur-Adm, or Atm-Re, was the first heavenly god of Egypt. Egyptian pharoahs of the earliest dynasties had *Magyar* names; and, continuing the theme of lost tribes, the 'Ur' title of 14 of the 29 kings of the Khatti-Pictish-Eskitas-Magyar tribes of Baratannia (Britain) is clearly of Phoeno-Huno-Sumerian-Magyar origin.

Abraham's journey south coincided with a Deluge that destroyed the city of Ur; and his arrival in Egypt coincided with *cataclysmic* events that occurred at the end of the Old Kingdom, c.1500 BC. The Egyptians have no record of Israelites escaping their country but they *do* have records of cataclysms and plagues matching those recorded in the Exodus. Cataclysms there certainly were!

Pertinent Egyptian records are the *Papyrus Ipuwer*, now in the Museum of Leiden, and the *Papyrus No.1116b Recto* in the Hermitage Museum of St. Petersburg. The Exodus coincided *only* with the tenth plague - mainly a series of major earthquakes - when Tutimaeus, or Tut-Meses (David-Moses?) was pharoah of Egypt. (The Hebrew for 'David' being 'Dwd' reads as 'Tut' in Egyptian).

The Ten Plagues

If the Egyptians have no record of the Israelites leaving Egypt – unless the latter are identical with the Ish-ra-el, or People of Ra, led by Tut-Moses – then either the emigrants were few in number or the Egyptians were occupied on more urgent matters than keeping records or numbers. The Bible mentions the emigrants included 600,000 men. Adding women and children a total of 3 million people can be estimated, a wholly insupportable host to wander about in desertland without food and water, and with livestock already decimated by the

Fifth plague. There is confusion in the Hebrew account about the numbers leaving Egypt. Midrashic and Talmudic rabbinical sources mention that *only one person in fifty of the Israelites survived the ten plagues.*

What physical phenomenon could explain the cause of the ten plagues, taking Hebrew, Egyptian, and Arabian records into account? The answer is revealed by identifying the realistic and logical sequence of the plagues, based on nothing less than interplanetary catastrophic events that gave rise to Pillars of Fire and Smoke and the raining down of manna, naphtha, brimstone and lethal radioactive ash. Here is what I accept of leading catastrophist Immanuel Velikovsky's sequential analysis of those events:

The First Plague: Rivers of blood, the Moon turning red, the fire and brimstone, were caused by red ferrous oxide, 'ashes of the furnace,' and sulphur-brimstone, falling from the sky.

The Second, Third, Fourth, and Eight Plagues: Involving plagues of frogs, gnats, flies, locusts, ants, lice, fleas, mice and other vermin, each group reacting – as they do today during earthquakes and volcanic eruptions, – to heat, toxic dust, earth tremors and excessive noise.

The Fifth Plague: Livestock died from choking, sulphurous fumes and, since the people were later instructed to roast meat and not boil it in water, there may have been radioactivity around from interplanetary 'blasts from heaven.' This caused the foetal and newly born of living things to be stillborn or spastic, and for the nails and hair of the populace to fall out.

The Sixth Plague: Burns, boils, skin cancer, and other eruptions would be caused by irritating radioactive dust.

The Seventh Plague: The word 'barad', traditionally interpreted as 'hail', means 'hot stones', in this case ferrous or iron meteorites, mingled with flames, making a tremendous 'din' when they struck the ground, killing every living thing they struck and destroying buildings.

The Ninth Plague: The recorded three days of darkness is not difficult to imagine, caused by the blotting out of the Sun and Moon by dust and ashes, blinding and choking the populace.

The Tenth Plague: On the 14th day of Aviv (April, the month of Venus), first month of the Hebrews, the unlucky 13th day of the Egyptians and Central Americans, the electromagnetic fields of Venus and the Earth as it crossed Venus's dust, ash and meteoritic tail – clashed! Two equally matched planetary forces, like magnets, sought to repel each other. A radioactive atmosphere of dust, sand, and ashes killed the *bchor*, the 'first-born' as well as most of the *bkhor*, or 'chosen.'

§§§

This logical sequence of plagues and events was the first phase of a cataclysmic story, followed by a second phase – *during the Exodus!*

During the desert sojourn 'miracles' were related to celestial phenomena that followed the plagues, such as the Pillar of Fire at night and the Pillar of Smoke during the day. '… a stretched out arm and great terrors.' Blasts of heavenly displeasure; streams of hot naphtha and petroleum running red with fire; various forms of cooling hydrocarbons, including *edible* manna - all of this dropping from the skies?

Across the world similar accounts of planetary cataclysms are registered in the Mayan Popul Vuh, Manuscript Quiche and the Annals of Cuauhtitlan, the Buddhist Visuddhi-Magga, the Scandinavian Kalevala, the Epic of Gilgamesh, the Iranian (Carian-Hurrian) Anugita and Bundahis; and, perhaps most importantly for western historians, the Egyptian Papyrus Ipuwer in Leiden. How much more evidence is needed?

Stolen Treasure of the Egyptians

A 'mixed multitude' of Egyptians accompanied the Exodus. Also, Exodus 12.36 states, *'In this way the Israelites carried away the wealth of the Egyptians.'* Did this wealth include an original, or design for, the Ark of the Covenant, plus the Tabernacle upon which it was placed, the Ten Commandments of (perhaps) Tut-Moses, and the more important, but lesser mentioned, Tables of Testimony, compiled by the 'Lord'? '… and I will give thee tablets of stone, and a law, and commandments which I have written…'(Exodus 24.12.) 'And thou shalt put into the Ark the testimony that I shall give thee.' (Exodus 25.16.)

The Ark, built, some say, to the specifications of an electric condenser powerful enough to kill a man, made of resinous wood, and double-plated with gold inside and out – was taken to Jerusalem by King David (Dwd/Tut) and later placed by Solomon and the Levite priests in the Holy of Holies of the Temple, built by master mason Hiram Abiff. Neither the Ark nor the Tables are listed in the registers of Nebuchadnezzar after his destructions of Jerusalem in 598 and 587 BC. Such important trophies would have headed the list, yet they were absent? Where did they go?

§§§

There is a story that between 1118 and 1127 AD the Knights Templar, with the help of their crusading partners the Priory of Sion and the Cistercian monks of St Bernard de Clairveaux obtained from a chamber below the Temple of Jerusalem the Ark and its contents, plus a considerable wealth of knowledge and other treasures. Summoned to France by St. Bernard to the Council at Troyes in 1128 the soon-to-become First Grand Master of the Knights Templar, Hugues de Payens, and a company of Knights, duly brought the treasure from Jerusalem, following which St. Bernard wrote:

'The work has been accomplished with our (Cistercian?) help and the Knights have been sent on a journey through France and Burgundy, under the protection of the Count of Champagne, where all precautions can be taken against all interference by public or ecclesiastical authority.' Evidently it was a clandestine operation.

At the meeting in Troyes St. Bernard was elected *Patron and Protector of the Knights Templars*. Some years earlier the Champagne Court of Troyes had auspiciated a College of Kabaalistic and Esoteric Studies whose task was to decipher the Jerusalem treasure scripts.

Shortly after this episode the Templar Order became extremely rich, expanding rapidly to dominate European commerce and banking including the introduction of the first chequeing accounts and the strengthening of associations with the Islamic Middle-East and North Africa.

Six centuries later, in 1956, a decipherment of the *Copper Scroll* - part of the famous Dead Sea Scrolls collection found at Qumran in 1947 - revealed that an 'indeterminable treasure' (the Ark and Tables?), including a vast amount of bullion and valuables had, in fact, been buried beneath the Temple in biblical times.

Did the Templars inherit this treasure? And, intriguingly, did it contain the 'wealth of the Egyptians' removed during the Exodus? Was it secretly taken from Paris and shipped out on the 18-ship Templar fleet berthed at La Rochelle in 1307 AD then, in the 15th century, moved again, this time to the vaults of the exquisite Templar Chapel at Roslin some 7 miles south of Edinburgh, presently the focus of growing interest in Templar lore?

There is another story that Grand Master of the Templars, Jacques de Molay (d.1314), received certain secrets from the Jewish Kabbalah and from the Essenes of Qumran, following which he was appointed custodian of *a treasure from Jerusalem*. Legend has it that upon his death at the hands of the Inquisition in 1307 much of the treasure did pass through the port of La Rochelle to Scotland under the care of one George Frederick Johnson, Provost-General of the Templar Order of Scottish Lords.

Coincidentally, the powerful but impoverished St.Clair (Sinclair) family of Scotland became very rich, which caused a lasting rift with the French Templars. The Sinclairs, best known for their stout defence of Scotland's sovereignty between the 14th and 17th centuries - from Edward I down to Oliver Cromwell - were, from the time of Robert the Bruce - famous Scottish king of Norman-Viking descent - protectors of the Scottish Templar tradition and subsequently custodians of its guise in Scottish Freemasonry.

St. Bernard of Clairvaux whilst head of the Cistercian Order rescued the ailing Celtic Church of Scotland and rebuilt the Columbian Monastery on the Isle of Iona. Legend states that when the Templars brought the treasure from Jerusalem in 1128 AD it was Bernard who masterminded into Europe the sacred geometry of King Solomon's hired masons. Under his guiding hand the magnificent Gothic architecture, as if dropped from the skies, exploded across Christendom.

Can there be any doubt that the archi-geometrical knowledge gifted to St. Bernard was a product of Islamic culture that expanded during the European Dark Ages; and that this knowledge had originated from a time 2000 years earlier, when Egyptian armies 'press-ganged' Syrian artisans – the builders of Baalbek - to work in Egypt, creating Egypt's highest peak of civilization.

Given the above accounts we boldly propose plausible links between 'the wealth of the Egyptians', the treasure of Jerusalem, and a Phoeno-Magyar background to the Egyptian dynasties.

Could the name Abraham (or Abram) have derived from 'A-Brahmam', possibly a Magyar-speaking Khattio-Brahman schooled at Tell-el-Mughier (Magyar), site of Ur of the Chaldees? Did he receive the oral Kabbalah from Indo-Sumerian priests, complete with the story of Sargon I - the 'Sakhar', or 'baptised one' - traditionally also abandoned in a basket in a river? The word 'Kabbalah' means to 'receive by oral tradition' and might have originated through the Indo-Khatti order of priests called the *Smriti*, which in Sanskrit also means 're-

ceived by tradition.'
But what has all this to do with the Mormon plates?

The 'New Egyptian' Language of Patriarch Lehi

The *Book of Mormon* is specific about the mother tongue of patriarch-chronicler Lehi c. 600 BC, as evidenced by the writings of his son Nephi, *'Yea, I make a record in the language of my father, which consists of the learning of the Jews and the language of the Egyptians'* (Nephi I, 4). Did the Egyptians who joined with the Exodus include the forefathers of Lehi?

The Hebraic word 'isra' means 'desert', and suggests the name 'Israel' could mean 'people of the desert'; but should not the elements *Is-ra-el* more correctly mean 'The People of Ra', that is, worshippers of Ra-Amon-Isis-Zedek-Jupiter?

Who were the Tutmoses pharoahs? Were the Egyptians actually the first to have a Davidic, or Tutic, royal line called the *Choshen* (Chosen?), a known Egyptian priestly sect? And did it extend to King David (Tut), father of Solomon (Zal-Amon?), c.1000 BC?

The Book of Mormon, in Mosiah I, 4, tells us, *'... for he (Lehi) having been taught in the language of the egyptians, therefore he could read these engravings and teach them to his children...'* And, later, in Mormon 9, 32, we read, *'And now, behold, we have written this record according to our knowledge, in the characters which are called among us the reformed Egyptian...'*

The Chester Beatty Papyrus, published in the 1930s by Sir Alan Gardiner and dating from the Egyptian New Kingdom period - around the time of Lehi - was also written in a Neo-Egyptian language. It may stretch a point to suggest it was identical to the language of Lehi but it does indicate a development of neo-egyptian dialects (a confusion of tongues?) by generations of traumatised Egyptian exiles following the cataclysmic end of the Old Kingdom, similar to the confusion of tongues in Babylon.

There are many crossroads twixt Judah, Egypt and Ethiopia that hint at shipments of secret treasures and archives in times of crisis, often during major cataclysms followed by invasions and migrations. There seems to be no reason why the Brass Plates of the Mormons could not have existed under the custodianship of Laban *'the* Joseph', and, later through a line of neo-Egyptian speaking 'Josephs', beginning with Lehi and Nephi.

Analysis of priest-names and place-names in the Book of Mormon strongly suggests an Amu-Amalekite-Hyksos background for the Egyptian connections of Lehi, his son Nephi, and the language of the brass plates. Personal names such as Amulek, Amaleki, Amoron, Amlici, Ammon, Amulon, also the tribe of Amalekites, the Amlicite faction of the Nephites, the Ammonites, the land and city of Ammonihah (possibly Egypt and Memphis?), seem self-explanatory.

The 7th century BC migrations of the Amalekite-Phoenician-Khatti federation eastward to India, the Kara Peninsula of Malaque-Malaysia, Indonesia, and westward with the Carian-Phoenicians through Carthage, Malaga (Amalaki), and Gades (Cadiz), to America, coincide in time with the flight of Lehi and his family from Jerusalem c. 600 BC, which offers a plausible historical grounding both for the brass plates appearing on the American Continent and the transplanting of an Order of Melchizedek.

The brass plates given to Joseph Smith by *angel-messenger* Moroni at Cumorah were spirited away around 1830, never to be seen again. However, a facsimile of written characters extracted by Smith and given to one Martin Harris, and by him to Professors Charles Anthon and Samuel Mitchell, is kept in the Office of the Church Historian in Salt Lake City, Utah. Smith took 60 days to translate the book of Mormon – some 250,000 words - from reformed Egyptian into English. Assuming 250 words per page being stamped on one side gives 1000 pages of brass plates. This must have been quite an endeavour mentally and physically. Unfortunately, it does not square either in number or volume with Smith's description of the discovery, which states, *'On the west side of the hill, not far from the top, under a stone of considerable size, lay the plates, deposited in a stone box…The box in which they lay was formed by laying stones together in some kind of cement. In the bottom of the box were laid two stones crosswise of the box, and on these stones lay the plates and the other things with them.'*

The chronology of events began with the first appearance of Angel Moroni to Joeph Smith in September 1823, followed by further meetings for purposes of instruction until September 1827 when the metal plates were temporarily entrusted to Smith. The translation by Smith was signed by witnesses and published in March 1830. The precise date when Smith returned the plates to Moroni is unknown.

Armed with the above information we can move on to the *Tayos* plates!

Moricz and the Authorities

3

A great deal of polemic and misunderstanding surround the relationship between Moricz and the Ecuadorian authorities regarding his 1969 expedition to the Cave of the Tayos. The reality can best be appreciated from the actual record of events between June and December of 1969. The following is a translation of a copy of the 'Memorandum of Facts' given to me by Moricz in the late 1970s in case anything should happen to him.

MEMORANDUM: presented to H.E. the President of the Republic of Ecuador, Dr. Jose Maria Velasco Ibarra, on the discovery made by Sr. Juan Moricz in the Caves of Los Tayos.

THE FACTS

1. On 24th June 1969, Sr. Juan Moricz, of Argentine nationality, reports to the Minister of Finance, and through him to His Excellency the President of the Republic and the whole Nation, his discovery at a point in the province of Morona-Santiago within the borders of Ecuador, of a system of caves and caverns within which there are precious objects of great cultural and historic value for Humanity. After the report is accepted by the Accountant General of the Nation, it is conveyed to the House of Ecuadorian Culture in official letter No. 3395 of 8th July 1969, to the attorney General of the Nation in letter No. 3394 of 8th July 1969, to CETURIS in letter No. 3501 of 11th July 1969 and to the Ministry of Industry and Commerce.

An authentic copy of the report, together with original signatures and initials of the compiler of the report, his lawyer, and the officials concerned, the administrative stamps and other measures involved in the acceptance and processing, was registered at the notary's office in the region of Guayaquil belonging to Dr. Gustavo Falconi Ledesma, on 21st July 1969.

2. On 8th July 1969, the discoverer Juan Moricz and Dr. Gerardo Peña Matheus obtain a personal audience with H.E. the President of Ecuador during which they explain to him the fact of the discovery and the report that has been presented. The Head of State asks for photographic proof that will permit him to appreciate the reality and magnitude of the discovery. He also states that it would be necessary to have the testimony of another person who would confirm visually the existence of the subterranean world and of the objects within it.

3. When the Ecuadorian Government Tourist Commission CETURIS is officially informed by the Ministry of Finance letter No. 3501 of the report and discovery it decides to finance an expedition which would inform the Executive Power as to the reality of the discovery. On 15th July 1969 CETURIS sends H.E. the President of the Republic letter No.1159 explaining the objectives of the expedition. The same corporation also sends a letter with similar purpose, No. 1154, of 14th July, to the Sub-secretary of Finance.

4. The expedition is organised under the leadership and management of the discoverer and titled: 'Expedition Moricz 1969.'

In accordance with the terms of the report it is planned to divide the expedition into two stages: (1) 'Caves of the Tayos': and (2) 'Taltosok Barlangja' All members of the expedition, from the moment they set off on the 26th July 1969, continually wear the expedition's badge, on which are inscribed its two stages.

5. The discoverer and leader of the group, Juan Moricz, to fulfil the aims of the first stage of the expedition, 'Caves of the Tayos', led the members of the expedition as far as the exact place where various caves and caverns are found which contain the objects that were discovered. When they arrived at the place, they established 'Camp Moricz' on the surface and went down into the bowels of the earth. They covered a few kilometres of the subterranean world, taking large numbers of photographs, film, and colour slides for projection. They confirmed the existence of archaeological remains, tunnels, passages, doors, cyclopean stones etc., which clearly demonstrated that they are the work of man. The film and photographic documents are in the possession of the Ecuadorian Government Tourist Commission.

6. When the first stage of 'Expedition Moricz 1969' was completed the discoverer remained in the forest region of eastern Ecuador until 12th September 1969, awaiting stores and provisions, so that he could continue with the substantiation of the discovery. Lacking support, he

was obliged to leave the camp and return to civilization.

7. When he left the forest he tried several times to obtain an audience with H.E. the President of the Republic to inform him directly of the results of the first stage of the expedition and of the requirements and organization of the second stage. All his attempts to obtain an interview with the President were fruitless.

8. In view of the futility of the attempts to obtain an audience and the danger that Ecuador might lose the historic privilege of supporting and bringing to the world's attention the partially confirmed discovery, Dr. Gerardo Peña Matheus sent the following telegram, dated 27th September 1969, to the office of the President of the Republic (H.E. Dr. Jose Velasco Ibarra):

'Moricz Expedition financed by Ceturis with official sponsorship of your Government has confirmed existence of fabulous system of caves and caverns in Ecuadorian territory and the existence within them of the remains of a very ancient culture as reported by investigator Moricz in your presence… STOP… Having returned from the eastern selvas the discoverer wishes to inform you directly and show you a plan and requirements for the second stage expedition and explain to you his ideas and findings connected with his discovery… STOP… An audience will allow you to have at your disposal details to support a Government declaration intended to prevent other countries relieving Ecuador of the credit of informing the world of the existence of a subterranean world thousands of years old… STOP… Evidence has been found to justify seriously considering the great significance of the Moricz report… STOP… If in agreement, I would be grateful if you could inform me of a new date and time when you could grant the discoverer an audience.'

(Note: In reply to the above solicitude an audience with the President was, on 1st October, postponed until 27th October 1969, followed by a cancellation due to official commitments and a suggestion to apply later. The desired meeting never materialised.)

9. On 28th September 1969, two of the more serious and prestigious newspapers of Ecuador, 'El Comercio' of Quito and 'El Telegrafo' of Guayaquil publish, in large headlines, news of the discovery of a subterranean world in eastern Ecuador made by the Argentine investigator Juan Moricz. El Comercio publishes the event on the front page… and El Telegrafo in its 3-colour supplement. Both publications are profusely illustrated with photographic material.

10. On 22nd October 1969, in the Hotel Colon International, in Quito, there was held a joint meeting of the Commanders-in-Chief of the three branches of the Armed Forces: Army Commander Edmundo Baquero Seilgade: Air Force Colonel Cesar Rhon: Navy Commander Jorge Couz Polanco. Also present were Dr. Gerardo Peña Matheus and the Aide-de-Camp of the Minister of Defence. Juan Moricz explained his discovery at length, its location, its consequences and the need to rely on the Armed Forces to preserve the objects discovered. The meeting did not produce any practical or positive result.

§§§

On 23rd October 1969, Juan Moricz and Dr. Gerardo Peña Matheus obtain an audience with the Minister of Foreign Affairs for the purpose of informing him of: (a) the facts; (b) the desirability of being present on the spot to confirm the national sovereignty of Ecuador over the discovery; and (c) the need to send official observers from other countries, archaeologists, anthropologists, sumerologists, geologists and investigators, to take part in the second stage of the expedition and to be witnesses of the confirmation of the discovery, since the discoverer insists on the presence of observers and scientists officially invited by the government before he will lead the expedition to the exact spot where the objects were discovered, a condition laid down in the (initial) report of the discovery dated 24th June 1969.

The Minister of Foreign Relations was prevented from attending personally because some foreign visitor had extended his stay unexpectedly, so the Sub-Secretary, Señor Don Alfonso Bamera Valverde, took his place. Showing great understanding of the possible international and diplomatic consequences of the discovery, Señor Bamera promised his presence with an official party from the Ministry of Foreign Relations at the site of the discovery.

The journey was to take place the moment that a helicopter could be made available to transport the party. It is most unfortunate that, to date, no such transport has been made available.

On 21st November 1969, the international magazine VISION, distinguished for its veracity and wide circulation throughout the continent, publishes on page 60B, under Archaeology, news of the discovery of a strange subterranean world in Ecuador by the hungarian-argentinian investigator, Sr. Juan Moricz.

In its December 1969 issue, the Ecuadorian magazine VISTAZO also announces the discovery of the subterranean world and the hardships and incidents of the Moricz Expedition 1969 in its journey through the forest.

In order to obtain the necessary support for the second stage, and in view of the impossibility of obtaining it directly from Ecuador, in spite of the time that had passed, actions taken, and articles published, the discoverer Juan Moricz sent an urgent telegram to the President of his country (Argentina) Señor Juan Carlos Ongama, asking for resources and assistance of a logistical, diplomatic, economic, scientific and legal nature.

As a consequence of this communication, the Argentine government agreed to send an official representative with the object of obtaining permission from the government of Ecuador for Argentine intervention and assistance.

§§§

REQUESTS AND REQUIREMENTS: (presented by Juan Moricz)

Considering the importance of the discovery of a system of caves and caverns which runs the length of the Continent from North to South and the existence within it of precious objects of incalculable cultural value for Humanity we believe there is good reason for bringing to the attention of the Ecuadorian Head of State the aspirations and wishes of the discoverer, Señor Juan Moricz, which may be stated in the following terms:

1.   The presence in person of the Head of State or his representative at the site to confirm the discovery officially.

2.   A declaration of the government before the accredited diplomatic corps announcing the existence of a sub-terranean world which extends the length of the South American continent from North to South and informing all American countries of the discovery.

3.   Acceptance of Argentine assistance and collaboration.

4.   Full facilities for the discoverer, so that investigations can proceed under his direction, and the appointment, with agreement from the Executive Power, of a mixed commission composed of notable persons, scientists and investigators, from Ecuador and from abroad, who will be responsible for ensuring the safety and preservation of

the objects discovered.

5. Convocation of an international congress of investigators and scientists to be organised by the Mixed Commission and sponsored by the Ministry of Foreign Relations.

6. The need to warn official bodies, ministries, authorities etc. which, for the duration of the investigations of Sr. Juan Moricz in the subterranean world, should not permit any other expedition, whether of Ecuadorian or foreign composition, to explore caves and caverns in the Republic. A Decree to be issued prohibiting explorations and expeditions of this type and authorising Sr. Juan Moricz to continue his investigations.

7. Appointment of an Ecuadorian citizen in the confidence of the Head of State to liaise constantly between the discoverer and the President of the Republic.

8. An aerial photographic survey of the zone of caves and caverns to be carried out by the Military Geographic Service and official publication of the discovery to be made by this institution.

9. A helicopter constantly at the disposal of the discoverer, which will permit the transport of persons and equipment from the Teniente Ortiz Military Base at Santiago to the campsite.

10. A permanent guard at the site composed of chosen personnel from the National Civil Police.

Confident that the patriotism and wide culture of H.E. President of the Republic, together with the knowledge that he already has of the facts, will enable him to give favourable consideration to the discoverer's aspirations, we remain, etc.,

(Signed by Dr. Gerardo Peña Matheus & Señor Juan Moricz)

§§§

The 'FACTS' indicate that on three separate occasions, despite the apparent importance and sincerity of the evidences presented to the Government of Ecuador, it proved impossible for Dr. Peña and Moricz to secure the assistance required. Why?

None of the offers made for the second stage of Moricz's project focuses on 'treasure', only on 'objects discovered' plus a commitment to lead an official expedition to 'the caves and caverns' already visited, a fact confirmed by his request for a helicopter to be based at the

Santiago Military Camp near the confluence of the rivers Santiago and Coangos.

Not surprisingly, offering what were judged by the authorities to be unreasonable conditions he ran into trouble. No geologists were present on the 1969 expeditions thus a professional opinion on the geological structure and formation of the caves was not forthcoming to counterbalance his claims of construction by human hand.

When other personalities are introduced into the story another picture emerges suggesting a concealed and somewhat desperate agenda behind Moricz's actions. Also, I have never seen a photograph of Moricz actually inside a Tayos cave despite his many expeditions, although Dr. Peña may have some.

Seven years were to pass before there was any follow-up to the Moricz Expedition 1969. For my part, beginning in 1975, securing a comprehensive dossier and reliable independent information to justify a British expedition proved to be a long and arduous process.

There is a magic about Ecuador that can mesmerise the inexperienced visitor, not only because it boasts every type of climate in the world and scores of divergent cultures but also in the diversity of its cities, towns and provinces. Like a tropical fever the rush to believe fantastic things in this most fantastic of countries invariably traps the unwary traveller from a developed country longing to escape mundanity. It can take decades - for some a lifetime - to understand how the heart of Ecuador beats, and to what rhythm, the same rhythm that seduced the Conquistadores and their descendants, truly a country too complex and hypnotic for the insincere to master.

Ecuador: Cradle of American Civilization

4

Ecuador is a unique place to investigate American prehistory, for the following reasons:

1. The country straddles the Equator at a unique north-south/east-west confluence of geography and history.

2. The Andes are at their narrowest close to Cuenca, where they touch the apex of the massive geological shield that curves round from Guyana down to Bolivia.

3. Prior to the Conquistadores, long-serving emperor Inca Huanya Capac planned to establish his birthplace, Tupipampa (Cuenca), as the northern capital of the Empire of Tayhuantinsuyu, dominating the shortest route between Amazonia and the Pacific and the rich gold and silver deposits of the Cañari nation settled west of the geological shield. His son Huascar was, like himself, also born in Tupipampa, which explains why the local Cañari allied with the Inca invaders and later paid a terrible price to the ultimately victorious Atahualpa.

4. The cold Humboldt Current from Antartica that creates the coastal deserts of Peru turns westward in southern Ecuador, where it collides with the warm El Niño current that created the fertile Ecuadorian coast, ideal for agriculture, aquaculture, and the development of early Amerindian formative communities dating from the end of the last Ice Age, c.7500 BC.

5. Ecuador has more live volcanoes to surface area than anywhere in the world, producing fertile land in its three principal climatic regions, as well as considerable polythermic and alluvial mineral potential. Quito, curiously, is surrounded by a diamond pattern of four major volcanoes.

6. Following the pattern of the volcanoes, there are also more indigenous groups to land area than anywhere in the world, some, like

their volcano counterparts, more explosive than others.

7. Metal craftsmanship on the coast dates from c.2000 BC to the time of the Conquest, the earliest work equal to the most advanced in the world. Their goldsmiths' skill at 'granulation' is matched only by the Sumerians of Mesopotamia.

8. An extensive subterranean cave system exists east of the Andes where the Pacific geological plates dipping under the Amazonian plates have pushed up three ranges of Cordilleras. The cave system has been formed by huge quantities of rainwater running off the granite and basalt of the high Andes into the softer Cordillera layers of limestone and sandstone.

9. Straddling the Equator, four ancient migration routes run east to west through the Andes, uniting Amazonia with the Pacific coastal plain.

10. Formative coastal cultures based on the planting and harvesting of corn predate Mexico by up to 2000 years, indicating an experimental and genetic development of agriculture from c.8000 BC.

11. The development of tobacco and chilli peppers points to early experimentation and domestication expanding from the eastern Cordilleras westwards through the narrowest Andean route to the coast, through Cuenca.

12. The chewing of dried coca leaf with lime is widespread among Andean peoples for alleviating pangs of hunger, thirst and fatigue, and was used in religious ceremonies as early as c.1500 BC. The coca bean was originally cultivated on the eastern slopes of the Andes, under the cool and moist conditions the plant demands.

13. Ecuador has produced the earliest known figurines in stone and clay in the New World, and many archaeologists are beginning to acknowledge that those of Meso-America originated in Ecuador.

14. Iridescent painting derives from ceramic experimentation. However, iridescent pottery found at Ocos in Central America had no such experimental period. Consequently, the conclusion is that the technique was transmitted fully developed from Ecuador.

15. Balsa wood for constructing rafts capable of travelling large distances across oceans is found *only* in Ecuador and was used extensively to carry commerce to northern, southern and possibly western regions of the Pacific. From Ecuadorian coasts in recent times Thor Hyderdhal and Vital Altzar constructed balsa craft that sailed thousands of miles across the Pacific Ocean.

16. Although Mexico is geographically closer to Central America, coastal Ecuador imposed the greatest formative influence on agriculture and technology in that region from c. 8000 BC onwards. Contact was exclusively by sea. Contrary to earlier belief that Ecuadorian coastal peoples were ignorant of ships and sailing they were demonstrably the 'phoenicians of the Pacific coast', presently opening up for historians new visions of coastal history and regional influence.

The Triangle of the Sacred Shell

5

The Olmec civilization of Central America dating from c.1500 BC was a precursor of the brilliant Maya. We find the Olmec art and Chavin art of the coastal plains of Peru and Ecuador based on identical cosmological myths, central to which were two marine molluscs – the spiny oyster *Spondylus Marinus* and the conchlike shells *Malea and Strombus*. Neither is found in the cold waters south of Ecuador and they are extremely difficult to obtain, the most prized Spondylus being found at depths of fifty feet or more.

Given the similarities in Olmec and Chavin practices it is surprising so little evidence exists of the use of these shells among the coastal communities of Ecuador, especially considering the universal dependence on these communities for supplies.

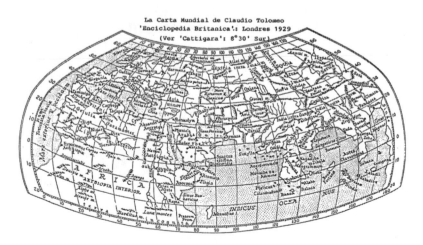

Ptolemy's World Map

By 600 BC Ecuadorian communities had declined as innovators in the New World but their unique balsa rafts continued to dominate the commercial routes of South and Central America.

§§§

We have covered sufficient historical background to encourage our story of exploration and discovery. We might well be on our way to discovering South America as the *missing page* of world prehistory and Ecuador as the *cradle* of American civilization. And where, we wonder, recalling Moricz's ideas on Magyar prehistory, might these factors stand in the formation of *global* civilization? The recent discovery of the 5000 year-old city of Caral some kilometres inland from the coast north of Lima, and my assertion published through Reuters News agency in 1992 that Chan Chan (lat. 8° 07' South), near Trujillo, sits on the site of Claudius Ptolemy's legendary city of *Cattigara*, might merit attention in this context.

The mirror through which I had been looking was changing into a window, facing across the Atlantic, up the Amazon headwaters and into the dark underworld of the Andes.

In March 1974 I decided to organize for 1977 an expedition of professionals to cross that narrow neck of the Andes. It would focus on scientific objectives and need protection from the running Moricz - von Daniken controversy. A quick assessment of my credibility and experience made any expedition to South America seem a long way off but it was a relief to concentrate so many years of global historical investigation into a practical objective. South America was surely the *missing page* and the ingredients for a great adventure were self-evident. Such euphoric ideas would soon transform into pushing a camel through the eye of a needle, but that would come later.

First Reconnaissance

6

January 1975, Scotland. With scientific objectives listed there remained the business of organization and methods. I put on my planning engineer's hat. In place of 20-storey buildings I had the Andes. Not a problem! Helicopters, vertical take-off jets. You name it - I considered it! Logistics? Simple! I contacted army Colonel Gordon Pender, Head of Army Recruitment and Training in Scotland, who happened to live across the street from my house in Dollar. We met at the nearby Muckhart Inn. He grasped my plan and immediately approached Army Headquarters in Edinburgh.

I was invited to meet with Major Alan Fisher to design a military team. As the magnitude of the venture became apparent it was suggested experience lay with the Joint Services Expedition Unit based at Salisbury, run by the ebullient Major John Blashford-Snell.

Convinced this arrangement would not work I insisted the expedition be organized in Edinburgh although adding that if Scottish Command, backed by the reputations of Scottish regiments, scientists, engineers and explorers felt it had to go south of the border for help then by all means go ahead! Amid rueful smiles I got my way.

The dominating factor was logistics. Captain Philip Maxwell of the Royal Highland Fusiliers was brought in. After a discussion over maps our budding expedition committee concluded an early reconnaissance was essential. It was February 1975. The expedition was programmed for July 1977 (later dramatically changed to July 1976). I would have to back my convictions by financing a reconnaissance visit.

Clearance to plan the expedition was authorised by the U.K. Ministry of Defence. The Foreign and Commonwealth Office opened negotiations with the Ecuadorian authorities and the British Embassy in Quito. Contact was made with a few Ecuadorians with knowledge of the target area. Meantime, I maintained contact with Moricz and Dr. Peña. All responses were encouraging and we began to feel we were onto a winner.

With archaeology a major element advice was sought from Dr. Elizabeth Carmichael of the Museum of Mankind in London and Dr. Warwick Bray of London University. Both had experience in Ecuador. Unfortunately, for reasons of timing, cost and availability efforts to bring them on board proved fruitless. The committee in Edinburgh decided there was no reason why I should not go since we were still in the early stages. The archaeologists could come from Ecuador.

§§§

Captain Maxwell and I arrived in Quito on separate flights. At breakfast in the Hotel Colon on the 20th April 1975 we formulated a programme for our two-week stay. Every expensive moment had to count. Ecuador, of course, had other ideas.

First stop was the British Embassy. First shock was that nobody was prepared for our arrival. Ambassador Norman Cox had not been briefed by the Foreign Office. However, he kindly arranged a lunch at his residence inviting the principals of all relevant scientific, government and military institutions.

Philip and I set up meetings with local archaeologist Olaf Holm in Guayaquil, Ing. Luis Alcivar Elizalde, Director of the government tourist agency Ceturis, Dr. Brian Kennerley, Head of the British Geological Mission in Ecuador, and others we believed could assist us.

Luis Alcivar happened to be staying at our Hotel and we arranged to meet for dinner. Speaking good English he provided background on the role of Ceturis in the 1969 Moricz Expedition, also presenting his vision of the Tayos Caves as the 'Machu Picchu' of Ecuador.

Surprisingly, he emphasised, 'If you return to Britain without consulting the key man in the story you will be criticised. I met Moricz for the first time two weeks ago and confess I found him most impressive. You should definitely meet him!'

'Okay!' I agreed. 'Provided you organize the meeting and discussion is confined to matters of planning and logistics.'

I began to realise I needed more flexibility in conducting the reconnaissance. Working in a latin-american environment appeared to involve more personal contact than was normal in Britain.

58

'Fine!' I heard my pompous pride whisper, 'We can meet with Moricz if we have time left at the end of our two-week visit. It might also help to clarify the Erich von Daniken story since we cannot ignore it.'

We requested from Ceturis copies of photographs of the Moricz Expedition and were told by Luis these should be in the company's Guayaquil office. During the next few days in Quito we met Arquitecto Hernán Crespo Toral, Director of the Museum of the Central Bank (later, Director of UNESCO) and General Antonio Morales, former Military Commander in the Morona Santiago zone. Gradually, a fuller picture emerged of what had occurred since the Moricz Expedition of 1969.

Happy with progress we requested through the Embassy permission to visit the Santiago military base near the target area. Awaiting a response from the military junta in power we flew to Guayaquil to meet archaeologist Olaf Holm, of Danish descent and a resident of Ecuador for more than thirty years. He immediately stressed the need to involve the Ecuadorian scientific and archaeological community.

Through Luis Alcivar we met with Gaston Fernández Borrero, former Director of Ceturis and participant in the 1969 Moricz Expedition who, surprisingly, was in personal possession of the expedition's photographic slides. He projected them onto a wall in our room at the Hotel Continental. With due permission Captain Maxwell photographed each one. These spectacular photographs and the personal reports of Gaston were our first solid evidence that the 'Cave of the Tayos' truly existed. Curiously, none of the photographs included Juan Moricz. We soon learnt there were many 'Tayos' caves. The photographs were of the main Tayos Cave system in the River Coangos area, the originals of those featured in *Gold of the Gods*. (Note: It is evident in a letter from Erich von Daniken dated 3rd February 1973 in Dr. Peña's possession that he had permission to use the photographs for purposes of fomenting interest in the 'Taltosok Barlanja' second phase of the 1969 expedition.)

Gaston suggested we meet with anthropologist Dr. Alfredo Costales Samaniego in Quito. Of particular note - knowing what I know now – was a second suggestion for a meeting with someone called Petronio Jaramillo who apparently 'knew something' of the story.

Conscious of our shortage of time and meetings already scheduled I declined his offers. Sixteen years after our 1976 Expedition I recall thinking that perhaps not meeting with Petronio Jaramillo was unfortunate, though excusable in the circumstances. My guardian angel had warned me risky contacts could compromise scientific objectives and turn the expedition into a disaster. No doubt, meeting Jaramillo would have dramatically changed my strategy, not regarding the expedition, but regarding Moricz, for reasons that will become clear further into our story.

Due to an inordinate delay getting clearance for our visit to Santiago precious time flew past, making us more and more concerned - enough to take drastic measures! Olaf Holm had a contact in SAVAC, a small airline that flew small packages into Cuenca and other cities in a five-seater Piper aircraft. We decided to waste no more time, contacting SAVAC to pick us up in Cuenca on Monday 28th April to fly to the Santiago miltary base, by which time we were confident official permission for the visit would be granted. Timing was critical. We had to be back in Quito for the Ambassador's lunch in a few days time.

Still without permission on the crucial day, we resolved to fly with Olaf over the Andes to Santiago on the assumption that the cause of delay was bureaucratic and not intentional.

Flying into Cuenca by national airline we met up with the two SAVAC pilots and flew eastwards. Initially the sky was clear but clouded over as we descended over the Cordilleras and the humidity increased.

With Philip Maxwell and Dr. Olaf Holm: Santiago Military Base 1975.

Though elated to be on our way we realised that none of us, including the pilots, had an accurate map. The British Geological Mission in Quito headed by Dr. Brian Kennerley was preparing maps from aerial photographs but it would be months before these were available. It dawned on us that despite the cavalier joviality of the pilots we were flying by the seat of our pants. They had never been in this part of the country.

The only information they had about the Santiago base area was that in wet weather - and we are talking about *wet* weather - one end of the runway was unserviceable… but which end?

Approaching in breaking cloud we were soon in verbal crossfire about the number of small airstrips we could see from the windows - but which one was ours? Thankfully, we spotted the military base. Landing safely in bright, dry weather but without previous warning we had no idea how the military in that strategic zone would react. Would they shoot first and ask questions later?

The suspicions of Base Commander Major Lamar abated when Olaf explained our situation. He was most courteous, promising collaboration should the expedition go ahead. Military patrols had reported a number of caves in the area and we agreed these could also be investigated.

Having arrived at the Santiago base the long-running border tension between Ecuador and Peru seemed of secondary importance. However, as national resentment for 150 years of opportunistic land-grabbing by neighbouring countries became clearer I began to appreciate why Ecuador had turned itself into a fortress, armed with 'considerable powers of dissuasion.'

It is little known that the ancient Kingdom of Kitus once stretched from the Pacific along the Amazon River as far as the delta at Belen. Some elderly inhabitants of Iquitus in the province of Loretto, Peru, nostalgically cherish their pre-1942 Ecuadorian cedulas of identification. Peru claimed Loretto was part of the old Empire of Tayhuantinsuyu centred in Cuzco, although Atahualpa, the victorious Shyri ruler based in Quito, might have asked who won the war. It is a curious phenomenon why so many wars are between neighbours!

Staring blissfully across the wide Santiago River to the sharp-peaked Cordilleras roofing the cave systems we were surprised by the suddenness with which the skies opened up. Thunder and lightning sent us streaking for shelter through sheets of rain, accompanied by gales of laughter from the soldiers. It was Amazonia's first warning of what the expedition could expect.

The downpour lasted four hours, each hour diminishing my wallet by $150 USD. When it faired the pilots prepared for take-off. Lining up at one end of a runway covered in muddy pools the plane pluckily roared forward a short distance before slewing sideways onto soft grass. We had wondered which end of the runway was unserviceable in the rain. Now we knew! Amid more hilarity, soldiers and local Shuar rushed to push us, and our red faces, onto firmer ground.

The second time, we bounced a long way down the runway, splashing through the pools. I resigned myself to the thought we were not going to make it. The pilots were gritting their teeth, not cracking jokes anymore. Then, triumphantly, we soared into the air, waving back, white-faced, at the still-laughing mob below who doubtless believed they were seeing the last of the crazy gringos.

We were in for more shocks. Our indomitable pilots decided it was too dangerous to fly back the way we had come, so they would look for a passage through the mountains to the north. I sensed internal panic. Find it *where*, exactly?

We flew north, then sharply west into mist-shrouded valleys, unable to climb straight because of the mountains - those fleeting, black shapes, occasionally too close for comfort, flashing past our windows. Forced to climb in spirals, flitting from one valley to the next, we were glee-fully reassured by highly pitched voices and half-crazed eyes that the

Skidding off the runway at Santiago

plane could go to 30,000 feet if necessary.

The end was nigh: I was sure of it. How could they find a way back through mist over an unmapped route? We would certainly crash and, even if we survived, no doubt be eaten by some lost tribe of cannibals, all as described in my boyhood adventure books. We had been mad to come in the first place. For sure, we were not going to make it back. Here I was in cloud, at 16,000 feet, being calmly asked if I would like an oxygen mask. Sick with fright, I could only sit there, breathless, white and nonchalant, nodding, shaking my head in response to inaudible questions, nursing thoughts of a doomed man and asking myself what the hell I was doing here.

Suddenly - so much seemed to happen *suddenly* - we were through the mountains and valleys and flying through low cloud into Cuenca. Hardly able to believe we had made it, I tottered out of the aircraft with a brave face, taking a deep breath of rarefied air before soberly paying the pilots as if I made such flights every day. Never again!

Philip and I parted with Olaf, thanking him profusely for getting us over the first hurdle. For my meagre resources it had been a costly, but successful, and certainly memorable, first reconnaissance. Through the

Padre Carlos Crespi: A lifetime of caring

euphoria of finding myself back in the real world I concentrated on determining where the expedition would be headed on the ground. The Santiago base offered an ideal supply base for the proposed camp-site at the Tayos Cave 20 minutes by helicopter to the south-west.

After booking into the Hotel El Dorado we set off to hire transport for a reconnaissance eastward to Limon Indanza so Philip could complete his logistics report. The transport did not transpire. We could find nobody who spoke English and our Spanish was limited to a few words. We had been told that some priests at the Cathedral Maria Auxiliadora spoke English. I knew of the legendary Padre Carlos Crespi from Von Daniken's book so brilliantly reasoned that wherever he was located, even if he spoke no English, we would find priests who did. Simply by asking the way to 'Padre Crespi?' in the street we must inevitably arrive at our objective.

The ruse worked. But of course we came face to face with the one priest we wished to avoid due to the von Daniken controversy – the venerable Padre Carlos Crespi! There he was, large as life, small of stature, his weather-beaten, oval face etched with a twinkling smile of welcome, quizzically peering at us behind a long, grey beard and droopy

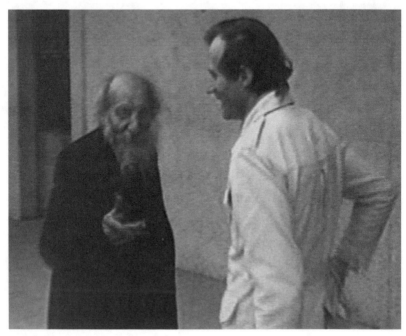

Tee-hee! Some believe I am Adolph Hitler

moustache, a picture of Old Father Time himself. Naturally he assumed we wanted to visit his museum containing some 70,000 artifacts, a few of which were illustrated in *Gold of the Gods*.

I laughed at the irony of falling into my own trap. As it transpired we would not have missed him for the world. Struck by his saintly warmth and kindness we respectfully looked at some metal objects he showed us before breaking off to continue searching for transport.

Our desired objective, Limon Indanza, was from where Moricz and his 1969 Expedition had travelled by mule to the Tayos Cave. Still we found nobody willing to hire a vehicle. One taxi driver seeing our 'green' ears offered the trip for $120 USD, too expensive for my purse. Travelling by bus would have taken too long. Finally, we abandoned all hope of a terrestrial reconnaissance: a disappointment, particularly for Captain Maxwell.

Crespi artifact of doubtful authenticity

By the skin of our teeth we arrived in Quito in time for the Ambassador's arranged lunch. We agreed not to bring up Moricz's name. After the meal the principals of key military and cultural institutes listened attentively as he outlined the purpose of our mission, following which Captain Maxwell, with the Ambassador translating, explained our plan in detail. Each party responded in turn, agreeing in principle to a venture with equal British and Ecuadorian participation.

Then came the first bombshell! We had visualised an expedition of moderate scale, but the Ecuadorians, anxious to lay the ghost of controversy, wanted it brought forward to July 1976. In a state of shock we heard ourselves agreeing to this, also to the fact there should be no publicity until the expedition had been officially authorised by the Ecuadorian Military Junta. In short, we had been given 15 months to make it all happen. The normal time needed for an expedition of this size was 3 to 4 years. I comforted myself by assuming we could depend on authorisation being granted quickly.

We left the meeting having established the viability of the expedition and the goodwill and support of the civil and military organisms. Thanks to Ambassador Cox and Military Attache Peter Wills we had achieved success beyond our expectations.

Crespi plate inscriptions

That evening at a cocktail party in his house Captain Wills brightly informed us in conversation with General Antonio Morales that permission had finally come through for our planned reconnaissance trip to Santiago. Philip and I exchanged fearful glances, realising we had to confess we had already been there. On my declaring this Captain Will's shocked countenance and our own embarrassment was skillfully neutralised by the general who gulped down his whisky before stating, with a broad, don't-ever-do-that-again, smile, 'Well! We are even! You went too early, but we gave permission too late.' I was going to enjoy working with people like him. We relaxed for the first time in days.

Luis Alcivar telephoned to confirm he had arranged the meeting with Moricz so next day we flew back to Guayaquil. Neither Luis nor Olaf felt they should attend in case their presence might inhibit Moricz. We met at 10 a.m. on the 1st May in the home of Dr. Gerardo Peña Matheus who, after the introductions, opened the conversation in perfect English.

'We understand you had a meeting in Quito with various authorities about your proposed expedition. May I ask, was Señor Moricz discussed?'

Crespi clay dome dated 900 AD

'No!' I replied, expecting the question, 'I assume responsibility for ensuring that Señor Moricz was not discussed; but please assure him we are not here to make judgments, only to seek facts. In that context he has as much credibility as anyone who sat at the Ambassador's table. Unfortunately, we cannot escape the fact that the controversy arising from Erich von Daniken's book also affects Señor Moricz.'

Moricz responded quietly, 'The victim suffers from the assailant!'

Dr. Peña continued, 'Why has it taken you two weeks before coming to see Señor Moricz?'

'Again, I am responsible! I am neither archaeologist, nor scientist nor soldier, but an engineer. I was already concerned about my credibility and it became apparent that any direct collaboration with Señor Moricz was not feasible. Only an independent, interdisciplinary scientific investigation with the caves as a focus of interest was possible, without depending on archaeological discoveries for its success. As far as this visit is concerned we thought Señor Moricz might be willing to assist Captain Maxwell with logistical advice based on his knowledge of the area, the local Indians, and the caves. We cannot get involved in any discussions about his discoveries or historical theories.'

Dr. Peña translated for Moricz.

'I will be happy to give what advice I can,' he smiled, glancing at me, 'but I am surprised you thought I might want to discuss my discoveries and theories with you.'

With these words Moricz made it clear what sort of individual we were dealing with. He sat, arms and legs crossed, leg swinging, an attitude he adopted, Dr. Peña later informed me, when he was suspicious of anyone who might be strolling around the edge of his kingdom. Nevertheless, he politely listened to all I said and seemed to enjoy our exchange.

For some time we concentrated on logistical problems. The conversation was lightened here and there with references to subjects in which the others, all of whom spoke English, could participate, such as British involvement in, and apparent abandonment of, South America. There was the death of 80% of the 6500-strong British Expeditionary Force (The Albion Brigade) sent to help the Independence movement of Simon Bolivar, and the almost total ignorance of the British public in relation to Britain's historical role in South America.

Moricz proved helpful, practical, unreserved in his advice, exposing the odd glimmer of enthusiasm. There was a moment when, gaining confidence in him and sympathising with difficulties he had had with the authorities, I asked whether he might consider using part of the expedition to reveal his discoveries on an official basis, taking advantage of logistical support unlikely to be on offer in the future. However, I added, it would be impossible for anyone on the British team to appoint him as leader.

Moricz declined the offer absolutely, explaining that he had laid down the conditions for his discoveries in a notarised document and would not deviate from that position. Thus it was left. Time to call it a day.

Captain Maxwell left the meeting mid-afternoon for Quito to catch his flight to the U.K. next day. Moricz became more relaxed. Mentally I summarised the position. Luis was right about Moricz being knowledgeable and intelligent. Now, free from logistical and military matters, our conversation spread into various historical fields. Such was the bond I developed with Moricz that our discussion continued all that evening and into the early hours of the following morning; sixteen hours, surely a world record for a first conversation through translators, the three of them working between short breaks, exhausting work, yet, every time I moved to leave, I was assured all were genuinely enjoying the exchange.

At no time did I confront Moricz further about his discoveries or

Roger St.John Hender, Moricz, Hall, Maxwell, Dr.G. Peña M. & Victor Pino.

theories, preferring to concentrate on assessing his personality, particularly noting his groundbreaking ideas on the origins of ancient Scythians and Magyars on the American continent.

His historical journey is a remarkable adventure by any standards. Single-minded dedication, physical and intellectual courage mingled with danger, mystery and intrigue, one man against the historical record, a lone ranger - and intractably stubborn! The more I learnt of his difficulties with the authorities the more the weakness of his position appeared. *First*, his refusal to reveal the location of the library, generating accusations that he was afraid to put his claims to the test. *Second*, being of Hungarian origin, his assertion that the language of the library was (in five developments of) ancient Magyar could be inherently biased. *Third*, since he had published only a short article on Scytho-Magyar migrations (for Guayaquil Historical Society, in the late 1960s), his theory of a South-American origin/diffusion for world civilization greatly depended on the alleged revelations in the metal library. *Fourth*, having put so much energy into strongly held convictions, was he guilty of fabricating answers that suited his claims?

Could I trust him? Could I expect him to trust me? Our historical ideas had parallels but would a working relationship be feasible? Moricz seemed too much a loner. These and other concerns flashed across my mind like fireworks.

Apparently - a word I came to use a lot - those who knew Moricz admired his high level of culture, knowledge and field ability. At our marathon meeting I had introduced everything I could think of dealing with comparative religion, philosophy, theosophy, prehistory, catastrophism, evolution, intercontinental migrations, folklore, world wars, here and there laying little traps - as I am sure he did with me. Apart from Hungarian, he was fluent in Spanish, Italian, German, French and, to a lesser extent, Russian – though, curiously, not English. His knowledge of ancient history and languages was impressive. In short, a brilliant man, calm in his arguments and convictions. Yet the same question kept coming back. Was he perhaps some kind of Rasputin, or Alisteir Crowley, able to mesmerise listeners into believing him through sheer force of personality? After all, I was using words like 'brilliance' just to get some perspective on his capacities and achievements.

Once again I stood up to leave, saying, 'Señor Moricz, it has been a pleasure talking with you. Unfortunately, our expedition has no mandate for co-operation on historical matters and despite what you say the archaeological community has advised us there is little possibility of important discoveries in the Rio Santiago area. In these circumstances a picture would be worth a thousand words.'

There was nothing I could expect him to offer. I was, after all, just another visitor with an idea for an expedition that might never happen: still a dreamer. It was natural he be cautious. Then, he surprised me again. Signalling me to sit down he stood and paced the floor a few times before fixing me with a penetrating gaze.

'We leave at 4.00 o'clock!' he exclaimed.

I thought, whatever his idea, he must be referring to 4.00 o'clock in the afternoon, and said so.

'No! Now!' he urged, 'I will take you to a place where there are large, inscribed standing stones, similar to those you have in Scotland, in singles and in groups. That should convince your archaeologists. We will take photographs and you will have my permission to use them any way you choose.'

'But that alone would be an important discovery.' I ventured in astonishment, feeling a little foolish at stating the obvious.

'They have no priority significance,' shrugged Moricz.

I glanced at one of the translators, Roger St. John Hender, a tall, eagle-nosed Englishman, one-time Adjutant to a Viceroy of India. He had lived in Guayaquil for many years after leaving Colombia, an old-guard military man who liked to reminisce about the times the regimental sergeant-major would take a troop 2000 miles to collect the regiment's beer ration. Shrugging his shoulders, with just the flicker of a smile, he replied encouragingly, 'Moricz has never made such an offer to anyone before. I think you should go. What can you lose?'

Feigning a moment to consider the offer and hide my enthusiasm I quickly realised the advantages outweighed the disadvantages. It meant re-scheduling my flight but I would be passing through Limon Indanza and could report on the route to Captain Maxwell. What a decision to make - with Moricz's eagle blue eyes fixed on me like a beast of prey - either to pack my bags for the U.K. or cross the Andes on a unique adventure.

Most of his detractors were academics. Few were close to him as a person and, because his historical ideas challenged the academic norm, the impasse with Ecuadorian institutions was total. My ideas on maritime migrations had much in common with Moricz and helped our intellectual bonding. I saw no difficulty in being with him given that

71

our mutual investigative interests were kept separate from expedition objectives.

Crespi metal plate. Magyar? Sanskrit? Pali?

Journey to the Stones

7

4.00 a.m., 3rd May, 1975, Hotel Atahualpa, Guayaquil. The telephone rang from the foyer downstairs. Moricz and Dr. Peña had arrived. Grabbing my bag I joined them and, after a quick breakfast, climbed aboard Moricz's famous 'Jeep.' A photographer friend, Virgilio H. Aviles, was in the back seat. We three 'musketeers' sat up front. With Moricz driving we set off along a potholed road towards the distant Andes. It was dark, hot and humid.

On the mountain route we stopped by an old Quechua lady friend of Moricz to buy some bread and cheese and stretch our legs. Dawn was breaking over the high peaks, the Sun's rays streaming along the foothills and valleys mingling with the sounds of a waking world.

By mid-day we had reached the flat *altiplano*. The altitude and lurching of the vehicle had taken its toll, especially on Dr. Peña. We stopped so he could climb out for a breather. Moricz drove some distance ahead, smiling mischievously. When the good doctor caught up with us, looking pale and weary, I sympathetically helped him into the jeep, following which Moricz drove on as if nothing had happened.

'Sr. Hall,' said Dr. Peña, smiling wryly, 'Now you see that Moricz *does* have a sense of humour.'

Suitably warned, I settled back to enjoy the journey. The variety of scenery and climate, beginning with the forests of the western slopes, across the sparse, stern altiplano, then down the eastern foothills into the rain forest, was breathtaking, stunning – a truly lost world! To think that, the day before, I could have chosen to fly back to the U.K. Moricz, an outdoor man, was in his element. Here was his other side - man of action, positive, decisive, in control!

By early afternoon we entered Limon Indanza, coming to a halt at the home of the Punin family, friends of Moricz. Invited for lunch we ate a simple cooked meal, which, for a poor family, was obviously stretching the larder. When we finished eating Moricz beckoned the father Alfredo outside. I leaned sideways for a better view of what was going on, only to see Moricz discreetly giving him money to cover the meal, plus something extra for a rainy day.

After arranging to return the next morning to collect Punin and one of his sons, Moricz drove further east to Mendez where we were to stay the night, arriving about 7.00 p.m. Fourteen hours had past since we left Guayaquil. Moricz had insisted on driving all the way.

'Moricz must be tired,' I said to Dr. Peña, himself exhausted. Looking at his tired countenance I was reminded that for the past three days he had played an amiable, generous, and unselfish role as host and translator. Virgilio and I were tired too, though with the excitement of the adventure my adrenalin was keeping me going. Dr. Peña smiled, shaking his head wearily, 'Sr.Hall! Moricz *never* gets tired!'

'Where has he gone now?' I queried, looking around.

'To repair some damage to the exhaust pipe. His jeep is more exhausted than he is, no?' Chuckling, he seemed pleased at such a comical remark erupting from his tired brain.

When Moricz returned we booked into Ruby's Hotel and were proudly shown some spartan, interior rooms; with few windows, the only light in my room coming from stars shining through holes in the roof. My eyes, becoming accustomed to the dark, fixed on a bedframe with a torn, straw mattress. Gratefully, I lay down. An overactive brain kept me awake for some time.

Being a jungle novice I imagined every rustle was some poisonous snake, scorpion, or tarantula. They *had* to be around somewhere! Vampire bats and fleas would suck me dry if I dared sleep. God, what was I doing here? I remembered I had said the same thing during the SAVAC flight. Slowly, the excitement of the adventure began to sink into my bones. At some moment in the still quiet darkness of that starlit night exhaustion finally overcame any determination to stay awake.

Next thing I remember was Moricz waking everyone to an early dawn. After breakfast we returned to Limon Indanza for Punin and his son. (I learnt that Punin was one of the first to accompany Moricz to the Cave of the Tayos in the mid-1960s.) Half-an-hour later there they stood accompanied by a third man, Luis Nivelo, patiently awaiting our arrival. We drove east a second time, the river Yanganitza racing us on our right.

Halfway back to Mendez Moricz stopped by a gorge and jumped out, peering at the raging river below. Our guides, following his instructions, led us steeply down by rope. Punin's son stayed behind to guard the jeep and guide us back.

The descent, with its projecting rock faces and foliage, was muddy

Mendez: Tayos prehistory in stone

and dangerous. We could hear the river roaring, like a hungry lion, waiting to gobble us up at the first slip. Suddenly, there was a scream. Above me, Virgilio Aviles, carrying heavy camera equipment, lost his footing and came hurtling down, yelling, with a pop-eyed expression that looked as if he were heading for Hell. Instinctively I grabbed a tree root, leaning across his path as he gathered momentum for a spectacular plunge into the torrent.

I grasped his arm and steered us both, with a twisting thud, into an earthen wall. There had been no time to consider whether the root would hold or whether we would both disappear into the gorge. Without a guardian angel holding the root we would have suffered injury or worse. Fortunately, Aviles, though shaken and stirred, was unhurt. The camera equipment also escaped damage.

Just above river level we came upon a Shuar trail (pica). Treading gingerly, we followed it up river until we arrived at a high overhanging cliff face over which cascaded a shower of crystal-clear water. At its base, to my astonishment, was a large, engraved standing stone. Unable to contain my excitement I joined Moricz to chalk in the ideographs whilst Aviles took photographs.

Nearby was a similar stone half-buried in the ground, its inscriptions more primitive. Leaving the group I started to dig around it with bare hands. Punin immediately cried out, waving his hands and shouting, 'Culebras! Culebras!'

'Snakes!' translated Moricz.

Amid laughter I leapt back as if bitten by the world's prize poisoner.

'Punin says he recently killed some snakes around here,' comforted Dr. Peña.

'When are we going home?' I smiled bravely.

An hour passed before we got back to the jeep, guided by repeated calls from Punin's son. Moricz suggested he and I be photographed, sticking a loaded revolver in my belt - to impress, he said, those back home. We set off back to Limon Indanza.

We were all tired from the climbing. Moricz, of course, was driving. A loud silence filled the jeep as it bounced across the potholes, everyone gathering thoughts about our adventure with the stones. To my mind, however, silence meant wasting time.

'Okay!' I blurted out, goodnaturedly, 'I have seen *two* inscribed stones and cannot afford the time to visit more. Dr. Peña, would you please ask Punin how many other stones he knows about?'

After calming the rush of answers from others, Punin replied, 'Stop the jeep here! We will take you to some stones at the top of this hill.' Others urged a visit to even bigger stones at the nearby community of Chiviaza. (Note: A decade later, I visited the latter stones, and rockfaces, also covered in pictographs.)

'Close by here,' said Moricz, showing amused interest in the discussion, 'there is an inscribed stone as big as a house. All around there are

Nivelo, Hall, Moricz, Peña & Punin 1975

hundreds of stones, spread over an area from Limon Indanza to the Tayos Caves. More are found in the Cordillera slopes to the north. They exist all the way from Venezuela to Peru. Had I known about them earlier, my work on the caves would have been easier.'

'All right!' I exclaimed, holding up my hands against the continuing onslaught of information. 'I am convinced! I am convinced!'

'They should be surveyed and mapped,' continued Moricz. 'Maybe your army engineers could make a start.'

As we bumped and joggled along the mountain path I felt pleased with my decision to join Moricz. One day in his company and an archaeological discovery related to the caves was already guaranteed. (Note: As it turned out on the expedition there was no time for mapping these stones. It is a serious project for some archaeologist.)

As well as a potential stones project we had copies of the 1969 Expedition photographs in Captain Maxwell's camera, including some of the follow-up September 1969 expedition, in which Gaston Fernández Borrero and General Antonio Morales Morales had participated without Moricz. Moricz said he had waited 52 days from July until September for this group to arrive with supplies but he left when they failed to come as planned. He had got back to Guayaquil, hungry and delirious, threatening to shoot those who had abandoned

The 'Hall Stone': So named by Moricz.

him, certain they had hoped he would come to grief so they could benefit from his discoveries. Dr. Peña calmed him down but it was the last time Moricz placed any confidence in the civilian or military authorities. Mutual mistrust set in, and it was in September of 1969 he publicised the results of the Moricz 1969 Expedition having in July registered his claim to the discovery.

The stones' adventure made me think… if only Captain Maxwell could see me now?

'When you get back to Scotland,' said Dr. Peña, 'nobody will believe you!'

'You're right, Dr. Peña! I can hardly believe it myself.'

It was the first of similar experiences I was to have in Ecuador over the years, one day confronting something amazing, the next day wondering whether the experience had been real or imagined, so removed from the normal world. It was vital to mentally register each event and be determined to defend its truth, however sceptics might react. Unfortunately it was also the domain of dreamers smitten by South America and who, adding to their fantasies with exaggerations, diminish the work of genuine investigators. However, as the saying goes, 'If you can't stand the heat, get out of the kitchen!'

In Limon Indanza we bid farewell to Punin and his companions. Before we moved on Moricz bought me a feathered Shuar headdress as a souvenir. Then, on our way out of the village, he pulled up by a two-storey house, beckoning Dr. Peña and myself to follow him inside.

Dr. Peña whispered, 'Moricz is visiting an old friend, Juan Perez, the first person ever to take him into the forest. He is very ill.'

Perez's wife Maria answered Moricz's quiet knock on the door. Never have I seen tears flow so suddenly. She embraced Moricz, who held her head to his shoulder, before leading us into a room where, lying on a bed, was the once 'tiger of the selva', Sergeant Perez, able to move only his head.

We stood back respectfully as Moricz approached, embracing the old man's arm weakly raised in silent welcome. Perez tried to bring up his other arm for a proper embrace but Moricz gently laid it back. His wife stood at my shoulder, smiling through tears. Moricz's visit clearly meant something special to them. Looking at me and nodding towards the bed, she whispered, 'Moricz! Moricz!'

I nodded in agreement, words being unnecessary. It was a moving moment. Months later, I was told Moricz had brought him the long journey by road to hospital in Guayaquil where, shortly afterwards, he died.

Because of his unique work and special nature Moricz was a solitary man. Seldom showing emotion despite the setbacks of the past, the loss of a loyal and trusted friend with whom he had shared so many experiences must have been painful for him.

By the time we were re-crossing the altiplano dusk was closing in and the temperature was dropping quickly. I asked Moricz to pull over for a moment. The misty mountain scenery had reminded me of the valley of Glencoe in Scotland. I had an impulse to stand inside the experience, perhaps unconsciously feeling a touch of home after being on another planet. Large billows of *neblina* were rushing down the mountainsides faster than a man could run. Moricz, ever with a sense of occasion, produced the bottle of Haig's whisky I had given him in Guayaquil. On that cold, *dreich* and desolate altiplano we drank a toast to 'SHE': Scotland, Hungary and Ecuador, small countries we imagined would play a key role in rediscovering *the missing page of prehistory*.

After our shared moment in the mist we set off again, visibility now diminished to a few metres. I watched Moricz's face as he negotiated the steep, sharp bends, clear blue eyes peering into the gloom, occasionally opening the side window to feel the cool air on his face. One lapse of concentration and we would disappear into the ravine far below. Dr. Peña and Virgilio had fallen asleep, their bodies bouncing from side to side with each jolt of the jeep. My mind was churning over too much to rest, and there was the possibility - I kidded myself - that I might need to grab the steering wheel should Moricz get tired. In those steady Hungarian eyes and resolute countenance I saw the qualities of intellect and resolve that had made him the stuff of legend to his friends. I finally dozed off to sleep confident he would get us home safely.

Arriving in Guayaquil around midnight Dr. Peña made sure I was booked back into the Hotel Atahualpa. Moricz and I looked at each other briefly before saying goodbye, who knows, for what might be the last time, conscious of the language barrier but intuitively communicating satisfaction with our shared adventure. We shook hands firmly, sensing a trusted friendship had been forged. Photographs of our trip to the stones, he assured me, would be sent on to Scotland.

Next day Dr. Peña drove me to the airport and we had a brief conversation, being alone with him for the first time. There was one key question I wanted to ask him.

'Dr. Peña! You are an educated man, experienced in European ways and attitudes; and your family is wellknown here, and has been close to Moricz for some years. Have you ever experienced moments of doubt about his historical claims?'

He sighed with understanding, leaning forward, hands clasped together, speaking thoughtfully.

'I remember when Moricz asked me to draft the legal documents for his discoveries. I could hardly believe what I was reading but decided to proceed. I remember once the pen fell from my hand, deeply questioning my involvement and the potential embarrassment for my family. I was young, just beginning my career. But the more I have listened to Moricz and come to know him, the more amazed I have become, and the more convinced that I am dealing with some kind of

Mendez: Returning from the Stones' site

genius. The metal library may be astounding - *but it is not his greatest discovery!*'

At that moment, as happens in all good adventure stories, Fate stepped in to cut our conversation with the announcement of the last call for my flight. We said a hurried goodbye. He and Moricz might never see me again, all the more admirable for the special efforts they had made. I recalled with gratitude that nearly all my conversations with Moricz had been translated by Dr. Peña who never once gave the impression of being molested by such an exhausting task.

On the flight back to the U.K. I contemplated how objectives might be adjusted to the developing situation. There could be no secret treasures associated with the expedition. Moricz, too, had made that clear. Looking out over the Andes I visualised a meeting of the minds of Darwin, Humboldt, Velikovsky and Moricz that might just harmonise the theories of evolution, creation, and what I considered to be the real missing link - *Catastrophism!*

'Señor Hall!' I recalled Moricz saying, 'It is either simple or impossible!'

Words of Immanuel Velikovsky also came back to me.

'Decide what part of the task is for you, then *dare!*'

§§§

With Dr. Peña and Moricz crossing the Altiplano 1975.

There were three principal objectives established for the expedition:

1. Locate the Tayos Cave in the Rio Coagnos Area.
2. Map as much of the cave system as possible.
3. Effect scientific investigations in and around the caves area.

I kept telling myself in disbelief that we only had
fifteen months left to get the expedition to Ecuador, a third of the time required.

First task was to form a joint military-scientific committee. Dr. David Saunders, Chairman of the Edinburgh University Expedition Council, was invited to Army HQ. The situation was explained to him and I blandly proposed he put together a multi-disciplinary team of the best available British and foreign scientists. His Council would have to assume responsibility for the recruitment and management of the scientific team. Specialist Army jungle units would supply logistic and organizational support. All scientists needed to be contacted before the start of the university vacation period in a few weeks time.

After I had outlined the plan Dr. Saunders inhaled deeply, before responding, 'This is not something we've done before!'

'Nor we!' I hastened, 'But if we can't win you over in the next thirty minutes the expedition will not take place.'

Dr. Saunders smiled. We sensed he wanted to help.

'I'll raise the matter with the Council and let you know within a few days,' he concluded, rising to leave.

Then, Captain Maxwell dropped a bombshell.

'I've been posted to the Middle-East. You will need a new military leader!'

My heart sank. His involvement had been crucial but the reality was that the expedition was in its infancy and his career was a priority. All we could do was search for a replacement – *fast*!

It was at this time the Army suggested I should take a leading role. Major Fisher would collaborate to integrate the civil and military elements. I was duly named Project Director and our resolve to succeed was reinstated.

With a multidisciplinary planning background the challenge did not worry me. It made sense to be involved with strategy and work to bridge the military and scientific efforts. For the Army and the scientists participation was routine, with clear ground rules. For me it was an extra task, costly, unpaid, and demanding at many levels. At one stage I had a fleeting image of the venture dissolving before my eyes. As it happened, my experiences in Ecuador, even the loss of Captain Maxwell, proved to be good training for heavier setbacks yet to come. It is worth recording the organizational events of the Tayos Expedition if only to encourage, or discourage, aspiring expeditionaries.

True to his promise we soon heard from Dr. Saunders. His Council had agreed to assist. Major Fisher and I glanced triumphantly at each other. It was all systems go!

Those were the halcyon days, with everything falling rapidly into place. Fisher called me in to meet Major Christopher Browne of the 1st Battalion the Royal Scots based in Edinburgh Castle. An amiable and gregarious communicator, Browne had recently returned from Borneo working with indigenous communities and was keenly interested in the Tayos expedition. Another problem solved!

Short of time and plagued with early uncertainties we again came under pressure from High Command to hand over the expedition to the Joint Forces Expedition Society run by Colonel John Blashford-Snell, specifically to a group which had been forced to abort its *White Lion* expedition to Ethiopia. I had served in the Royal Air Force in the late 1950s, but the surprises of the military decision process during the build-up to the Tayos expedition always shook me. The difference in character between military and civilian elements was a constant concern, needing all my interdisciplinary acumen. I was learning that military intransigence and self-interest has no hesitation in sacrificing non-military elements.

When Major Alan Kennedy of the Royal Ordnance Corps came on board we knew we had landed one of the British Army's most experienced ordnance specialists. The organizational web now came together quickly and, by September 1975, less than 6 months after the 1st Reconnaissance visit, we had recruited a rank and file contingent of 60 British soldiers, scientists and caving experts. In addition, the whole King Edward's 2nd Battalion of the Royal Gurka Regiment volunteered after recent guard duty at Buckingham Palace. With their renowned jungle skills and resemblance to the indigenous Shuar of Ecuador I saw them as a positive addition to the project but, disappointingly, their participation did not materialise.

First Expedition Conference

8

Edinburgh, 16th September 1975. A round-table conference of military officers and scientists, BBC Television team, and British Caledonian Airways - which planned to include the expedition in its planned inaugural flight to Ecuador - was convened in the offices of Consulting Engineers, Blyth and Blyth. This company, through partner and friend James F.G. Gunn, consistently offered encouragement, providing office facilities and a magnificent conference room for formal meetings.

Our strategy was to charter a Caledonian Boeing 727 and sell surplus seats at economic rates to the extra passengers. With a concession from the airline, sale of tickets, and by generally acquiring those things for which money was needed instead of the money itself, we aimed to reduce expedition costs to zero.

Highlights at the Edinburgh meeting made it the best day of the project so far. UNESCO in London indicated interest in contributing two scientists then on contract to the Andean Pact. Anthony Isaacs of the BBC declared that of all expeditions in which they had participated the Tayos expedition was by far the best organized. Each party present produced glowing reports of progress. All were congratulating themselves when I stood up to read out a letter from Neil A. Armstrong, then professor of Aerospace and Applied Mechanics at the University of Cincinnati, in which he accepted our invitation to be Honorary President of the expedition; and, time permitting, he hoped to actively participate. Since the planned July 1976 date would coincide with the United States Bicentennial, his participation was a spectacular coup.

Then came the downside!

§§§

The Ministry of Defence, due to a recent rabies scare in Britain and the classification of Ecuador by the World Health Organization as an endemic rabies area, cancelled all military expeditions involving caves.

Stunned by the news in the middle of things going so well it seemed the end of our world had come. However, as tends to happen after an initial shock, there followed a determination to strike back. First question? What was the scientific evidence behind the Army decision? Consulting our scientists and cavers produced the glimmer of a way out. Why not invite rabies specialists from the British Medical Research Council to join us? They would have scores of volunteers to take the new rabies vaccine then under study in Britain, already accepted in the U.S.A. and France. Bingo! In a short time, with a rabies-histoplasmosis team on board, we convinced the Army to make an exception. We were back on course, with an additional safety bonus for the expedition.

Next problem! Concern was growing over the delay in securing authorisation from Ecuador. To our horror Olaf Holm wrote in October 1975 asking why no official request for authorisation had been issued from the Embassy in Quito. Warning bells began to ring. On contacting the Embassy we were informed about a failed political coup in September and that we would have to begin again from scratch. Most of the officials with whom we had been dealing had either been replaced or jailed. Worse still, the Embassy did not want to see any more reconnaissance missions until further notice.

How would we ever get permission on time? Why had the Embassy not set the process in motion immediately after our visit in April, six months previously? Why had I not insisted on being kept better informed? I could blame nobody but myself!

Now, those with experience of Embassy-speak know that a message can sometimes mean the opposite of what is said or written. Then, I had no experience, but I soon learnt that under its superficial affability the main purpose of an Embassy is to administer, inform, and retain authority whilst discarding responsibility and accountability - and absolutely bury any suggestion of creativity! My background held these four elements were inseparable. It took a crisis and a desperate shortage of time to learn facts the hard way. The military and scientists in the expedition could do nothing. So, if *responsibility* and *accountability* (mine) were to be ignored it was time to substitute *creativity*. Rules would have to be bent, the Embassy now being viewed purely as a 'stopper.' If no stopper occurred a presumption of tacit approval would be assumed for any creative action taken by us. We had no other option and needed to get a 2nd Reconnaissance to Ecuador immediately. Without firm authorisation raising sponsorship would be impossible. Who would pay for the second reconnaissance? Who else?

Second
Reconnaissance

9

4th December, 1975. Major Fisher, Lieutenant Michael Stewart, Danish scientist Dr. Vagn Mejdahl (of Glozel Tablets fame), Dr. David Saunders, and myself flew at 24 hours notice from Swindon, England in a Hercules aircraft taking supplies for the troubles in Belize occasioned by sabre-rattling in Guatemala.

Landing at Gander Airport, Nova Scotia, in a snowstorm we were surprised to see a British Airways Concorde parked in the blizzard. After the storm abated we took off for Nassau in the Bahamas. Not long into our journey the pilot calmly announced the heating system was not functioning, nevertheless he had to climb to 30,000 feet to avoid a military exercise in the Atlantic.

A ventilation duct began blasting out cold air directly above me forcing me to suffer the journey with a sweater over my head and legs tucked inside a plastic bag stacked with newspapers. We staggered from the rear of the aircraft onto the tarmac at Nassau hardly able to catch our breath in the rush of hot air. Casually, we were informed the Hercules would be grounded until a new engine was flown out from Britain. Army and RAF personnel would be put up in a local 5-star hotel but, unfortunately, there was no such procedure for civilians.

We were two days in that millionaires' playground, waiting for the officers to leave for Belize on the Hercules. We civilians agreed the best option would be to meet up in Panama. Arrangements were made through a helpful off-duty British Airways official in Nassau and that night we stayed in Panama City, before reuniting with our military colleagues and flying on to Ecuador, having lost three days at no small cost.

In Quito we re-established contacts. The Embassy was surprised by our 'commando raid' but soon entered into the spirit of our determination. Once more we were back on course. In a country where there had been twenty-seven attempted coups in the same number of years how many more upheavals could be expected before the expedition took place. Clearly a 3-4 year organizational period would have had little meaning with the destination being Latin America. Attempted coups, sudden and frequent changes of government, earthquakes, and volcano eruptions, need to be matched by intelligent creativity. The expedition would clearly never take place if left to the mercy of military and political criteria. Equally, the scientists could never do it alone.

Our British officers persuaded the U.S. Landstat Aerial Survey unit attached to the Instituto Geográfica Militar to assist us by flying over the caves' area in Morona Santiago, providing invaluable photographs of the mountain and jungle terrain. American families, too, arranged a barbeque for us at the home of U.S. Mission Chief Colonel Dougherty, where we were warmly welcomed. Should anyone from those families be reading this book please accept on record our gratitude for the generosity and kindness shown to the 1976 British Tayos Mission. Creative American assistance and hospitality in those difficult days provided an invaluable boost to morale and strengthened my decision to have American representation on the expedition in the U.S.A. Bicentennial Year.

I can still hear Colonel Dougherty's words.

'Goddammit! Here we're thinkin' that old 'aircraft carrier' off the coast of Europe is sinkin' below the waves and you guys turn up with that old British pioneering spirit. Goddam!'

The scientists and I flew to meet Olaf Holm in Guayaquil, where I also hoped to re-unite with Moricz and Dr. Peña. It was satisfying to see Danish compatriots Holm and Vagn Mejdahl seated at the 'Raffles style' Hotel Humboldt, animatedly discussing archaeology and dating techniques.

Suddenly, Moricz and Dr. Peña, as if by magic, appeared in the Hotel bar. Both had a friendly relationship with Olaf who was about to leave. I introduced them to Dr. Vagn Mejdahl and after an hour or so it was clear Moricz and Mejdahl were getting on well. Later, I asked Mejdhal for his impressions of Moricz.

'He is an impressive man! I was particularly struck by his composure and confidence. He has all the airs of someone who really has made an important discovery. Otherwise there is no logical explanation why such an intelligent and knowledgeable man should dedicate so much energy to his work.'

On the flight back to Quito we worked on the draft letter to be sent by the Embassy to the Military Junta, seeking authorizations and collaboration with national institutions. On the 16th of December we flew out of Quito reasonably content with results but still harbouring concerns, mainly due to past experiences. We were to learn in the U.K. that the official request for authorization was despatched from the Embassy on the 24th of December 1975. Christmas Eve, of course, was the worst possible date to deliver correspondence. Just getting the request written had taken eight months. We had six months remaining.

Due to the political crisis in Belize we were stranded for a week. Frequently morning reveille was provided by RAF Harrier 'jump-jets' landing in clouds of dust around the camp buildings.

My visit to Belize was memorable for sharing a beer with Dr. Alan Jones, the legendary intelligence adviser to Winston Churchill during the Second World War and later professor at Aberdeen University. He happened to be 'on holiday' with his daughter and grandchildren. Showing great interest in our venture he offered me advice on how to trace Commander George M. Dyott, the vanished British explorer contracted by Lloyds Insurance Company to investigate the fate of Colonel Percy Fawcett. Dyott had apparently become something of a recluse, one more victim to the magic of Ecuador. We discover later that he was a principal player in the search for Atahualpa's treasure in the Llanganati Mountains, also how his story interrelates with that of Juan Moricz and other key protagonists.

We arrived in Scotland on Xmas Eve praying that the request for authorisation sent that same day would arrive safely. The cancellation date set for the expedition was the 31st of December. The departure date of 30th June 1976 remained unchanged.

As the days passed questions tortured my mind. Should I call the whole thing off? To the military mind cancellation meant no more than an aborted training exercise. I was more concerned about the scientists and cavers who normally fixed programmes two years in advance. Many had switched plans to join the Tayos expedition.

I felt like a pilot who could eject only if he let the plane crash with the passengers inside. My determination that the expedition would go was tempered with feelings of guilt. There seemed little choice but to sit tight whilst the wings fell off, the fuel ran out and the passengers stayed blissfully unaware of the danger. Perhaps my guardian angel would reach down and somehow get the fuselage to its destination. Inspirational words like Velikovsky's 'Dare!' and Moricz's 'Simple or impossible', now paled in the cold light of reality.

What helped to keep me going was remembering the unfair ridicule heaped on Velikovsky's ideas, and the dangers faced by Moricz for more than a decade. During the 2nd Reconnaissance I had visited Moricz's mining operations at Cumbaratza in the eastern Cordilleras, also the nearby convent at Zamora managed by his friend, Sister Laura Theresa. Experiences like these were counterpoints to concerns that might otherwise have proved too much to bear.

Zamora
Interlude

10

December 1975, Zamora, province of Morona-Santiago. I never thought I could be beaten at table-tennis by a nun but that was what Sister Laura Theresa had just done, my vision of her a beaming smile amid a greyish blur firing plastic bullets past my bright red ears.

We had arrived tired and sweaty after a day trekking around Moricz's mining operations with consultants Klochner of Germany, stunned by evidence of the valuable alluvial and hardrock minerals in the Cumbaratza concessions. Moricz had rented rooms at the convent until his offices and laboratories were ready at Nambija.

Felix Blasco, an Argentinian scholar and friend of Moricz who taught at the school, had been watching with undisguised amusement my demolition by Sister Theresa.

'Never mind!' he sympathised. 'Maybe that game is too tiring for you. Better we show you how to play darts.'

'Okay!' I replied defiantly. 'In Scotland, I often play darts.'

There were six of us. We formed two teams. Dr. Raimund Klein-Herring, head of the Klochner team, Sister Theresa (I wanted her on my side) and myself, against Moricz, Sr. Blasco and Dr. Peña. I was holding the darts for a practice throw when Sr. Blasco cried out, 'No, señor! Here, we play Cumbaratza darts.'

He cleared some chairs out of the way before standing about twice the normal distance from the dartboard for a practice throw.

The loud cheers that erupted when I occasionally hit the dartboard were only superseded by the uproarious laughter each time I missed, but I never enjoyed a game so much. I could not put my finger on it but there was something magical about the atmosphere in that convent games room. Maybe it was the camaradie, combined with the way the sisters alternated so easily joining in the fun and attending to their duties, always smiling.

A Shuar girl about ten years old and her four-year-old brother had been standing quietly outside, just within the light of the doorway. Sister Theresa, smiling recognition, invited them inside but they were too shy. They had come to see Moricz.

He walked over and crouched down beside them, asking the girl whether she had finished the job he had given her. She nodded, so he gave her some money. She smiled down at her little brother as Moricz asked him the same question. He nodded shyly, so Moricz paid him something too but, after close examination, he complained it was not enough. Asked to explain why, he gave his reason. Moricz, to my surprise, refused to pay him one sucre more. The child, near to tears, stamped his foot in frustration but Moricz was adamant and argued back; a true re-enactment of David and Goliath, though it appeared, this time, that Goliath had won the day.

I was fascinated by the tussle. Finally, by way of a back door, Moricz arranged another task for his little friend, this time exaggerating its value and overpaying him in advance. To this day I cannot make up my mind which of them really won the argument.

Curious, I questioned Moricz on his actions. He answered soberly.

'Soon, our so-called civilization will descend upon these children. It is better they grow up understanding that they do not get anything for nothing.'

As the evening passed, bathed in the good-natured banter. But always behind the laughter of Moricz one sensed his underlying commitment to a serious mission.

Relaxing on the verandah I spoke with Dr. Klein-Herring.

'I know you have been working with Moricz for three months now. What is your impression of him?'

He thought for a moment before replying.

'This might sound strange, but you need to be 'at least German' to understand someone like Moricz. He is from typically high, aristocratic, Hungarian military background.'

Then he said something revealing.

'That means it is almost impossible for him to tell a lie. You can see his background in everything he does. I understand he is involved in some controversial historical project but I know little about that. His workers know that if they steal something they might be forgiven once but, if they steal a second time, no amount of tears or pleading will get them back into his trust, even allowing for differences in cultural standards.

'An incident I experienced will highlight what I am trying to say. One evening about 7 p.m. - it was dark - Moricz came in from work, dusty, tired and ready for his meal. He found the sisters and the children distressed in the games room. A youth from Loja visiting the convent that day had stolen one of a set of darts.

'Moricz listened to the story then, without a word, climbed into his jeep for the two-hour journey to Loja. The mountain track is dangerous enough in daylight, as you know, but, in the dark, alone, anything could happen. He found the youth in a café, showing off his dart trophy to friends. Grabbing him by the collar Moricz took him to his father whom he then proceeded to chastise for bringing up his son so badly. Then he drove back to the convent, put the dart in its place, washed, changed his clothes, and sat down to his meal, around midnight.

'Moricz has become something of a patriarch in this area. He has done a lot for the convent and the Sisters think highly of him.'

At that moment Dr. Peña joined us.

'Yes!' added Dr. Peña. 'That sounds like Moricz. I could tell you similar stories. Some years ago we were in Cuenca. I had a lady friend with me. She and I were walking in the street, talking. Moricz, not wanting to be a gooseberry, was looking in a shop window.

'Suddenly, a thief grabbed my friend's handbag and ran off. I was not built for running. Moricz, seeing the commotion, set off after him. It seemed hopeless yet, a few minutes later, he re-appeared holding the poor thief in a state of collapse. Pushing him towards me Moricz said: 'Take care of him!' - and returned to the shop window. The thief was twenty-three years old, half Moricz's age. Observing that he was being pursued by such an elderly man he had made the mistake of turning on him.'

From the verandah we looked down the Zamora river valley on one of the most beautiful night skies I had ever seen, the seven stars of Ursa Major just above the horizon, shining so brilliantly I commented that I had never seen stars look so much like lanterns.

We moved inside for dinner and the evening again filled with fun, especially the infectious laughter of Sister Theresa. I noted the fencing of words between her and Moricz. They shared a closeness that seemed to override differences of opinion, perhaps because it came from a shared spiritual fountain.

Next morning we drove down the river valley to Cumbaratza. (All roads in this region are actually paved with gold-rich alluvial deposits extracted from the river.) Moricz had made arrangements with some Jivaro-Shuar for a canoe trip, keen to show me a river and land route to the Tayos caves.

Peering through dust billowing around the vehicle I spotted on our right a long strip of cleared ground.

Moricz, with a serious expression, called out, 'We are now passing Cumbaratza International Airport.'

Heavy rain began to fall and he voiced concern. Too much rain would quickly raise the level of the river and prevent us getting to the canoe. In the end we were forced to call off our little expedition. The problems did not end there.

'Landslides!' Moricz shouted, pointing up the valley slopes. ' We have to be careful on the way back.'

Flash floods and landslides were common and adjacent slopes were dotted with the clearings these had made. Mountain tracks were often blocked and Shuar settlers frequently washed away because they had cut the stabilising hillside forest to build their homes, or had built them where a slide had swept away a previous family. Removing the shallow-rooted trees binding the soil was a recipe for disaster. A family of five had disappeared the previous week, engulfed in an avalanche of mud and undergrowth now transformed into a silent, unmarked tomb.

Later, on the way back to Zamora, we stopped by a stationary pick-up carrying a Shuar teenager whose head was swollen like a football from snakebite. Her tearful father explained it had happened whilst she was collecting water from a hillside stream, the snake reacting when her long hair became entangled in a bush.

The poor man was despondent.

'If we are blocked by a landslide between here and Loja she will die,' he wailed.

I looked at her swollen, silent face. Standing in the rain I thought how helpless humans were at the mercy of this relentless, untamed environment. There was little we could do but drive on and help clear any landslide up ahead. At times like these, human hope expects the gods will be kind – but, sadly, it was not to be!

Right on cue we found the track blocked by a large slide we had just missed coming through earlier. A small bulldozer was busy pushing it into the gorge, the driver under constant threat of further falls from the weakened slopes above him.

Working alone in the downpour he was in no hurry, until we told him about the stricken girl. Then, whether with commendable courage or gross naivety he redoubled his efforts, swirling his machine around like a toy driven by a madman. Such action would normally win an award for gallantry. The rain continued to fall in sheets as he gambled between aggravating the slide and slipping over the edge in his little machine. From his poker face we could tell nothing but, amid the numbing fatalism of his daily existence, there had sprung a spark of determination to help the youngster beat the elements.

Sweating and exhausted, he managed to clear the path just before the pickup arrived and we, too, continued on our way. I often wondered if the girl survived and, if so, whether or not she would ever know how much was owed to her little angel of the Andes.

We stayed at the convent another night. Next day, after saying goodbye to the Sisters and Felix Blasco, we headed west through the mountains to Loja where Dr. Klein-Herring and I had to catch a bus for Guayaquil – the latter a twelve-hour, overnight trip I was not looking forward to!

In Loja, Moricz stopped to quickly visit to some friends. A Quechua girl in full traditional dress answered the door. Looking as learned as I could I enquired about the significance of her large, beautifully coloured, bead necklace.

'Oh, it's just the latest fashion!' she laughed, letting Moricz pass before closing the door.

Among the thronging melee at the bus station I again said goodbye to Moricz. As usual, he had taken care of everything, including the fares. When it came to money there were always three things I identified with him. First, he would never accept payment for anything whilst you were his guest. Second, he constantly refused to generate a single dollar from his sensational story, considering it unethical to do so. Third, and probably most important, he was one of those rare human beings who cannot be bought. Some had tried, sometimes when he most needed help, and failed.

The arrival of the bus in the square was the signal for the quiet, detached demeanour of the passengers to change to a frenzied embarkation of people, pigs, chickens and kitchen sinks. It was now dark, I was tired, my one thought amid the bedlam being to get a seat at the back of the bus, away from the chattering driver and blaring radio which was usually tuned to keep himself and everybody else awake.

I climbed into a back corner seat and settled in for a good nap. The bus moved off. Ten minutes of bliss passed before I almost hit the roof from a sudden blast of *mariachi* music coming from two speakers just above my head. *C'est la vie!*

I sat amid the bumps from countless potholes in the road, trying to offset the noise with dreamy thoughts of the last few days. I thought of Moricz, the laughter at the convent, the sorrow of the desperate father battling through the rain to save his daughter's life, of the bulldozer driver's brave efforts to clear the way on time. Then, despite the music, I fell asleep.

I awoke later to see lights focussed on a landslide blocking the road. Looking to the right I saw it was a long way down to the river shining in the gorge. One slip of the back wheel and all my efforts would be brought to a tragic end.

Of course, the real dangers were not so honest and obvious. The biggest obstacle lay closer to home, in a place I had assumed was the most dependable of all – *the British Foreign Office!*

Countdown

11

Expeditions are vulnerable to political climates, mainly in the country of destination. What seems good one day can change to a nightmare of delays, extra costs and re-organization. The Tayos expedition was no exception.

The British Ambassador and Ecuadorian authorities shared the view the expedition venture should be promoted by both governments. However, the Foreign Office in London decided it would be a private affair it would assist in 'administering.' When the going got rough it held to this view despite having placed itself at the head of the British contingent. The policy was control without responsibility or accountability.

The key requirement remained unresolved - authorisation from the Ecuadorian government. By the end of March 1976 there was still no sign of it. Worse! - no action from the Embassy!

Finally, on the 4th of April 1976, authorisation was granted. Securing this crucial piece of paper had taken 12 of the 15 months available, with publicity prohibited until authorisation was confirmed. Any sensible person would have walked away.

The following three months run-up to the June 30th deadline can only be described as traumatic. Authorisation had come too late - for the BBC team, British Caledonian Airways, the sponsorship campaign. I was left with a fuselage – no wings, no fuel, no film team, no transport, with commitments to expedition members and now with the Ecuadorian government commitment to honour.

The Ecuadorian Ambassador in London wrote, ominously

'As far as my government is concerned, a formal proposal for a major joint scientific and military project has been submitted by the British government through its Ambassador in Quito. This proposal has been duly considered and approved and

we now expect the British government to honour its commitment.'

Early in May 1976, the FCO and MOD held a meeting to consider the consequences of cancellation. They concluded that with the expedition being a private affair, responsibility would fall on private parties - in short, *me!* A withdrawal of military support would underline this strategy and the MOD and FCO would neatly avoid any embarrassment. As one Army officer commented: 'They have produced a negative-negative!'

Seven weeks before the deadline I was called to Army HQ in Edinburgh and politely confronted with an ultimatum. Unless the cost of equipment and air flights for the military contingent could be guaranteed by 15th May the MOD would be forced to withdraw military support.

Consultation with the scientists was not an option. They were being shielded until the last moment. Army officers who had staunchly defended my position throughout the rollercoaster of crisis periods - especially the ever loyal and effervescent Major Alan Fisher – were powerless to help. I was on my own!

I could not bring myself to criticise the government agencies, pre ferring as usual to blame myself. However, I was learning lessons at the speed of light.

Examining stark facts, I made a decision. The expedition would *go* – regardless of cost and consequences! Whatever happened would be my responsibility. In grand style I murmured what Marshall Fey reported to Napoleon at Waterloo: *'My left falters, my right is weak, my centre crumbles. I am attacking!'*

Having made the decision, anxiety was quickly subordinated. I toiled to get as much sponsorship as possible; found a film team willing to go at short notice and got the 70-strong British contingent to Canning House in London for a conference and briefing.

The departure date of 30th June coincided with an anniversary of the famous London debate on Charles Darwin's theory of evolution prompted by his *Beagle* voyage to the Galapagos Isles in the mid-19th Century. As a student of catastrophism, I wondered whether Darwin's ghost was behind all this frustration?

None of the expedition group happily milling around London's Heathrow Airport on that fateful morning of the 30th June had any idea of the drama being acted out in a nearby office where Major Fisher and I sat by an ominous-looking black telephone awaiting a call from the British Airways directorate - to confirm whether or not the Tayos Expedition could depart for Quito!

It was 10.30 a.m. Departure time was 11 a.m. Long minutes ticked by. I was surprised at how calm I felt, but I had already passed the pain barrier. The previous ten months had been like walking through a First World War battlefield: 'God!' said the generals, 'Is this what our men have to face?' Where were my halcyon days of September 1975, when everything was running so smoothly? What had made the difference? More particularly - who would stand by me now?

A flight delay of one hour was announced. A godsend! Was that a click I heard? It was like playing Russian roulette.

Then, Major Fisher, a source of encouragement throughout, stood up, smiling painfully, excusing himself with the words, 'Sorry, Stan! I can't stand the tension of waiting on that bloody phone ringing. I'll go off and mix for awhile.'

For me there was no escape. I waited an hour more. Click! The deadline passed. No further delay was announced. Still no telephone call! Maybe everyone had gone home? My mind's eye concentrated on a small white dot at the end of a long dark tunnel. Another click! Mentally composed, possibly from latent anger, I was prepared for the worst.

Suddenly, the telephone screamed. *Drrrrring! Drrrrring! Drrrrring!* I consciously let it ring three times.

'Yes!' a voice said. 'The expedition can go!'

I thanked the caller, replaced the telephone carefully, then, waiting a moment to let the message sink in, set off to join Bunny Fisher standing at the bar. My stoney expression gave nothing away. I placed an order for two beers. He screamed softly through clenched teeth, 'Well?'

I screamed back softly, 'Let's have our beer before we tell them to get on the plane. Cheers!' Both of us were emotionally drained, maybe a little hysterical. Perhaps no two beers ever tasted better.

The announcement came to board the plane. At the embarkation point we wished each of the exhuberant expeditionaries goodluck as they were roll-called through to the waiting area by none less than Lieutenant the Lord David Balgonie. They took off at 1.00 p.m., two hours behind schedule.

Bunny and I watched the huge Jumbo jet lift them off on their great adventure. I was smiling inwardly at the irony of being the only one left behind. It mattered little now whether or not I had made the right decisions. There was no going back! *'The woods were lovely dark and deep, but I had promises to keep.'*

On the 7th July I was summoned to an urgent meeting with officials of the Foreign Office. A telex message from the Ecuadorian government had placed them in a state of quiet desperation. It stated two last-minute conditions: *a) that the expedition was to be a joint government operation with costs to be shared; and b) that the Ecuadorian government would not sign any agreement with a private party, only with Her Britannic Majesty's Government.*

The FCO insisted I fly immediately to Ecuador and assist the Embassy persuade the Ecuadorian government to change these conditions. I was back in the eye of the hurricane!

Tunnels below the Andes

12

On arrival in Quito the expedition was accelerated through Customs and Excise as previously arranged, lessons having been learnt from problems faced by the British-Brazilian Survey Expedition of 1969.

The sudden appearance of a large expedition in Ecuador produced sensational reports in the national media. The British contingent joined up with its Ecuadorian counterpart and, after a day of official receptions, a detailed logistics programme was finalised for the assault on the caves.

6.30 a.m., 2nd July, 1976. Three of the eight-man caving team flew south in a Twin Otter passing the majestic volcanoes of Cotopaxi, Ruminahui, Condorazo and Tungurahua, the peaks of which reach

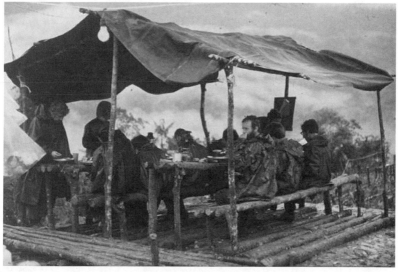

Tayos dining facility

some 2000 metres further out into space than Mount Everest.

During the planning stage earth tectonics in Ecuador had been considered a possible danger. In April 1975 we heard that an eruption of Cotopaxi - or *Cutupacshi*, in Quechua meaning 'Great Father' - was imminent. The volcanoes of Ecuador are aligned north-south on geological fault lines stretching from the San Andreas region of California. When tremors occur they give the impression of a country on the move. I had visions of the expedition trapped in the caves when an earthquake struck. (Cotopaxi did not erupt but, on the 12th of August 1976, when the expedition was at Mariscal Sucre Airport in Quito awaiting the flight back to Britain - mount Sangay *did*! There is a saying in Ecuador that when Pichincha coughs, Cotopaxi will sneeze and Tunguragua will vomit, the lava flutes being connected underground. Sangay, too, might be an extension of this group.)

The original plan of routing the expedition through Cuenca and Limon Indanza was abandoned. On the 2nd of July the main body travelled south by road, past the city of Baños – a former spa for the Quitenian Shyri-Inca aristocracy – to the military base at Shell Mera-Puyo in the eastern province of Pastaza. There followed four days of organizing 23 trips flying equipment and personnel further south to the Santiago base. Four days of apparent chaos, quiet efficiency - and *rain*!

Santiago: Tayos 1976 helipad

At Santiago an advance party had powered its way up the River Santiago in Gemini rubber boats to its confluence with the river Coangos; but rising water levels, strong currents and submerged tree trunks proved this method of transport too dangerous for the main group. On the morning of the 6th of July a Puma helicopter roared over the southern horn of the Cordillera de Cutucu (Cutucu offers good potential for archaeological investigation). That day, 76 personnel and their equipment were flown into the Tayos cave location.

For two weeks the Ecuadorian Special Forces had been denuding an area of forest for the scientific and military camps, plus a heliport. Felled timbers were used for pathways, bases for kitchens, latrines, platforms for radio equipment, and similar purposes.

Amid the growing buzz of activity Dr. David Judson, head of the caving team, accompanied by Arthur Champion – then joint holder of the world depth record in caves - quietly collected their gear and wound their way down a narrow, muddy track to the yawning mouth of the legendary Tayos cave situated 810 metres above sea level.

The atmosphere at the entrance was silent and foreboding, almost primeval. Shafts of sunlight piercing through the foliage illuminated a shower of water cascading from the overhanging cliff-face. Cautiously, they lowered themselves into the abyss. From its bowels came the

Tayos underworld: Coangos 1976

clicking sounds of hundreds of oilbirds - the so-called Tayos - spiritual guardians of the Andean caves, alleged by Moricz to be the *Turul*, sacred royal birds of the Seven Hordas of the Scytho-Magyar nations.

The depth of the cave was difficult to judge. A wire ladder touched bottom at 165 feet. Also dropped was a 200-foot nylon rope, procured by Neil Armstrong and picked up by the cavers passing through Miami. They descended slowly, gardening the edges. Near the bottom pink eyes stared unblinkingly from the darkness. The eyes moved. A large, rat-like creature shuffled off into some fallen rocks.

Venturing inside they entered a rifted gallery with ledges and fissures through which streamed shafts of pale green sunlight. Climbing over a pile of rocks they came across a rectangular passageway and entrance to a second passageway. More pale light filtered in from the far right. They moved towards this, scrambling over mounds of bird and bat *guano* containing pips and kernels dropped by winged cave dwellers returning from nocturnal excursions. Over the mounds scampered rats, tarantulas and scorpions, startled by these two-legged, strange-smelling intruders.

Frightened bats flapped around in the pale light coming from a roof entrance 200 feet above them, festooned with *liana* (vines) and other greenery. Sun-kissed water dripped down to nourish the unique plant life sprouting from the fertile cave floor.

Sector of the Tayos campsite

The massive scale of the cave system was confirmed. Rock strata generally inclined towards the southwest, varying in thickness according to whether the layers were of clay, sedimentary limestone, or harder greenish andesite. The two cavers had already seen enough to be sure of exciting their companions tramping around above them.

During their absence the campsite was being erected to get everything and everyone under cover before darkness. Kitchens, stores, longdrop latrines and pathways were in an urgency of construction, together with a pathway leading down to a stone dam built for laundry and bathing purposes.

Then came a major setback! Bad weather postponed helicopter flights for five days. After three days food ran out. It became necessary to buy from local Shuar families, already suspicious of the intrusion into their territory. A pig was purchased and voraciously consumed despite pleas for caution from the medical team.

Whilst awaiting a favourable break in the weather a gantry platform was constructed over the cave mouth and a petrol-powered generator and winch installed. Timber logs, some weighing more than 200 kilograms, had to be felled, dragged and manipulated into place. The cliff was drilled to fix metal pins and heavy cable was threaded through the winch and pulleys into the shaft. The end result was a slow, but safe,

Typical campsite weather

chairlift facility operating at 14 feet per minute, taking about 15 minutes to reach the cave floor. Over four weeks more than 200 vertical sorties were made, with a total of 45,000 feet of cable passing through the winch - twice the altitude of Mount Sangay!

Meanwhile, a curious event occurred. Vestiges of a stone wall were unearthed at the campsite. An enthusiastic Ecuadorian archaeologist –

Monster Tayos stalactite

coincidentally a vociferous critic of Moricz - had British soldiers toiling on it for hours in the rain. Amidst the euphoria a local Shuar walked out of the forest, curious to see what was happening. The archaeologist pounced, explaining that the wall had most likely been built by his forefathers. The Shuar, after listening patiently to the speech, responded with a wry smile, 'That wall was built by Juan Moricz in 1969 to support his flagpole.' He continued on his way no doubt satisfied he had little to learn from these intruders. The comments of the soldiers are not recorded.

With the campsite complete the machinery of expedition swung into action. Scientists and military fanned out in every direction, inside the caves and over a large area of surrounding jungle, including the Cordillera ridges whenever a heliocpter was available.

It was the rainy season, which happened, perhaps unfortunately, to coincide with the university vacation period in Europe when most scientists are available. The weather grew steadily worse. Mud was everywhere, including the tunnel entrances of the tents. The adverse climate and lack of a dry, warm area to socialise in the evenings dimin-

Hauling up equipment

ished the incentive each morning to set off into the caves and forest. But the work had to be done, and an excellent kitchen helped to keep spirits up.

Added to the trying conditions was the increasing dependency on the cavers even though, of all those on the expedition, they were among the most physically and mentally prepared. Cavers at this level, like their mountaineering cousins, are focussed, dedicated individuals, used to operating alongside dependable colleagues. Here they faced a unique challenge. As well as working on a detailed survey of 5 kilometres of the cave system, they were responsible for the safe conduct of expedition members and a stream of visiting V.I.Ps, television crews and military personnel. They spent three days underground with film crews, running cables, hauling lighting equipment – including large 2nd World War searchlights and batteries brought by the Army - dragging everything over piles of rocks, bird guano, and waterfalls. Given they had never had this level of responsibility before their contribution to the Tayos expedition can only be described as immense. In particular, the contribution of Dr. John Frankland, cave-rescue specialist, behavioural expert and medical practicioner, was incalculable, ably assisted by British Nurse of the Year, Claire Trevor. Every member of the Tayos expedition stretched their limits of physical and professional endurance, yet none would have missed it for the world!

Discovery in the Caves

13

20th July 1976, 11.25 a.m., seven years to the day since Neil Armstrong's left foot made that 'first small step for man' on the Moon. Jim Campbell, a young scientist from the University of Glasgow, was kneeling on a pile of guano molesting a scuttling beetle with a twig when he scraped across a shard of pottery. By rare good fortune archaeologist Padre Pedro Porras and his team from the Universidad Católica, also the expedition film team, were down in the caves that day. Responding to excited calls echoing around the chambers they were quickly on the scene.

Not by human hand

Tayos 'Amphitheatre' (above)
Padre Pedro Porras G.: Tomb Discovery (right)

Padre Porras, examining the shard, noticed a pile of rocks adjacent to the cave wall of a different material from the wall face. Excitedly he called for more light. Soon, busy hands were removing the rocks and, to everyone's delight, they uncovered an ancient burial chamber. The entrance was cleared enough for a student to squeeze through and report. Army caver Sergeant Pete Holden also took a turn.

Inside the tomb was an extremely fragile, decomposed cadaver, in

a seated position, surrounded by an array of pottery shards and shell ornaments, about 70 pieces in all. Later, they were dated to c. 1500 BC. The cadaver, as if surprised by the sudden intrusion after so many lonely centuries, crumbled to dust when touched. It must have been someone of rank to be so ceremoniously interred in such a difficult and unique location. It was too much to expect the cadaver might have been the legendary *Nunkui*, who inhabited these sacred caves amid great luxury at the beginning of Shuar time. It was an important

Tayos Tomb Cave 1976. Tomb located top of right bank

discovery - and Fate had the film team and archaeologists on hand to record it live!

In classic expedition mode some present at the discovery were struck down by a mysterious illness. Body temperatures soared to 106 F° and the medical team, baffled and concerned, had neither antidote nor diagnosis to combat it. After spending a week covered with cool, damp blankets on bare skin, all of them, fortunately, recovered. An obvious parallel was drawn with the Curse of Tutankhamun that allegedly struck 27 members of the Caernarvon - Carter team within 12 years of opening the tomb in November 1922. In both instances, the cause was probably 'histoplasmosis', a fungal disease of the lungs caused by contaminated spores from bat, bird and animal droppings in dry conditions, also from old books - *and decomposing cadavers!*

The medical team had been busy since the expedition arrived. Gastroenteritis -locally called *Atahualpa's Revenge* - struck down many in the expedition, and everyone was plagued by insect bites that caused supurating sores, the female contingent being particularly distressed by this.

Shuar families, overcoming their distrust – especially after watching soldiers chasing butterflies – began visiting the camp for medical treatment, some travelling up to 50 kilometres. Another common, some-

British Caving and Medical Teams

times fatal, illness was recognizable by symptoms similar to tubercolosis, caused by eating raw crayfish. One young life was saved due to quick diagnosis by an Ecuadorian medic and follow-up action by the expedition medical team.

A 'barefoot doctor' programme implemented by British Medical Council associate Dr. Karl Nicholson was also successful. Less than 15% of people in developing countries receive basic medical treatment. The Tayos expedition offered an opportunity to test equipment sufficiently lightweight to be carried by one person, trained in a few hours. Expedition members volunteered to take the new rabies vaccine that two years later would contribute to it being declared medically safe for use in the United Kingdom.

Of 400 plant species collected by the botanists about 20% were entirely new to science. Various specimens were dispatched globally to more than thirty specialist centres. 36 species of termite were found, twice the number previously discovered in Ecuador. Other achievements included 7 new species of bat and 400 species of butterfly. Four archaeological sites - excluding the Tayos Cave tomb - were discovered in and around the indigenous communities.

This level of attainment was reflected throughout all fields of the scientific work. As an archaeological and scientific project in hostile

Ecuadorian Special Forces at the Cave site

territory, and as an exercise in collaboration between military, scientists, and the indigenous population, the expedition could hardly have been more successful. Though sparsely publicised because of the *Gold of the Gods* controversy and delay with authorisation the Tayos expedition is today considered one of the most successful multi-disciplinary scientific enterprises ever undertaken, its aggregated value incalculable.

For those who believed the expedition was clandestinely searching for gold treasures, lost civilizations, extraterrestrial life, oil storage reservoirs or atom bomb shelters, it proved disappointing. Everyone enjoys a lost civilization and treasure story but, if it cannot be made a reality, imagination and fantasy soon fill the vacuum.

The expedition also took on another dimension. Few of the scientists and soldiers beavering away in their microcosmic world of jungle

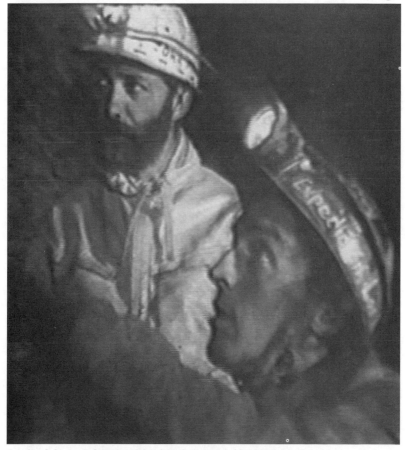

Medical doctor John Frankland with Pete Holden at tomb discovery

sounds and echoing caverns would imagine they were on a spaceship spinning at 1000 miles per hour, speeding around the Sun at 65,000 miles per hour and streaking out into space at 900,000 miles per hour. However, to one man about to join them on their fantastic journeys, such mind, time and space parameters were nothing new.

Tayos tomb artifacts now in the Universidad Catolica de Quito

Neil Armstrong: A Second Small Step

14

Neil Armstrong sent a message saying he would arrive in Quito on the 1st of August and asking for advice on how to get to the caves. 1976 was the USA Bicentennial, when demands on national heroes could be expected. For that reason alone I had always felt he would be unable to join us in Ecuador. To complicate matters the expedition radioed me in Quito advising that, due to bad weather, a shuttle programme to airlift everyone from the caves to the Santiago base by 27th July was underway. Armstrong stood to miss out on a cave visit! However, when I radioed back his impending arrival things began to buzz and a programme was feverishly resolved. The cavers, as usual, came to the

Riverboat crews

rescue.

A welcoming task unit was set up. There were technical inconveniences but these had technical solutions. The film-crew would not be available, having moved out. Critically, the cave winch would be gone, together with the power generator, lighting and telecommunications equipment. The only way down would be by a 6-inch wire ladder free-hanging 165 feet in space. Lighting would be provided using Davy headlamps and torches, aided by occasional shafts of light piercing the gloom.

The weather had truly taken its toll. Many were tired, some were ill,

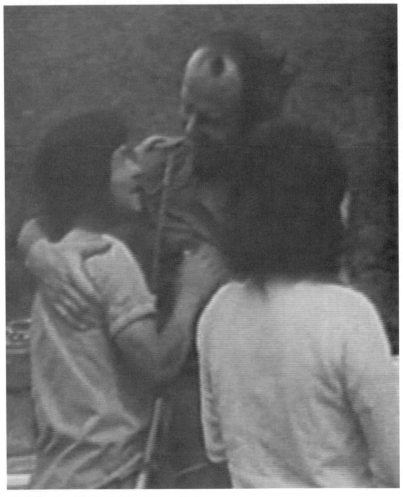

Goodbye from biologist Dr. Dieter Pedersen

and everyone needed rest. Would the volunteer cavers find the energy for a few more days of toil and heavy responsibility? What would happen if America's favourite son had an accident, fell down a shaft, or was bitten by a poisonous beastie? Would war come?

In Quito I set about organizing his accommodation. Being the Conference season the larger hotels were fully booked. I reserved rooms in the Santa Maria, a modest family-run hotel with a glorious view up the Avenida Mariana de Jesus to the volcano Guagua Pichincha. Dr. Vagn Mcjdahl was arriving on the same plane and could also stay there. (I had sent for Mejdahl the day the tomb was discovered.) Both would find each other stimulating company and I could more conveniently update them on progress to-date.

This neat little plan for cosy chats was quickly torpedoed when British, American and Ecuadorian officials miraculously came up with

Botanist Dr. Brindsley Burbridge and Dr. George d'Argente

the best suite in the five-star Hotel Colon International. Preparations to receive Armstrong moved into top gear, the Ecuadorians in particular wanted to make the most of his visit.

With the situation swirling out of my hands I was introduced at the English Pub to a tall, quiet Scotsman named Alan Miller, a retired forestry consultant domiciled in Ecuador for many years, curiously the proud owner of the only Rolls Royce in the country - a 1937, recently refurbished, cream coloured, open-fronted beauty. Having little faith in the transport arrangements for Armstrong going smoothly at the airport I persuaded Alan to postpone his weekend arrangements and park himself outside the VIP lounge, without any guarantee he would be needed. Up for the challenge he was delighted to accept, although

Entomologist Dr. Mark Collins

I sidestepped his offer to appear in Scottish kilt and bagpipes, arguing it might frighten Armstrong back onto the plane.

Next morning I had a local tailor make me a suit in a record time of four hours and, at the appointed hour, observed Alan parking as discreetly as a classic Rolls Royce would allow to await my prearranged signal to stay or go home. News of Armstrong's arrival had leaked and half the population of Quito was at the airport. Commotion rippled through the crowd as the colourful Boeing 727 of Aerolinea Ecuatoriana floated majestically down from a bright, cloudy sky, proudly roaring out its arrival.

As I listened to the engines whining down a strange stillness came over me, like I was suspended somewhere between past and future; appropriate, I thought, to the surreal circumstances in which I found myself twixt moonlandings and Tayos caves.

A stir in the crowd became a voluble crescendo as, suddenly, flanked by two beaming airhostesses, there he was, smiling and waving to the cheering multitude. I had not believed we would actually see him in

Zoologist Dr. Tjitte de Vries

Ecuador, just as I began to accept after my lonely experience at Heathrow that I was destined never to see the Tayos caves. Now, Fate was conspiring to get me there with the first man on the Moon. My guardian angel had not deserted me yet!

Somewhere in the flurry of introductions, with my no-time-for-a-haircut thatch blowing in the wind, my four-hours-to-make-suit fitting tolerably, the cheering crowd as a backdrop, Captain Peter Wills introduced us. We shook hands. Yes, he was *real!* Hearing my name, hardly audible in the noise, he hesitated a moment and nodded before being whisked off to the VIP salon, packed with army, embassy and airport officials and media crews. Eager laughing faces were soon grotesquely pressed against closed glass doors.

A respectful silence descended for him to say a few words, following which a soon-to-be shamefaced reporter asked how he was coping with the altitude. Hoots of laughter anticipated his answer.

'I'm quite used to altitude!' he smiled.

The amusing incident broke the ice and, after finishing his short speech, in which he mentioned a previous visit to Ecuador after the

Botanist Dr. George d'Argente with ornithologist Dr.Barbara Snow

Moon landing, he opened the glass doors to let some children in for autographs. There was a ripple of panic in the room that heralded an overwhelming stampede, but the good-natured crowd respected his thoughtful gesture of providing a few 'moonstruck' children with a memorable moment in their lives.

What happened next was no surprise to me. Captain Wills discreetly asked if I knew anything about the transport arrangements. Naturally, everyone thought that particular responsibility lay with some other party. My guardian angel gracefully swung my arm to signal Alan, who glided the vintage Rolls Royce over to the main entrance, his impressive nose suitably tilted for the occasion. The surprise appearance of the magnificent duo distracted the crowd long enough for officials to usher their illustrious guest into the front seat and myself into the back, presumably congratulating themselves on their transport department having made such a spectacular arrangement.

Later, standing beside him in the elevator of the Hotel Colon International, I felt uneasy. The scientific and logistic credibility of the expedition was sound. It had been an outstanding success, even though for a month the media had enjoyed a field day with the controversy. Peo-

Musical welcome from Tayos shaman 'Geronimo'

ple will always believe what they prefer to believe. What would happen now that the first man on the Moon had arrived?

From the welcome he received I realised he was no longer an ordinary American citizen. The world had adopted him, as it had done with Yuri Gargarin. He had been to the Moon, but not just for America. Here was one of the most tried, tested and trusted human beings in history, one of an elite breed pioneering Mankind into the future.

I had been too busy to worry about his visit but there in the elevator responsibility began to weigh heavily, less for any concern about his welfare than for his right to privacy.

I had done some research on the pre-1976 astronauts, almost all of them - with the notable exception of Armstrong - freemasons and sons of freemasons. It had been interesting to discover how many had

Ecuadorian archaeologist Presley Norton

found it difficult to come to terms with life on Earth after their experiences in space.

My concerns diminished when, after eyeing the well-stocked bar in the suite, he poured a stiff whisky and sat back on the bed to relax. His attitude was simple and direct, not affected by controversy provided expedition objectives were clear, reports were factual and any attempt to reflect his personal opinions was avoided. I understood his fears about exploitation and sensationalism; on the other hand, as his escape from the experimental 'flying bedstead' and captaincy of the 1967 Gemini 8 had demonstrated, he was not one to expect a smooth passage.

Thanks to a magnificent team the expedition was free of serious hiccups. I simply had to stay cool, honour his trust and take things one at a time. He was his own best defence, knowing the pursuit of knowledge never bows to controversy. I felt more confident after that first meeting, still wary of gremlins that might appear, but content! Both of us were descended from the Armstrong clan of Langholm in Scotland (I on my mother's side). Curiously, we also shared the rare blood group Rh Negative O. The O Positive Blood Group covers 95% of the indigenous communities of North and South America. Interestingly, some Japanese scientists consider the O Group to be the oldest in the world. We agreed to donate blood to each other in any emergency and the medical team was duly informed.

Alan Miller picked me up at the Hotel Santa Maria and we collected Neil for the planned reception at Captain Wills' residence. A starlit sky hung over Quito. I felt relaxed for the first time in months. It began to dawn on me I had produced a winner.

Apart from Juan Moricz there was another key personality at that very moment closely monitoring the expedition, although it would be 16 years before a meeting with him would produce a surprising development, details of which will be disclosed in a later chapter.

On that beautiful August night I told myself: 'Stan! Your guardian angel is steering your ship well!' Gazing up at the bright equatorial Moon, Armstrong might well have experienced flashbacks from his 1969 Apollo XI mission. I imagined telling a story in some fisherman's hough in Scotland, something like: *'Once upon a time I was at the centre of the world with the first man on the Moon in a Rolls Royce. We flew over the Andes into the Amazon jungle and descended into a vast subterranean world where the lost history of mankind is inscribed in the Gold Library of Atlantis.'*

'Och aye!' I could hear the reply. 'That's the best joke since the one aboot the Loch Ness Monster runnin' up and doon Ben Nevis tae slim for the tourist season?'

At the reception discussion on the expedition was animated since it continued to be reported daily in the media. Neil, possibly unaware of the mystique surrounding his visit, was enjoying himself. Possibly some 'men in black' were present but a few glasses of whisky soon made them invisible. I almost felt guilty that I was not a man of mystery since some, no doubt, were suspicious why such an ordinary person was doing such extraordinary things. In fact, my objectives were far beyond their world of Ian Fleming, Maxwell Knight, Puharich, Schaller or Crowley.

When I returned to the Hotel Santa Maria a message was waiting

Caving expert Arhur Champion

from Dr. Julio Goyen Aguado, an Argentinian caving specialist and friend of Moricz. He had booked into the hotel. We met up next morning, when he showed me a film of a 1968 caves expedition with Moricz made by anthropologist Paul R. Cheesman of Brigham Young University, Utah. (The Mormon Church maintained a keen interest in Moricz's claims about a metal library, especially after his meeting with President Spencer W. Kimball in Salt Lake City in the mid-1970s.) The doctor and I experienced difficulty with language but we managed. Apparently, he had been in contact with the Ecuadorian Ministry of Foreign Relations with the object of joining the expedition. Dr. Peña had also telephoned to ask me, on Moricz's behalf, if I could receive and assist him.

'In 1968, we did not go to the Tayos Cave on the Rio Coangos,' commented Dr. Goyen. 'Moricz took us further east to caves on the Yaupi and Nangaritza rivers. Inside one Yaupi cave was a rectangular panel with inscriptions in Phoenician characters.'

Moricz had confided this story to me in Guayaquil so it was satisfy-

Geo-scientist Dr. G. Jeffries

ing to have it confirmed. I enjoyed the film, feeling free from the flurry of expedition engagements. It was good to see Moricz standing there on a raft, hurtling through the rapids of the Nangaritza, looking every bit the intrepid explorer, crowned with an old straw hat and smoking - surprisingly - a long-stemmed pipe. There, too, was his old friend Perez, sadly no longer with us.

In the comfort of the hotel room, with my senses responding to the changing scenes of the film, I thought more profoundly about Moricz and his unique investigations. I had never met anyone who cared so much about the enigmas and errors of history, or who dedicated so much energy to fieldwork in such difficult circumstances. Most investigators were academics accustomed to working in the more comfortable regions of the globe, financed by personal or institutional patrons. Moricz was doing it the hard way, armed with a brilliant mind and wide knowledge of ancient languages and history, steadfastly refusing any offers of financial support with conditions attached.

Aside from any dramatic discoveries here was a great human adventure story, one man against the world. His visible treasures were his ideas and theories about the American origins of Humanity and his insistence that the 'Taltosok Barlangue', Magyar for 'Language of the Taltos (Gods)', was the mother language of civilization – also the language of the metal library!

Dr. Goyen, of Basque origin, believed the work of Moricz was of critical importance for Basques.

Curiously, an english-speaking Cuban professor, in the cafeteria for breakfast, apologised for overhearing our conversation and suggested he might join us as translator since we were obviously having communication problems. We happily invited him to our table.

Dr. Goyen then surprised me by saying, 'Señor Hall, I have known Moricz for many years but he told me yesterday that if ever he had ever found someone to whom he would reveal the metal library it was Stanley Hall. I want you to know I am prepared to give up everything to help you with your work.'

By the time we finished the Cuban professor had also volunteered his collaboration, but I was truly too preoccupied with expedition matters to take such offers on board.

Into the Tayos Caves

15

1.30 p.m., Sunday 2nd of August, 1976, Quito Airport. I joined Neil, Vagn Mejdahl, Goyen, various VIPs, some Ecuadorian generals and military representatives from the British and American embassies, for the flight south via Shell Mera. From there we flew to Santiago where

Armstrong, Hall & Col. Alan Kennedy

the base battalion was paraded to welcome us in the blazing sun.

After the formalities we set off on the twenty-minute helicopter flight to the Tayos Cave campsite. Everything was happening so fast, though perhaps from the cavers' point of view not fast enough. The suspended platform that had witnessed four weeks of archaeological and scientific activity was still in place.

An entourage of civil and military personnel, including local Shuar elders who had arranged a speech of welcome, wound slowly down

Capt.Luis Hernandez (1995 'Hero of Tiwintza'), with Armstrong

the now well-worn pathway to the cave mouth. With the verbal pre-
liminaries over, a senior Ecuadorian general was good-naturedly held
back from approaching the cave. Armstrong calmly moved forward.
Once safely harnessed he stepped unhesitatingly onto the swinging wire
ladder and began to descend. A mere nine months had passed since he

Neil Armstrong: Second small step

had been named Honorary President of the expedition. Now he was a participant!

Everyone watched him make yet another 'small step for Man'… and, who knows, perhaps also for Mankind! Such steps only occur on sacred ground, certainly sacred at that moment to the silent, watching Shuar. The symbolic similarity with his ladder descent onto the Moon was self-evident.

As Armstrong reached the cave floor Arthur Champion grabbed my arm, peering into my pale face – akin to that of a condemned prisoner - with a sympathetic smile.

'How much caving have you done?' he whispered, tightening my harness.

'None!' I replied defiantly, with the same self-hypnosis I had used as a youngster jumping off the Olympic diving board at Blackpool rather than withdraw when the attendant blew his whistle.

'Never mind, we'll look after you. Take it easy and you'll be fine!'

Stepping gingerly onto the ladder I began the long, lonely descent. Water was dripping from the overhanging cliff. I could hear the clicking of the oilbirds.

Seldom can a ladder have been so cursed, as it swayed beneath and away from me with every inexperienced step. The slowly receding mouth of the cave, the bobbing headlamps below, the calls of encouragement, the mixture of fear and excitement in the dark, primeval interior, culminated in an exhilarating sensation. What was I complain-

Armstrong with ace army caver Pete Holden

ing about? Did I not relish risk and daring? Well, here it was! Repeatedly I asked myself: 'Am I really doing this?' With each step I counted a milestone since the decision to initiate the expedition, with the disc of daylight above reminding me of the 'light in the tunnel' at Heathrow airport a month earlier.

Drs. Van Mejdahl and Goyen followed me down. Two cavers set off with Neil to where the cave system bottomed out. The rest of us headed for the tomb cave found a week earlier, passing a number of features recognisable from Von Daniken's book. The tomb artifacts had already been removed by Padre Porras and his team. At the moment of the filmed discovery he had announced gleefully in his limited english, 'Twenty-five years in archaeology and never I see something like this!'

I calculated that at the June equinox some six weeks earlier the sun's rays streaming through the roof of this cave would have shone directly onto the tomb. (Later, Moricz was to ask me if anyone had seen the skeleton of a jaguar which, shortly before his 1969 expedition, had fallen 200-feet trying to claw down oilbirds as they emerged from the cave.)

On the way back Goyen and I took a wrong turning and were soon lost. My carbide headlamp fizzled out and Goyen's flickered ominously. Fortunately we heard voices and headed towards them.

Armstrong with Major Chris Browne

Nearing the cave exit I passed Neil wearily reclining his legs against a rock to let water run out of his caving suit.

'Resting?' I enquired.

'Draining!' he smiled.

Whilst the cavers organized us for the ascent to the platform we shared some food. Recalling the descent, I was not looking forward to the climb back up. Neil went first. After a few minutes, reluctantly, I followed.

With a rope under my armpits and the slack taken up by the platform I grasped the rungs of the aluminium ladder from behind and started to climb.

Then, the inevitable happened. Whilst seeking a foot and finger-hold the rope jerked upwards and I went flying into space, twisting backwards, sideways, swinging about, stifling a cry of 'Jesus Christ!' Spinning like a trapeze artist, now behind, now in front of the ladder, praying nobody would let go to see what the trouble was. Finally, I reached out and clutched the infernal wire ladder for dear life.

After some deep breaths to calm my nerves I recommenced the climb, feeling nausea, helpless and useless. 15 metres from the top I almost fainted from exhaustion. Concentrating my mind with eyes closed tightly, my body somehow responded.

Armstrong with Holden: Deepest part of the cave system

I called to the platform to take it easy. They realised something was wrong and let me rest every step. If only I could have slept – or died! Finally, strong hands hauled me aboard and the nightmare was ended. I lay face down on wet and muddy timbers covered in footprints, unable to move, drained of energy. But I was alive and quickly bundled aside for the next person to follow on up.

Normally a fairly fit person, I was truly shocked by my physical condition.

When our little group returned to the campsite we made our way down to the bathing pond, there providing a neo-classical scene in the primitive jungle setting, with laughter, splashing water, and the first sounds of Nature's afternoon orchestra all around us. After a good meal we sat around the campfire drinking warm beer and firewater and trading yarns before heading to the tents for a well-earned slumber.

Next morning, everyone except a skeleton guard was shuttled out to Santiago. As the helicopter took off and rose above the Cordillera del Condor, I looked back at the disappearing campsite. The expedition was over. We were on our way home!

I spent that afternoon with Van Mejdahl visiting some discovered archaeological sites in the Santiago area. Later that evening, seated with

Hall and Armstrong at Santiago

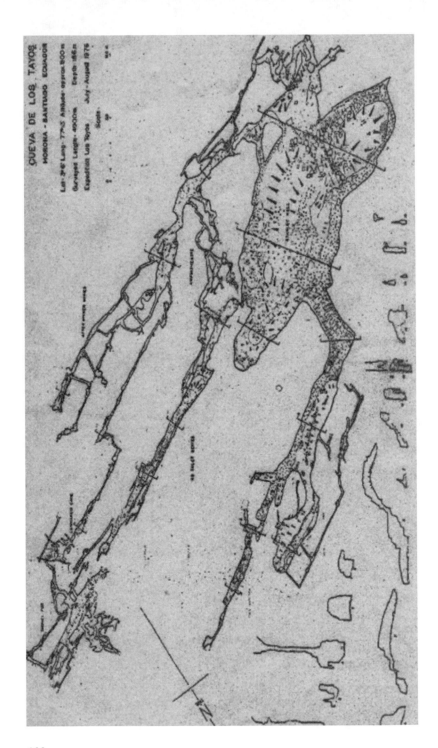

138

Neil and others, I broke my resolution not to ask any questions about the Moon landing.

'Tell us, Neil, what was your first thought when your foot touched the surface of the Moon?'

'My first thought was the first job I had to do,' he replied. 'I was too intent on that to consider anything else.'

'What about your thoughts in the capsule, looking out at the Earth, the Sun, the Moon and the stars?'

'I was thinking not so much about these but what was further *out there* in space.'

The voyages of the astronauts, beyond ordinary experience and comprehension, can only be matched by the inner journey each one of them must have experienced - a kind of 'marriage in heaven.' No amount of training can prepare the mind for such mental and physical journeys into the unknown. To look back on the world and its achievements as a grain of magnetised dust; to experience an at-one-ment with vast, unfathomable dimensions; to feel the soul emblazoned with the light of its own beginning and, later, condemned to return to the desolation of Mankind's greed and stupidity. Few minds can cope with thoughts like these. Those best prepared are born with special qualities. Neil Armstrong was one of them!

Evening arrived, full of moonlight, moths, dreams and heavy eyelids when suddenly the sound of scurrying feet on the wooden verandah caught my attention. Dr. Philip Ashmole, Director of the British Scientific Team, was looking for me.

'An indian has appeared out of the forest asking for you.' he said.

My face must have registered disbelief.

'He says he's a friend of yours.'

I jumped from my bunk to follow him certain there must be some mistake. Who did I know out there in the jungle?

To my surprise the 'indian' turned out to be Luis Nivelo, friend of Alfredo Punin and companion on our expedition to the 'stones' the previous year. Informed by Moricz of my arrival in Santiago, he had walked from Limon Indanza to the Tayos Cave site. Finding I had left, he had made his way through the forest and across the river, a journey across jungle and Cordillera of some 30 kilometres. Cordially, he declined my offer of food and shelter, saying he had achieved his objec-

Tayos Cave Map: 1976 (left)

tive of finding and welcoming me and would advise Moricz accordingly. Amazed, and not a little curious, I watched him walk briskly off into the darkness having quietly informed me that Moricz wanted to guard a nearby cave until the expedition left the area.

I smiled, recalling Moricz's love of practical jokes, including his promise to drop in on us by balsa raft for tea, dressed as a Shuar chief and accompanied by some elders. Accustomed to his tomfoolery, I did not take Nivelo's comment seriously. It was Moricz's way of partici-

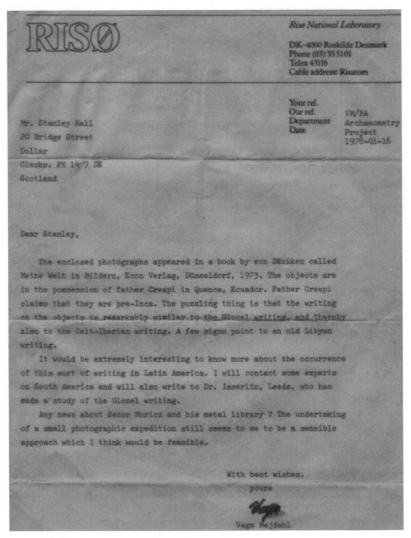

Vagn Mejdahl letter regarding Crespi Museum Inscriptions

pating in my adventure and his way of sending best wishes for a successful outcome.

Next day I took the first flight to Shell Mera with two companions. From there we hitched a lift on a pick-up truck heading for Quito. Neil stayed behind to spend a few days relaxing at Santiago where a farewell barbecue was arranged for his 46th birthday. I never saw him again but by all accounts he had greatly enjoyed his Tayos adventure.

A Scottish border clan, the Armstrongs, as their name and emblem indicate, were makers of weaponry, their leaders often advisers to royalty. In the late 13th Century, when the strongest army in Europe was that of Edward I with 27,000 men under arms, the Armstrongs boasted a force of 3000 mounted cavalry, employed to protect their lands against the Scots marching south and the English marching north.

When treacherously betrayed in the 17th Century only a few fiery and independent souls survived, but the exploits of their most famous son are testament to their stature.

Arq. Hernan Crespo Toral

Treasure of the Incas

16

Francisco Pizarro and his half-brothers Hernando, Gonzalo, Juan and other mercenaries, by destroying the Empire of Tayhuantinsuyu, perpetrated a crime of immeasurable historical consequence. Their barbarous acts, following on the destruction of the Aztec and Maya empires by Hernan Cortes a decade earlier, effectively obliterated the prehistory of the American continent.

In 1532, a few hundred adventurers in Central America, encouraged by rumours that a southern tribe called the Ibiru (from which Peru derives its name) inhabited a land of gold, sailed forth and landed at Tumbez on the border of modern Ecuador and Peru. A few weeks later they advanced into the mountainous hinterland with a strategy based on four debilitating factors affecting the Inca dynasty.

1. The empire was weak from civil war in which Atahualpa, Shyri ruler of the northern territory centred in Quito, had triumphed over his Inca half-brother Huascar based in Cuzco, capital of the southern part of the empire.

2. An Inca emperor, like an Egyptian pharaoh, was an absolute and divine ruler, without whom the structure of the empire would fall like a pack of cards.

3. The Spaniards were informed that their arrival from the sea in armour 'that shone like the Sun' fulfilled an ancient prophecy of the coming of fair and bearded gods from across the ocean. (The account is hotly contested by scholars who argue the myth was usurped by the Spaniards.)

4. The rumours of a golden empire were proving to be accurate, judging by evidence of treasure in abundance at Tumbez.

Atahualpa, unafraid because his men vastly outnumbered the visitors, met the 'conquistadores' at Cajamarca in northern Peru. Any excuse for a Spanish attack would have sufficed, especially since those accompanying the emperor were lightly armed. The Spanish claim that they were incensed by Atahualpa's scornful rejection of 'The Requirement of Conquest' presented by Padre Vicente Valverde, a document read to potential subjects of the Spanish Crown, failing acceptance of which they were threatened with force. According to chronicler Juan Ruiz de Arce, Valverde walked back from his confrontation with Atahualpa: 'weeping and calling upon God.' Was it because his soul was afflicted or because he knew what was going to happen next? Either way, he was the catalyst for the massacre that followed. To the blood-curling battle cry of 'Santiago!' the natives were savagely attacked and butchered, and the Emperor was quickly captured.

It has been asserted by more than one historian that the natives had weapons but were obeying to the death an order from Atahualpa that the visitors should not be harmed. Atahualpa's conquering army would clearly not be occupying enemy territory unarmed. The main body of his army was parked outside Cajamarca. The Spanish attack was sudden and savage.

Many indians had their hands cut off but continued to support their ruler's litter with their shoulders... those who were carrying the litter, and those who escorted, never abandoned him: all died around him. Within a few hours, seven thousand indians lay dead, and many more had their arms cut off and other appalling wounds, including scores of counsellors, lords and commanders.'

The chronicler Mena wrote, *'Truly, it was not accomplished by our own forces for there were so few of us. It was by the grace of God.'*

History records many cruelties justified 'by the grace of God.' It is unlikely that 7000 native veterans fresh from victorious battlefields were so easily defeated by so few. Most likely the majority of natives around Atahualpa at the time were unarmed townsfolk out to pay homage to the emperor.

Atahualpa was held to ransom with the deadline for payment in gold and silver being the time it took for messengers to reach Cuzco and instruct his commander Quisquis to bring it to Cajamarca. The Shyri emperor was anxious to secure his release quickly in order to overwhelm the invaders before they left the area.

In Cuzco, Quisquis was suspicious that Atahualpa had fallen to so few soldiers and, for a time, the ransom was not forthcoming. Worried about the delay, Atahualpa sent a relative with three Spanish officers to oversee the operation, with a condition that the temples of his father, Inca Huanya Capac, would not be defiled. For the temples of Huascar, he cared little. He was also as anxious as the Spaniards to make sure Huascar's priests were prevented from removing temple treasures.

Quisquis directed this second mission to the sacred temple of Curicancha, described as buildings: '… sheathed in gold, in large plates, on the side where the Sun rises, but on the side that was more shaded from the Sun the gold in them was more debased.'

Spain boasted one of the best mining fraternities in the world, skilled in prospecting and the use of mercury from southwest Spain for amalgamation and extraction processes.

With copper crowbars, the Spaniards prised off 3000lbs of gold plate from the temple walls. Only the sheer weight, shortage of time, and the fact they were 200 miles from Cajamarca, discouraged them from taking more. They were amazed at the amount of gold in the temples, evidence that fears of the possible removal of treasures by the priests were well founded. Who could doubt, following a tragic defeat and news of the Spaniards' interest in gold, that the priesthood would urgently seek to protect their heritage, it being a first priority of any nation to guard its sacred relics and archives.

The Spanish envoys arrived back in Cajamarca on the 13th of June 1533, leading 225 llamas laden with gold and silver. A further 60 loads arrived a few days later. The total ransom would be worth at today's value around 50 million dollars.

The departure from Cajamarca of Atahualpa's two most likely protectors, Hernando Pizarro and Hernando de Soto, sealed his fate. On the 26th of July 1533 (a date contested by scholars but considered by this writer to be the most exact), Francisco Pizarro ordered death by strangulation, cynically honouring his promise that 'not a drop of Atahualpa's blood would be spilled.' The emperor had told his followers that if he were not burned at the stake he would return to this world, which explains why his resurrection is awaited by the indigenous people of the Andes to this day.

Hoping to save his two sons and close family, the emperor allowed himself to be baptised. He was given a Christian burial, which Valverde planned would help the conversion of his followers. Atahualpa's wives, sisters, and loved ones were denied the honour of being buried alive in order to accompany him into the next world. When they realised he had not been burned at the stake, two sisters entered his abode, softly calling out his name, searching for him in vain.

Years later, soldier-priest Pedro Ciezo de Leon, considered one of the more reliable chroniclers of the Conquest, would write:

If the Spaniards, when they entered Cuzco, had not behaved with such cruelty, and slaughtered Atahualpa, who knows how many ships might have been needed to carry to Spain treasures which now lie buried in the bowels of the earth...'

The words: '... treasures which now lie buried in the bowels of the earth' are revealing in relation to treasures in the Tayos caves. Writer Harold Wilkins referred to orders given: '... *for treasures to be securely hidden in secret caves, to which mystic hieroglyphs, whose key is possessed by only one descendant of the Inca royal line in each generation, give the open sesame.'*

Are we not reminded here of the ideographic standing stones and treasures of Moricz?

The Spaniards heard a rumour that Atahualpa had sent convoys of captured treasure north to Tupipampa (Cuenca), also to Quito, which rivalled Cuzco in wealth. Later, his commanders were to be tortured to death in Quito rather than disclose the whereabouts of the royal treasures – except to indicate they were located in the eastern regions. So grew the legend of the fabulous lost treasure of Atahualpa, still sought today by a stream of adventurers in the Llanganatis and Quiñara-Vilcabamba regions of the Ecuadorian Sierra.

Many are the romantic tales about locations of Inca treasures. Yet, a number of forest tribes were vassals and allies of Atahualpa. They had little interest in gold and silver. Clearly the more probable locations for hiding treasure would be the Tayos Caves, conveniently protected by forest tribes and impenetrable rainforests. It is also logical that natives of the Sierra loyal to Atahualpa would hide treasure before the Spaniards arrived on their doorstep: but it would be illogical to hide it all in one place. This might explain the confusion surrounding possible locations of Atahualpa's hoard, variously called the treasure of the Incas, Rumiñahui's treasure, the treasure of El Dorado, and so on. One certainty is that if such treasures exist they will never be found by anyone not versed in the history of the Empire of Tayhuantinsuyu.

Like Rome of old all roads led to Cuzco; but the victorious Atahualpa was based in Quito, capital of the northern part of the empire. Following his conquests he planned to move power from Cuzco to Tupipampa (Cuenca) - birthplace of his father, Huanya Capac, a Cañari Indian, and also Huascar. Among other advantages this move would strengthen control over the mineral wealth of the Cañari. Huascar was taken by Huanya Capac from Tupipampa to Cuzco when he was six years old. He was 14 years old when he accompanied the first punitive expedition from Cuzco into the northern territories.

During the civil war, Atahualpa's ruthless general Rumiñahui exacted terrible revenge on the Cañari for siding with Huascar. Today, descendants of the Cañari mainly live in and around Chordeleg, where they still control the industry of gold and silver, much of it now coming from the Nambija region.

A topographical map of South America shows the Andes at their narrowest where the huge geological shield curving down from Guyana collides with the eastern Cordilleras of Ecuador, creating, as discovered by the Spaniards and later by Juan Moricz, rich mineralized areas in the provinces of Azuay and Morona-Santiago. Situated on the Pacific coast west of Cuenca is Guayaquil (named after Guaya and Kil, a legendary couple who ruled the powerful Huancavilca tribe), the largest port on the west coast of South America. Cuenca lies on the apex of the Guyana-Bolivian geological shield, midway between Guayaquil and the gold-drenched eastern Cordilleras.

As a solar and stellar civilization, the Incas and earlier indigenous peoples selected hiding places for sacred treasures in accordance with determined geographical and astronomical alignments. In this context, the volcano Sangay in south-east Ecuador is considered a holy mountain to local Shuar tribes.

Other craftsmen in competition with the Cañari were concentrated in the northern sierra and coastal regions of Tayhuantinsuyu, the coastal Manabi of Ecuador and the Chibcha of Colombia being particularly skilled, ranking with the best in the world. Writer Peter Kolosimo informs us:

'Returning to the Chibchas, we may note that they were not the only masters of the goldsmith's art. Among their chief rivals were the Manabi Indians, coast dwellers of northern Ecuador who, despite the lack of optical instruments, fashioned ornaments out of little grains of gold half the size of a pin's head, which they sometimes interspersed with even smaller, hollowed-out granules. The perfection of these works of art can only be appreciated by studying them through a strong magnifying glass. The process used was a technique known as 'granulation' rediscovered not many years ago by a German expert, Frau Treskow. It is so intricate and ingenious that scholars are convinced that it could not have been invented by several peoples independently of each other.... It is to be supposed, therefore, that the technique spread all over the world from the place where it was first invented.'

The lost treasure of Atahualpa, like the gold of El Dorado, retains its everlasting allure, and adventurers will continue to face hardship and death in the search for it. Natives, bearded mariners and wily worthies have for centuries traded 'genuine' maps and 'inside' information with an endless list of gullible, wide-eyed treasure detectives. Yet, none of their wild imaginings could surpass the astonishing tale I am about to relate concerning the mysterious treasure of Atahualpa and the treasure of the Tayos!

Percy H. Fawcett and George M. Dyott!

17

The following seminal account in our story is so amazing that if I did not frequently review the notes I made at the time I could not believe it.

As a youngster I had been fascinated by the Amazon journeys of Colonel Percy Fawcett and Commander George Miller Dyott in the 1920s and 1930s. With an abiding faith in their spirit of enquiry I could not believe men of such ability could waste their lives chasing moonbeams. Of course, the 'South American Disease', that inexorable attraction to exotic places and chases, was something to be wary of, as I learnt from experience.

Fawcett disappeared in 1925 searching for relics of Atlantis in the Amazon jungle. Before leaving on his last trip he wrote;

'Whether we succeed in penetrating the jungle, and come out alive, or whether we leave our bones there, of this I am certain - the key to the mystery of ancient South America and perhaps the whole of prehistory can be found if we are able to locate these old cities of the solar civilization and open them up to science.'

His disappearance remains controversial. Notes from an earlier expedition indicate he may have vanished in central Brazil, with more than one tribe claiming responsibility for his death. However, like most explorers, he was adept at laying false trails. Personally, I think he stumbled upon the notorious Amazonian rubber plantations managed by brutal Bolivian and Jamaican supervisors, whose cruelty extended to feeding natives to their dogs and who would not wish such treatment reported back to British investors. No doubt they also took advantage of their isolation to develop a drug trafficking operation. Even today, the last thing any explorer would want to cross is a path used by drug barons.

Fawcett's mention of a 'solar civilization' indicates he was heading for the Andes. It would be illogical to search for ancient solar cities in flat jungle that falls a mere 800 metres over a distance of 3000 miles between the Cordilleras and the mouth of the Amazon. Far more

Col. Percy Harrison Fawcett

practical to construct buildings above 1000 metres; close to mosquito-free, fast flowing, clean water shedding off the Andes, comfortable temperature and humidity levels, fertile soil, better defences, with spacious and ventilated subterranean caves available with fresh running water. And, importantly, with a clear view of the rising Sun!

Was his solar civilization the figment of a fertile imagination or did he have 'inside' information. We might never have known were it not for the Saleisian Fraternity based at Macas and Sucua in Morona Santiago. Tayos expedition archaeologist Padre Pedro Porras of the Catholic University in Quito heard about a large complex of pyramid mounds and pathways situated at c.1200 metres altitude near the headwaters of the Upano (Shuar: Kanús) river, in the foothills of Mount Sangay. During a few expeditions with his students, he cleared some of the area and published in 1985 a report, map and plan of the Sangay (more correctly 'Huapola') complex. Some years later after Padre Porras died the project ran out of resources. OSTROM, a French government sponsored organization for archaeological investigation in the Andes, continued with a programme which has to-date revealed more than two dozen archaeological sites in the area.

In the 1930s, Commander Dyott, an associate of the Royal Geographic Society, was commissioned by the North American News Agency and Lloyds Insurance Group to search for Fawcett in order to establish whether or not he was still alive. Subsequently, he reported finding a bag belonging to Fawcett, which served to support a life insurance claim by Fawcett's family. The only certainty is that Fawcett vanished without trace somewhere in the vast expanse of the Amazon jungle. No solid evidence of his whereabouts or the time and place of his death has ever been found.

Dyott's other investigations were concentrated in Ecuador, where he effectively disappeared from the public stage for some decades. What was *he* up to?

February 1978, in Guayaquil. I was dining out one evening with Moricz, Dr. Peña, Roger St. John Hender and some other friends when three men entered the restaurant, one of whom Moricz greeted with a wave. Excusing himself a moment, he approached their table. Soon, both groups were seated together.

Moricz introduced me to Don Andrés Fernández-Salvador Zaldumbide, a well-known Ecuadorian businessman, savant, athlete and, interestingly, leading pioneer in the search for the treasure of

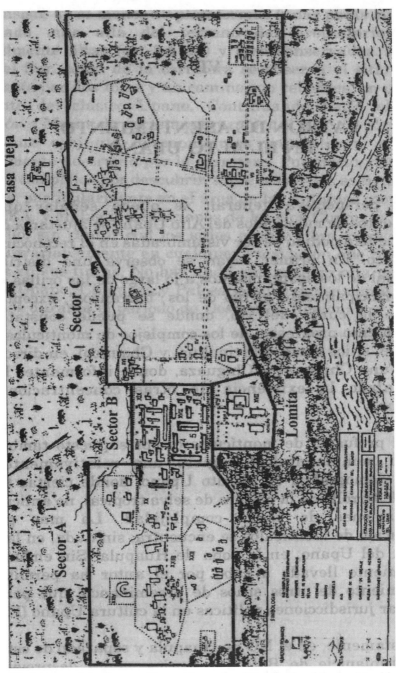

2Km² Sector of the Sangay (Huapulo) complex. Plan developed from original by Padre Pedro Porras, PUCE, Quito

Atahualpa! Our very international body of personalities was soon engaged in a lively discussion about the early explorers.

Suddenly, I was startled by Don Andrés declaring in his good English, 'History shows that the Spaniards produced some of the greatest explorers, but the British just have the edge on them - and the greatest explorer who ever lived was Commander George M. Dyott!'

I could hardly believe my ears.

'What do you know of Commander Dyott?' I enquired eagerly.

'He was my close friend and mentor for many years, a distant relative of the British Royal Family, agent of British Naval Intelligence, and explorer extraordinary. It was Dyott who, during the First World War, discovered that the hulls of German submarines were being constructed with a special wood found in Chile, and he was directly responsible for arranging an embargo on its supply. In the Second World War, the same wood was employed for the fuselage of the Mosquito fighter-bomber of the Royal Air Force.'

I sat enthralled as he expanded on the exploits of Dyott, sometimes in English, other times, frustratingly for me, in Spanish. Waiting my chance, I popped the question I had been most eager to ask.

'Why do you say he was the greatest explorer who ever lived? That is quite a statement! Apart from undertaking an unsuccessful expedition to find Fawcett and being a prolific writer, the world knows little of any significant exploration venture by Dyott.'

I had prodded him deliberately. He glanced at Moricz as if to seek some assurance about me. To my chagrin, somebody broke the thread of conversation with an irrelevant comment and the discussion moved away from Dyott. I could see Don Andrés was initially relieved by the interruption, as if he had already said too much. Then, to my surprise, he stood up, muttered something about being insulted by the interruption and promptly left the restaurant, leaving us all staring in amazement.

Secretly, I was exhilarated. I had got closer to the Dyott mystery. My growing conviction that Dyott had taken over the mantle of Fawcett was taking root. What I understood from Don Andrés was that Dyott had been living in Ecuador for many years, part recluse, part investigator of something to do with Atahualpa's treasure. Had he found it, or something else? I was determined to stay on the trail. Meanwhile, my excitement would have to face withdrawal symptoms since I would be flying back to Scotland next day.

One year later, precisely 9 p.m., 17th of February, 1979, Guayaquil. I rang the doorbell of a large house in the district of Urdesa. A servant answered and led me into the salon. My host appeared, smiling recognition, bidding me a warm welcome as he shook my hand.

'I am sorry we could not meet earlier,' Don Andrés apologised. 'I have been working late.'

We sat down and with teasing reference to my Scottish background he poured two large whiskies. (I wondered why people imagine Scots drink whisky like others drink tea.) The memory of our first discussion in Guayaquil was still on my mind, as if it had taken place yesterday. It seemed best to make my intentions clear from the start. I clarified my role in the 1976 Tayos expedition, my interest in Fawcett and Dyott, and my friendship with Juan Moricz and Dr. Gerardo Peña Matheus.

There followed a wide-ranging, get-to-know-each-other conversation for about an hour, covering philosophy, exploration, history, and the involvement of explorers in such esoteric fields such as Theosophy, Freemasonry and Rosicrucianism. Then, we spoke about Moricz.

'Moricz is a brilliant, but stubborn, man!' he exclaimed. 'In my opinion, he lacked diplomacy in dealing with the Ecuadorian authorities in 1969 and that is why, apart from his being a foreigner, he was bound to face difficulties.'

George M. Dyott in his early aviation days

'What is your opinion on his theories of relationships between the Mayas of Central America and the Magyars of Hungary, the Caras and Colorados of ancient Ecuador, and his alleged discovery of a metal library in the Tayos caves?'

Looking at me intently for a few seconds he said with a sigh, 'Let me tell you an interesting story. Soon after I heard about Moricz's claims that tribes of this region spoke a language related to the Magyars I contacted a cultured friend of mine, a Hungarian lady. She was, of course, astounded at the claims of Moricz who, amongst other things, claimed he had spoken Magyar with the Tscachi-Caranki (Colorados of Santo Domingo, midway between Quito and the coast). Personally, she was not prepared to visit the tribe but knew of a Hungarian engineer working in the area and made arrangements for him to investigate. Later, she told me his investigation confirmed the claims. I was very surprised but could take nothing away from Moricz. I had set out to call his bluff, to discredit him, but had to admit I failed.'

Andrés then followed with another incredible story.

'About 15 years ago - I believe it was 1964 - I was in Quito one evening when I received a telephone call. A German by the name of Alfredo Moebius introduced himself, insisting he had met me some years ago. He sounded excited, apologised for calling so late, but was anxious I visit him immediately. Assuming the matter to be important I told him I would be there in an hour.

'His house was like a fortress, with a steel-plated front door. I heard half-a-dozen bolts being drawn then a servant led me inside. In the hallway stood two more servants holding back a pair of snarling Doberman Pinchers. It was quite a welcome.

'Moebius appeared and, waving the servants away, led me into the sitting room where he excused himself to make a telephone call, addressing his contact with words I remember very clearly: 'He has arrived! You can come over now!'

'We were talking for only a few minutes when the doorbell rang. The visitor was introduced to me as Sr. Patricio Jaramillo. (Don Andrés, understandably, gave me a false first name.)

'He seemed nervous and unsure of himself until Moebius spoke: 'Now, Sr. Jaramillo, please tell your story again.' Jaramillo looked apprehensively at Moebius, then at me.

'It's alright!' Moebius encouraged him. 'You may speak freely!'

'Jaramillo then told me a sensational story. Years ago he had been an

Army recruitment officer in the Oriente. One day, passing through a Shuar village, someone called out his name, saying he had once lived with Jaramillo's family under an educational programme for Shuar children. Jaramillo recognized him and that evening they met to discuss old times.

'During the conversation the Shuar confided he would like to share a secret with Jaramillo, as an old friend. It was agreed they would visit the location next day. Early next morning they set off and entered a cave that led straight in from the banks of a river. Some distance inside they came across a rod placed diagonally across a passageway. Continuing by the light of his small army torch he was amazed to be shown a great treasure of artifacts, including a large metal library whose leaves were covered – or rather, embossed - with strange inscriptions and geometric designs.

'Passing into other chambers, there were more metal books and artifacts. They spent the whole day in the treasure cave and slept there overnight. Next day, on leaving the cave the Shuar, who was by now acting afraid, insisted Jaramillo must forget what he had seen and promise never to reveal the location.

'Moebius, at that moment, interrupted, declaring, 'We want *you*, Don Andrés, to organize an expedition to the treasure cave. You are the only man experienced enough to do it!'

'Despite the temptation I turned down the invitation, partly because I did not want to get involved in what appeared a risky adventure but mainly because I was planning another expedition to the Llanganatis to look for Atahualpa's treasure.'

Stunned, I interrupted him.

'Are you saying that you believe the metal library *exists*?'

'Yes! There is no doubt about it in my mind! I told Moricz about it (Ding! I made a clear note of these words), knowing he would be interested. Interested? My god! He was elated! I can still see his face lit up in amazement: 'That's it! That's it!' he cried out. 'That is what I have been looking for!'

'At that time, of course, Moricz could not make any claims about a library inscribed in the Magyar language, simply because he had not yet seen it. That claim came some years later.'

Here, I realised, was an important new development. It was interesting that Moricz had pursued an independent path to Ecuador on the language front but had known nothing about Jaramillo until he spoke with Andrés, just as I was doing that night.

To my mind, Don Andrés was telling the story as it happened. It was not something you forget easily and was too fantastic to be invented. I mentally calculated that the date of his meeting with Moebius and Jaramillo was shortly after Moricz arrived in Ecuador in 1964.

The development of the Tayos story between the time Moricz was informed by Andrés and his announcements to the media in September 1969 covers a period of four-five years. Not until I met Jaramillo in 1991, followed by innumerable conversations before his untimely death in May 1998, was it confirmed that Moricz had also met with Moebius and Jaramillo *after* he received the contact information from Andrés.

Present at Moricz's meeting was Moebius's daughter acting as translator, and an Italian-born Count, a former special forces' intelligence officer called Pino Turolla. Unknown to Jaramillo, Turolla was associated with what can best be described as an extraterrestial 'channeling' group based in the U.S.A. The group was led by Dr. Andrija Puharich, an inventor, parapsychologist, hypnotist, CIA intelligence adviser and creator of 'belief systems' who, some believe, seriously influenced world events in the late 20th Century. The mysterious connection with Turolla might explain the frustration and aggression the latter later directed at Jaramillo.

I looked quizzically across at Andrés, my amiable, multi-faceted host. His story seemed too fantastic but, added to other pieces in the jigsaw puzzle, it would become even more so. The evening was passing too quickly and I needed to get back to the subject of Dyott.

'You told Moebius and Jaramillo you could not mount an expedition because you were working on some important project with Dyott. He was my main reason for contacting you. Can you tell me what project you had in mind?'

He sat back in his chair, fingering his whisky. Would he volunteer the information or show me the door? Should it be the latter I might never find out about Dyott and would the story of his time in Ecuador ever come out?

After a long pause, he spoke.

'Dyott lived discreetly in Ecuador for many years. One of his projects was investigating Atahualpa's treasure. You may know it is also called the treasure of El Dorado, the treasure of Rumiñahui, or of the Incas, for centuries sought by adventurers including your own Sir Walter

Raleigh.

'Dyott made a number of trips into the Oriente, each time risking danger. Once, he was caught by the Shuar and imprisoned in a wooden cage hanging from a tree. He escaped, was captured again and, finally, escaped at his third attempt. At 63 years of age he was still making trips into the jungle. Quite an amazing man!'

I said nothing, but it puzzled me why Dyott had made dangerous trips into the Oriente when the Atahualpa treasure was traditionally located in the forbidding Llanganati Sierra east of Ambato. What had he been looking for so far to the east?

'What was your role with him?' I enquired.

'As I said, he was my mentor and a highly respected man. Being much younger than him I became his work-horse.'

'You believe the treasure of Atahualpa also exists?'

'Yes! That may surprise you, but I will tell you something even more astonishing. It has been found at least twice already. A number of people have died; first a priest called Father Longo in the 1790s, then a botanist called Anatasio – or Anastacio – Guzman, then an English sailor called George Edwin Chapman, and a Scotsman, a Captain Erskine Loch, who, suffering from cancer and depression and disappointment, shot himself.'

I was becoming impressed by, and thankful for, Don Andrés's phenomenal memory. He poured us another whisky then sat down again, his penetrating brown eyes peering straight through me.

'There is, in the historical archives of Quito,' he began, 'an account, centuries old, written by a priest-soldier called Valverde Leggio(?). The document contains no maps but describes his journey into the Llanganatis and the discovery of Atahualpa's treasure. When, years later, he lay dying in Spain, he donated the document, now referred to as the 'Derrotero of Valverde', to the Spanish Crown (probably Philip II).

'About 15 years ago in Quito I received an urgent call from Dyott. He showed me maps and a letter from a family in Nova Scotia. Apparently the family had years previously received a letter from a British Merchant Navy officer called Bartholomew Blake. The letter stated that following the recommendation of a mutual friend he was entrusting to them important information about the lost treasure of the Incas. Only upon Blake's death was this information to be passed on to someone selected by the family.

'Blake died in mysterious circumstances at sea – one account being that he disappeared overboard after a drunken argument, on a ship bound for New York. Someone advised the family in Nova Scotia to contact Commander Dyott in Ecuador. Dyott was informed that in the latter part of the 19th century Blake and a fellow officer, George Edwin Chapman, were on a ship that docked in Guayaquil for repairs. Discovering the repairs would take some weeks they decided to have an adventure looking for the fabled treasure of Atahualpa. Whilst in the Llanganatis Chapman died and Blake reported that he buried him with a wooden cross on the grave.

'Caught in a violent storm and weak from exhaustion Blake sheltered in a cave entrance. Venturing inside he was astonished to discover a huge treasure. Fortunately he had the presence of mind to draw a map of the area. With difficulty he made it to safety, carrying some gold pieces which some say he proposed to deposit with the Smithsonian Institution in Washington D.C., others, with the British Museum. Presumably, if the story is true, they should be registered under his name.

'The letter from Nova Scotia also said it would be necessary to visit another family in Vermont, giving an address but no further details. Dyott made the trip to Vermont only to find the house occupied by a family of another name that knew nothing of the matter. Nevertheless, a search was made in the attic and a dusty bible was discovered. A note fell out, upon which was written: 'Look for Knapsacks and Rifles.' Despite a thorough search, no knapsacks or rifles were found!

'Dyott returned to Ecuador convinced he had been the victim of a hoax. Then, the following year there came a startling development. A letter from the family in Vermont informed him that whilst cleaning out the attic they had found a book... Its title?'

I voiced the answer, *'Knapsacks and Rifles!'*

'Right! And inside the book was a map with instructions. It showed a small island off the coast of Maine, opposite Nova Scotia, with directions to dig at a certain spot marked 'X', like all good treasure maps. So! Dyott went to Nova Scotia!'

'An expedition to the island was organized, the spot duly located and, after digging about six feet down - You won't believe this! - they found a green bottle. Inside was Bartholomew Blake's map of the location of Atahualpa's treasure in the Llanganatis.'

My thoughts can be imagined. Even if it were a hoax it had me on the edge of my seat ready to shoot off to the Llanganatis just to be part of this fantastic story. Within a few hours I had been on some amazing journeys. Was it all fantasy? If so, Don Andrés had to be one of the world's best storytellers!

He continued warming to memories that came flooding back.

'Dyott called me to Quito because he wanted me to take Blake's map and find the treasure. There were in fact two maps. I suggested I take both but Dyott was convinced one was a fake. Anyway, I organized an expedition to the Llanganatis. I located some of the places on the map Dyott had selected and they *did* match descriptions in Valverde's Derrotero, but I did not find the cave or the treasure!

'Returning to Quito I studied the second map and persuaded Dyott I should search with both maps. I set off again and my suspicions were confirmed. Both maps proved to be genuine and I soon found most of Blake's reference points – unfortunately not enough, so, again disappointed, I returned to Quito empty handed. We left the venture aside for some time.

'About 12 years ago, I persuaded the Army to provide a helicopter to take some aerial photographs of key areas in the Llanganatis. However, flying low in bad weather, we crashed. Injured and suffering from dysentry, the pilot and I waited a month before our smoke signals were spotted. The media, it seemed, had given us up for lost. Spares for the helicopter were parachuted in and we repaired it, managing to take off and fly home. It was a miracle we survived!

Again he paused, his mind's eye visualising those exciting but desperate days.

'What is the position now regarding your search for the treasure?' I ventured.

'When you and I met with Moricz in Guayaquil last year I was 99% sure of its location. Then, a breakthrough! Many times I had checked the aerial photographs. Always there had been one photograph I kept laying aside convinced it did not belong in the pile. Just when I thought of giving up the whole venture, I picked up that photograph and examined it closely for the first time. Turning it round slowly, I cried out…'Eureka!' All the time I'd been looking at it the wrong way round. There, before my eyes, was the final clue - the *Inca Path*!

'In July 1977, I made a trip to confirm its authenticity and there was no doubt about it.'

'So now you are 100% sure of the location?'

'To within one kilometre! The locations on Blake's map and description in Valverde's account coincide: the spectacle lakes, the quaking bog, the three Cerros \ridges], the reclining lady, the Inca path and the other clues all fit perfectly. *Now, I want to invite you to organize an expedition to locate the treasure!'*

Did I hear those last words correctly? I had heard the words 'expedition' and 'treasure' so often during the previous hours that I wondered who was now organizing which expedition where. Maybe it was mental exhaustion, but more and more it appeared like a game of musical chairs to determine whom among the amazing characters in this story would find the fairy treasure. However, I had heard too many stunning things that evening to be taken aback by his sudden invitation.

I parried with a question, 'Why not organize your own expedition since it is you who has come so far?'

He stood up, walking around to demonstrate a limp, a result of the helicopter crash.

'It would take four people to carry me on a stretcher,' he laughed. 'And there is another reason. It might sound strange but after being so long on the Llanganati search I feel my part is done. I wanted to overcome a challenge and, now that I am near the end, it all seems something of an anti-climax. Also, I am facing the moral question of whether our society has the right to such priceless objects.'

'I can understand that,' I sympathised. 'Moricz said something similar when he felt so many people had turned against him. There was at least once during the 1976 Tayos Expedition when I, too, felt the same way.'

Wavering on his invitation I replied that I would try to get the Royal Geographical Society interested on my return to Britain. (As expected, the Society declined on the basis that it never gets involved in hunting treasures.)

Thus, an amazing evening came to an end. I had no idea that years later the whole scenario described by Andrés would cross my path again. I had made allowances for the fact he had probably not told me everything, was perhaps hiding a few details and flaws. That was understandable; after all, I was still much of a stranger to him.

Time had flown by. It was 5.30 a.m. I had a flashback to Dr. Peña's words on our Stones Expedition four years earlier: 'Señor Hall, when you return to Britain and tell your story, nobody will believe you!' His voice was now wringing loudly in my ears. If his words were true then, how much more so they would prove to be in the future.

Thanks to Andrés I now possessed a credible update on who truly were the key protagonists in the Atahualpa and Tayos treasure sagas. Both he and, to a lesser extent, Gastón Fernandez Borrero four years earlier, had mentioned the Jaramillo role, but why had not Jaramillo spoken publicly during the controversies in the media between 1969 and 1976? Apart from the fact I had no idea where to find him it was unethical to think of approaching Jaramillo over the head of Moricz.

I began to wonder if there were *two* parts of the treasure of Tayhuantinsuyu? On the way to the hotel I instructed my tired brain to register the fact that when I awoke in a few hours' time I had not dreamed the whole extraordinary experience. I spent the afternoon of the next day writing notes and letting the stupendous story of Dyott, Andrés, Atahualpa's treasure, and the Metal Library, fix itself clearly in my mind. The details were complex and I felt a responsibility to get them right.

At one stage in our conversation Andrés had mentioned an acquaintance of Dyott's in Quito called Paul Williams Snr. Two days later I paid him a short visit. He told me that Dyott, after giving up the search for the Atahualpa treasure, had settled on a small hacienda by Santo Domingo, intending, amongst other ventures, to develop a disease-resistant strain of cacao, which ultimately failed. He became something of a recluse and – to add to the mystery - was rumoured to guard a wooden chest so obsessively that he slept on it. One can imagine the chest full of old maps, photographs and manuscripts for publication or some further dreamed-of expedition - or maybe concealing relics of Atahualpa's treasure he had never shared with anyone? With half-knowledge, the possibilities for fantasy are endless.

The Explorers Club in New York informed me Dyott had died in 1972. Through Paul Williams I contacted his son Michael Henry Dyott in Palm Springs, California. I emphasised the importance of collecting as many of his father's papers as possible. Years later he informed me by telephone he had done exactly that. Consequently, I suggested he collaborate with the Explorers Club (I had been elected a Fellow International in 1993) for their publication but lost contact until 1995 when fate brought us together in Ecuador. It happened by coincidence at the *Hacienda Pacaritambo* owned by Andrés near Balzar. Michael arrived out of the blue with Llanganati explorer Diego Arias, a former son-in-law of Andrés. All the ingredients were present for a great discussion but, unfortunately, as can happen with strong personalities in charged circumstances, things did not go as well as I had hoped. Dyott Jnr. did confirm his intention to have his father's papers published but, since that meeting, I have heard nothing and, to my knowledge, no publication has appeared. (Please Michael! You do have a responsibility to make this happen!)

Valverde's Treasure

18

Close scrutiny of the *Derrotero of Valverde*, a copy being discovered, translated and brought to England in the 1850s by botanist Richard Spruce and read to the Royal Geographical Society, highlights *in one particular paragraph* why the legendary Atahualpa treasure of the Llanganati region has never been found.

The Christian name and precise identification of the Valverde of Derrotero fame, who lived in the 16th Century, is lost to history. Valverde was a surname not uncommon in the Sierra cities of Latacunga and Ambato, yet nobody in the region with that surname has ever claimed to be his descendant.

If the story of his marriage with the daughter of a grateful *cacique* - whose life Valverde supposedly saved in return for information on the Llanganati treasure - is true, then he may have been, c. 1530, a certain priest-soldier of fortune who, remorseful of the treatment being meted out to the native population, is reputed to have married and settled in Latacunga during the *early* consolidation of the Conquest, from 1535 to 1541. Andrés had mentioned, rightly or wrongly, one possible name of this man as Valverde Leggio.

He may or may not have been related to the notorious Dominican Friar Vicente de Valverde who in 1532 inflamed the Spaniards to commit the Cajamarca massacre and was in 1541 captured and eaten by natives on the Isle of Puna off Guayaquil whilst fleeing to Panama after the assassination of Francisco Pizarro in Lima. Or he may have been related to one Don Pedro Valverde who, on the 29th July 1538, obtained a certificate from the Council of Quito to develop a pig-farm near Latacunga. Perhaps the latter was the same Pedro de Valverde elevated to the position of Royal Accountant and Paymaster in Quito from 1576 until his death in 1579: and, curiously, since the will and testament of this Valverde has never been found, it is tempting to speculate that he might have received his Crown position after giving King Philip II the famous Derrotero.

Copies of Valverde's Derrotero that re-surfaced in the late 18th Century contain a suspicious break in the flow of the text. Geographical features are described in laudable detail for the march of about three days ending at a rocky bluff called the Margasitas (pyrites), after which, just when the clues should be getting *more* precise, it becomes impossible to deduce with certainty which direction to take.

Mining experts visiting the Llanganatis region have confirmed the opportunities for goldmining but viability is thwarted by the treacherous climate and access. Leading Ecuadorian geologist Diego Benalcazar discovered there indications of a gold *skarn* mineralization he believed could an extension of Cumbaratza's rich Nambija skarn to the south first discovered by Basque miners in 1564; and other clues point to copper and silver mines dating to pre-colonial times.

Veteran mountaineer Hamish McInnes has reported stone-built ruins east of the Llanganatis, including a stone channel and trough. Such settlements are frequently found close to mineral deposits so the ruins are conceivably part of an old mining operation. Old mines are logical places to hide treasure.

Dr. Michel Merlyn, an experienced Belgian geologist based in Ecua-

The 4PL Llanganati clue found by geologist Dr. Michel Merlyn

dor, described to me his discovery, a (geologist's) day-and-a-half march into the Llanganatis, of a cave about 30 metres long. At the end of one of two branches is a large oval stone, weighing about two tons, of a granite material *alien to that of the surrounding rock face.* Its surface, he said, is surprisingly smooth and, curiously, although there are stalactite-stalagmite pillars in the other branch, there are none in the branch leading to the stone.

During the Napoleonic Wars much intrigue about treasures took place in many strange parlours. The cargo and destination of the *El Pensamiento* which sailed from Lambayeque in Peru shortly after the *Peace of Amiens* began in May 1802, captained by American John Fanning as far as Panama, then by Scotsman John Doig to Edinburgh, presents an interesting challenge for history sleuths. Neither Doig nor Fanning have ever been identified but there are two lines of inquiry I believe will provide the answers. One trail should lead to the grandfather of Peruvian naval hero John Fanning The other should lead to John Doig, eleventh child of an immigrant Scots-French Doig family of Antigua. Doigs and Fannings of both families were living in Lambayque. Dates, locations, activities and sympathies fit nicely. The overall guiding hand behind the disappearance of the fortune should prove to be none other than famous Scottish banker, financier, and 'burner of documentary evidences', Thomas Coutts, whose sympathy with the British and French crowns, and the abandoned Spanish aristocrary in Central and South America, can hardly be questioned. Both the Coutts and Doigs came from the smuggling town of Montrose, on the east coast of Scotland.

I am pleased to have collaborated with the late Jim Gilhooley of Edinburgh on this matter and more recently with Dr. Merlyn in Quito. My personal belief at time of writing is there was probably roundtable collusion between the then Lambayeque residents, Antonio Pastor de Marin y Segura, ex-Corregidor de Ambato, and the neighbouring Doigs and Fannings. The *El Pensamiento* treasure, which allegedly arrived in Leith Harbour in Edinburgh on Xmas Eve of 1802, most likely belonged to the family of Pastor's second, and wealthy, wife Doña Narcisa Martinez de Tejada, accrued by her family over decades from, or in collusion with, the many robber-*huaqueros* of *Sipan* tombs and adjacent sites close to Lambayeque.

The legend of the lost treasure of Atahualpa sleeps safe in the knowledge that, as long as men dream dreams, the Llanganatis will safeguard its mysterious treasure and continue to welcome the naïve and unwary into its unmerciful clutches.

§§§

The Richard Spruce Account

The following is a transcript of the the discourse given by Richard Spruce to the Royal Geographical Society in London, followed by his translation of the Derrotero:

'In the month of July 1857 I reached Baños where I learnt that the snowy points I had observed from Puca-yacu, between Tungurahua

Richard Spruce, 1889

and Cotopaxi, were the summits of a group of mountains called Llanganati from which ran down to Pastaza the densely-wooded ridges I saw to northward. I was further informed that these mountains abounded in all sorts of metals, and that it was universally believed the Incas had deposited an immense quantity of gold in an artificial lake on the flanks of one of the peaks at the time of the Spanish Conquest. They spoke also of one Valverde [of the 16th century], a Spaniard who, from being poor, had suddenly become very rich, which was attributed to his having married an indian girl. The father showed him where the treasure was hidden and accompanied him on various occasions to bring away portions of it; and that Valverde returned to Spain and, when on his deathbed, bequeathed the secret of his riches to the King. Many expeditions, public and private, had followed the track indicated by Valverde but nobody had succeeded in reaching its terminus... I obtained, however, indisputable evidence that the Derrotero or Guide to the Llanganati of Valverde had been sent [in the late 18th century] by the King [Carlos IV] of Spain to the Corrigedors of Tacunga and Ambato, along with a Cedula Real [Royal Warrant] commanding those functionaries to use every diligence in seeking out the treasure of the Incas...

The Derrotero was found to correspond so exactly with actual localities that only a person imtimately acquainted with them could have drawn them up; that it could have been fabricated by a person who had never been out of Spain was an impossibility. The Cedula Real and Derrotero were deposited in the archives of Tacunga, [from] whence they disappeared about twenty years ago... I made unceasing enquiries for the map and at last ascertained that the actual possessor was a gentleman of Ambato, Señor Salvador Ortega, to whom I made application for it, and he had the kindness to have it brought immediately from Quito, where it was deposited, and placed in my hands. I am therefore indebted to that gentleman's kindness for the pleasure of being able to lay the accompanying copy of the map before the Royal Geographical Society. The original map is formed of eight small sheets of paper of unequal size (those of my copy correspond exactly to these, pasted to a piece of coarse calico [cotton cloth], the whole size being 3 feet 10 inches by 2 feet 9 inches.

TITLE: THE GUIDE OR ROUTE WHICH VALVERDE LEFT IN SPAIN WHERE DEATH OVERTOOK HIM, HAVING GONE FROM THE MOUNTAINS OF THE LLANGANATI, WHICH HE ENTERED MANY TIMES, AND CARRIED OFF A GREAT QUANTITY OF GOLD: AND THE KING COMMANDED CORREGIDORS OF TACUNGA AND AMBATO TO SEARCH FOR THE TREASURE: WHICH ORDER AND GUIDE ARE PRESERVED IN ONE OF THE OFFICES OF TACUNGA.

'Placed in the town of Pillaro, ask for the farm of Moya, and sleep (the first night) a good distance above it: and ask for the mountain of Guapa, from whose top, if the day be fine, look to the east, so that the back be towards the town of Ambato, and from thence thou shalt perceive the three Cerros Llanganati, in the form of a triangle, on whose declivity there is a lake, made by hand, into which the ancients threw the gold they had prepared for the ransom of the Inca when they heard of his death. From the same Cerro Guapa thou mayst see the forest, and in it a clump of Sangurimas standing out of the said forest, and another clump, which they call flechas [arrows], and these clumps are the principal mark for which thou shalt aim, leaving them a little on the left hand. Go forward from Guapa in that direction and, with the signals indicated, and, a good way ahead, having passed some cattle farms, thou shalt come to a wide morass, over which thou must cross and, coming out on the other side, thou shalt see on the left hand, a short way off, a jucal, on a hillside, through which thou must pass. Having got through the jucal, thou wilt see two small lakes called the Anteojos [spectacles], from having between them a point of land like a nose.

'From this point thou mayst again discern the Cerros Llanganati, the same as thou sawest them from the top of the Guapa, and I warn thee to leave the said lakes on the left, and that in front of the point, or nose, there is a plain, which is the sleeping place. There thou must leave thy horses, for they can go no further. Following now on foot in the same direction, thou shalt come on a great black lake, the which leave on thy left hand and, beyond it, seek to descend along the hillside in such a way that thou mayst reach a ravine, down which comes a waterfall: and here, thou shalt find a bridge of three poles or, if it does not still exist, thou shalt put another in the most convenient place and pass over it. And, having gone a little way in the forest, seek out the hut which serves to sleep in, or the remains of it. Having passed the night there, go on thy way the following day through the forest in the same direction till thou reach another deep, dry ravine, across which thou must throw a bridge and pass over it slowly and cautiously, for the ravine is very deep; that is, if thou succeed not in finding the path that exists. Go forward, and look for the signs of another sleeping place which, I assure thee, thou canst not fail to see, in the fragments of pottery and other marks, because the Indians are continually passing along there. Go on thy way, and thou shalt see a mountain, which is full of Margasitas (Pyrites), the which leave on thy left hand, and I warn thee that thou must go round it in this fashion. On this side, thou wilt find a Pajonal [pasture] in a small plain which, having crossed, thou wilt come on a canyon between two hills, which is the Way of the Inca.

(Writer: *At this point, the admirably accurate information, confirmed by many explorers who followed it, becomes extremely hazy, just at the point where it should become more precisely detailed in order to reach the treasure cave.*)

'From thence, as thou goest along, thou shalt see the entrance of the socabon [cave entrance], which is in the form of a church porch. Having come through the canyon and gone a good distance beyond thou wilt perceive a cascade which descends from an offshoot of the Cerro Llanganati and runs into a quaking bog on the right hand; and, without passing the stream, in the said bog there is much gold, so that, by putting on thy hand, what thou shalt gather at the bottom is grains of gold. To ascend the mountain, leave the bog and go along to the right, and pass over the cascade, going round the offshoot of the mountain.

And, if by chance the mouth of the socabon be closed with certain herbs, which they call 'Salvaje,' remove them, and thou wilt find the entrance. At the left-hand side of the mountain thou mayst see the 'Guayra' (for thus the ancients called the furnace where they founded metals) which is sprinkled with gold. And to reach the third mountain, if thou canst not pass in front of the socabon, it is the same thing to pass behind it, for the water of the lake falls into it.

'If thou lose thyself in the forest, seek the river, and follow it on the right bank; lower down, take to the beach, and thou wilt reach the canyon in such sort that, although thou seek to pass it, thou wilt not find where; climb, therefore, the mountain on the right hand, and, in this manner, thou canst by no means miss thy way.'

Analysis

It is known that a major geological upheaval of the altiplano of Ecuador, including the Llanganati Range, occurred within the last few centuries. It may have been during this, or another, upheaval when
Liribamba, the old Riobamba, was completely destroyed, together
with the royal centre of the Shyris at nearby Cacha, allegedly located in
the middle of a lake that was emptied by the upheavals. For this reason, caution is required in interpreting the Valverde Derrotero, compiled before the upheaval(s) took place. With this in mind, the following factors should be considered carefully.

1. There is no specific mention in the Spruce account of where a
searcher is supposed to reach (A lake? A cave?), or what reward might
await whoever climbs the (third?) mountain.

2. Significantly, there is confusion arising from three separate, but
interspersed, references to the socabon, as if they had been interchanged
- perhaps in a coded manner - to confuse investigators. We must assume that all mention of 'the socabon' refers to the same socabon,
otherwise the existence of more than one would be clarified at this
important part of the text.

3. We would expect to find a logical relationship of proximity between the grains of gold in the bog, the guayra and the socabon mine-
tunnel.

4. Lastly, the various references to mountains such as the Cerro
Llanganati, or the mountain, or the third mountain, without mentioning a first or second mountain, is deliberate or irresponsible.

Having, over 20 years, spent many hours with various explorers
pouring over maps - including Blake's map - aerial photographs, and
other related information, I hereby offer a reconstructed version of
the section that ends at the 'Margasitas', in a way I believe to be a
correct juxtaposition of the passages dealing with the canyon, the
mountain, the socabon, and the relationship of the latter with the grains
of gold and the guayra; and which better explains the true path taken
by Valverde.

It should be remembered that the copy extracted by Spruce was
compiled from 8 separate pieces of cotton cloth that comprised the
whole Derrotero, therefore it is not impossible this might have been a

source of confusion in the formulation of the transcript.

(Italics or parentheses used in the rewritten version are added to assist clarification.)

Writer's Version: (Using exactly the same phrases contained in the post-Margasitas section of the Richard Spruce copy of the Derrotero, but relocating them in a more logical and practical manner in relation to the following four key issues.)

1. 'On this side, thou wilt find a Pajonal [*pasture*] in a small plain which, having crossed, thou wilt come on a canyon between two hills, which is the Way of the Inca. If thou lose thyself in the forest, seek the river, and follow it on the right bank; lower down, take to the beach, and thou wilt reach the canyon in such sort that, although you seek to pass it, thou wilt not find where.

2. 'Having come through the canyon and gone a good distance beyond, thou wilt perceive a cascade which descends from an offshoot of the Cerro Llanganati [*probably the Yana Urcu – the Black Mountain*] and runs into a quaking bog on the right hand; and, without passing the stream, in the said bog there is much gold, so that, by putting in thy hand, what thou shalt gather at the bottom is grains of gold.

3. 'To ascend the mountain [*Yana Urcu*], leave the bog and go along to the right, and pass above the cascade, going round the offshoot of the mountain. On the left-hand side of the mountain thou mayst see the 'Guayra' (for thus the ancients called the furnace where they founded metals), which is sprinkled with gold. [*It would be logical for gold dust to be sprinkled around the guayra*].

4. 'From thence, as thou goest along, thou shalt see the entrance of the socabon (mine tunnel) which is in the form of a church porch [*also the description given by Dr. Michel Merlyn of the entrance to the cave he recently discovered*]. And, if by chance the mouth of the socabon be closed with certain herbs, which they call 'Salvaje', remove them, and thou wilt find the entrance. And to reach the third (?) mountain [*there is no mention of a previous, second mountain*], if thou canst not pass in front of the socabon, it is the same thing as to pass behind it, for the water of the lake falls into it. Climb, therefore, the mountain on the right hand, and, in this manner, thou canst by no means miss thy way.'

Completing
the Jigsaw

19

Never in my wildest boyhood fantasies, fed weekly by adventure stories from those unforgettable publications of the D.C.Thomson Publishing Group of Dundee - *the Wizard, Hotspur, Adventure and Rover* - or roaming John Muir's storm-lashed rocky shores and Lammermuir Hills around my hometown Dunbar, could I have imagined such an astounding story of investigation and discovery, nor that so many enigmas could be kaleidescoped into a single, simple, coherent picture. As part of the whole, few theories on the origins of civilization could match those of Juan Moricz:

First, a library of metal books containing the history and scientific knowledge of an unknown advanced civilization which spoke Magyar, the mother language of Cara Maya, Euskara, Quechua, Sumerian, Sanskrit and their derivatives, hidden in a subterranean world of the Andes.

Second, proof of the existence of the civilization of the *Atl Antis*, the Old Andes.

Third, his alleged discovery of 'irrefutable proof' within the metal library of the extra-terrestrial origins of the Atl Antis/Magyar language in the constellation Ursa Major. ('Some day, Sr. Hall,' said Moricz. 'I will give you the name of the town, the name of street and the number on the door!')

Fourth, proof of interoceanic migrations of Scytho-Magyar-Hunos nations, supporting the findings of celebrated Spanish chronicler Fray. Gregorio Garcia.

But, *were all these things true?*

After the Tayos 1976 Expedition was ended, apart from two short visits to Ecuador, it was in September 1982 my interest was reawakened by a strange incident in London that led to my boarding a flight to Ecuador three weeks later.

In the middle of dinner at my flat with a lady friend she suddenly stopped eating, laid down her knife and fork, and said, 'You have to call Ecuador!'

Surprised, I smiled and asked why, since Ecuador had been no part of the conversation and I had been out of touch for 4 years – at which point she became agitated.

'You must call immediately! Right now! Leave your dinner!'

Such was her insistence, I reacted with a flourish of hands, 'Okay! Okay! Don't panic!'

Mumbling about a wasted dinner and the cost of telephoning I checked the time difference and, by coincidence, noted it would be 4.30 p.m. in Ecuador, when Dr. Peña was normally in his office in Guayaquil. I dialled and, to my surprise, he answered personally, on an unusually clear line, with words that left me speechless.

'Stanley, I cannot believe your call! Señor Moricz has just arrived and we are talking about you. He wants you to come to Ecuador and bring a British Mining company. He has found a mountain of gold. We are preparing a telex message for you and will be dispatching some samples with someone returning to Britain.'

How could I forget the amazing spark of intercontinental intuition demonstrated that evening by my friend, who knew nobody in Ecuador and certainly had no way of knowing of the dramatic events taking place at that very moment in the office of Dr.Peña.

As the mining world now knows, Moricz had rediscovered the Nambija skarn deposit in the province of Morona-Santiago, one of the major gold finds of the 20th Century in South America.

Dr. Peña repeated what became a catch phrase in relation to Juan Moricz.

'Moricz never does anything in a small way!'

From September to November 1982, with the mineralised gold samples in my pocket, I interested mining groups such as Rio Tinto Zinc, Consolidated Goldfields, BP Minerals, Charterhouse, Lonrho, and Burnett and Hallamshire; a difficult task since, although I had great samples, I had no Feasibility Study.

By the 22nd November I arrived in Guayaquil with representatives of a British mining group. The mineral deposits Moricz showed at the Yacuambi and Nambija concessions were extraordinary. Unfortunately, contrary to an agreement that the mining company would let me review their draft proposal to assess the possible reaction of Moricz they sent it direct. Moricz threw it to the floor after reading the first page.

The company Chairman telephoned me. I suggested he should offer Moricz what he asked for but add an escape clause to the effect that if the gold values did not match the claims the offer would be reduced accordingly. This was agreed. Other companies also became involved which resulted in the most outstanding offer for a 'grass-roots' project in the history of goldmining; $25 million US dollars for 25% of the shares, an option to purchase another 24% within the 6 months of preliminary trenching and drilling, $100 million US committed to 1st Phase development of the hardrock and alluvial concession(s), and $1 million US up front to defray costs to date, which included the 5-months study by Klochner of Germany in 1975.

After agreement in principle was reached negotiations were dramatically terminated at a celebration lunch in the elegant Club Union in Guayaquil. I was not present. The group included Placer Dome of Canada, San Francisco Mining, and Burnett and Hallamshire of the UK and South Africa. The reason for the break would be impossible to understand were not Moricz's unique character already highlighted. Prior to our planned meeting with him that evening Dr. Peña told me what had happened, adding wearily he hoped he would never have to go through such an experience again.

My jaw dropped as the details unfolded. Apparently, during the general conviviality of the conversations, Moricz, in a reflective moment, had raised the question of the participation of Stanley Hall. To cut the sordid details short the reaction was basically: 'Stanley Who?' followed by someone's thoughtful offer to pay my flight back to Britain. Moricz had given a furious karate chop to the dinner table, spilling large brandies in all directions and calling them something akin to a bunch of shameless bandits. *The mining negotiations were over!*

How could a mining consortium having made such a huge offer be expected to understand rejection based on a question of honour and loyalty? To their minds, what could be more important? Well, now it understood in no uncertain manner!

Later that evening, in calmer mood, Moricz smiled in response to my fervent pleas to forget me and seal the deal.

'Señor Hall! Don't worry about it! The decision was simple. If that's the way they treat you, imagine how they would treat *me!*'

Four years earlier, in 1978, chief geologist for Rio Tinto Zinc Ltd., Dr. Christopher Morrissey had been unable to meet me at Nambija as planned due a serious back injury in Brazil where he had located the largest alluvial deposit in South America. There were times I thought the ghost of Atahualpa had placed a protective curse on Moricz's gold of El Dorado, which fabled land I was by now convinced by geology stretched from the Llanganatis in Ecuador to northern Peru. Gold ore deposits draw human settlers, a fact amply supported by the archaeology in the Ecuadorian Oriente.

Nambija was swamped by thousands of illegal miners who later formed an alliance with government, military, and private groups to wrest ownership from the Cumbaratza Mining Company. The battle for the prize Nambija concession wallowed in legal wrangles until 15 years after the death of Moricz in 1991. Law enforcement is practically non-existent and the chances of Nambija ever being allowed to operate in peace are extremely doubtful.

Such is the sad story of my part in the gold of El Dorado, beginning with a flash of female intuition in London and ending on a point of honour in Guayaquil. Moricz continued with his mining interests to the end, always insisting that he had even better prospects than Nambija but inevitably hampered by his stubborn streak and unrealistic attitude to business. I reminded him that of 50,000 miners who trekked to Alaska during the mid-nineteenth century Gold Rush, there remained only a few large mining groups. Big fish eat little fish!

Sadly, on the 13th of August 1984 (I call it Black Monday), in Olmo's Restaurant, Guayaquil, an incident occurred that separated Moricz and myself for four years. I had again given him my Tayos manuscript to review, a point of honour on my part; but, that day, he chose to accuse me of using historical information from his library (true), from his personal knowledge (true), and of invading his intellectual realm (partly true.) He simply said he was not going to return my manuscript.

THEN, A LANDMARK REALISATION DAWNED ON ME! WAS THE MAIN REASON MORICZ TOOK MY MANUSCRIPT BECAUSE IT CONTAINED MY RECORD OF THE MEETING BETWEEN ANDRÉS FERNANDEZ-SALVADOR AND PETRONIO JARAMILLO?

In typical Moricz style he said we could continue collaborating on the mining projects to which I replied we would collaborate on all or nothing. Thus ended our eventful decade of association.

Knowing him so well there seemed little point in asking how he could so badly treat someone who had sacrificed so much to assist him. As far as the manuscript was concerned all he had to do was ask me not to publish or maybe delete parts he held in contention.

The manuscript incident coincided with a low point in my life. Ill with Hepatitis B from surviving on biscuits, sardines and mineral water far too long, not knowing where my next meal was coming from, dispirited at the events surrounding my manuscript. To cap it all, news came that my brother had died in Scotland. I awoke one morning genuinely surprised to be alive, believing my rapid weight loss and dark urinal discharge must mean I was terminally ill.

Following some urgent medical treatment my convalescence in Guayaquil was rigidly controlled by an Argentinian lady whose husband owned a restaurant in Avenue 9 de Octubre. Probably I owe her my life. Years earlier she, too, had survived hepatitis after an illness of 9 months. Worried about my age, she would not allow anyone else to prepare my food. Twice a day for three weeks she sent meals - of course, most of it tasteless and bland - to my rented room in Las Peñas in Guayaquil.

It was during this convalescence that I resolved, like Scarlet O'Hara

Hall traversing Moricz's gold concession at Nambija (Cumbaratza) 1982

179

in 'Gone With The Wind', 'As God is my witness, I will never go hungry again!'

Step by step I climbed physically and mentally back into the real world, having experienced many worlds. I acquired an old copy of my manuscript from Britain, began to update it, and began another manuscript on missing world history. In October 1985 I married for the second time an Ecuadorian treasure and moved to live in Quito.

For a few years I struggled with the intrigues and beaurocracies of the mining business, invariably defending Moricz's rights on Nambija whenever the subject came up. I did renew contact with him in 1989 following a telephone conversation with Dr.Peña whom I understood, to his great credit, had made it clear to Moricz that he would not take sides.

For old times sake we all met for a 'no hard feelings' lunch in the Grand Hotel in Guayaquil. Frankly, I still harboured a grudge but there was no vestige of animosity in the conversation, rather a mutual aware-ness of the needless loss of years of contact and friendship.

'Well, Stanley!' Moricz mused mischievously. 'You followed me into history and now you are following me into mining!'

'Yes, Juan!' I smiled ruefully. 'I have not forgotten where my Ecua-dorian roots lie - nor that my ventures with you cost me everything I had. Maybe if you had not been so damned honourable I would be rich and famous by now.'

At the Cumbaratza mining camp 1983

'Soon,' he continued pensively, taking a sip from his coffee, 'I am making a trip to Hungary, to bring back some scholars.'

'For what purpose?' I queried, already knowing the answer.

'To help with the translation of the library,' he replied calmly, without the hint of a smile.

A surge of painful memories welled up inside me then quickly ebbed away. I resisted developing the theme except to say, 'Juan, please, this time don't tell anyone - just do it!'

'Of course!' he retorted quietly, before downing the last of his coffee.

As we said goodbye we shook hands warmly, a reminder of our first goodbye in Guayaquil in May 1975, then so full of expectations. It was the last I ever saw of him.

On the 26th of July 1989, anniversary [in my opinion] of the death of Atahualpa, and the 20th anniversary of the Moricz Expedition 1969, I telephoned him to say that, despite the trials and troubles over the years, it was my privilege to have known him; though I hoped the next 20 years for both of us might be more fruitful than the last. He was delighted with the call, saying that our differences were a thing of the past and adding with customary self-confidence that I would only get rich with him. I doubted *that*, but his amazing story is now a legend and, to say the least, life with him was never dull. Culturally and intellectually he may have been the richest man I ever knew. In that sense I can say, yes - I *was* enriched!

On the morning of the 27th February 1991, Juan arrived at his office feeling unwell and, at the insistence of friends, reluctantly had a medical check-up. His heart and lungs were fine but after reading the blood tests the doctor came rushing in to insist he lie down immediately. There was not a drop of potassium in his body. Stubborn as usual, and not wanting to appear weak and helpless, he asked for the prescription, breezily declaring he would take the medicine after lunch, otherwise the taste would kill his appetite. It was a life or death decision. A few hours later, alone in his room at the Sanders Hotel, he collapsed and died, and the world lost one of the most knowledgeable investigators of prehistory who ever lived. We may never know whether he made his fabulous discoveries in the Tayos Caves *or perhaps whether his real intention was to pave the way for someone else*. I will have more to say on that subject.

How I miss that amazing man, Juan Moricz Opos. God bless him

– although by now he is probably giving God a hard time – and his infuriating stubbornness, for he was the stuff great adventure stories are made of.

Over the years in Ecuador I met many adventurous spirits who sought the excitement of exploration. Restless souls, prepared to risk life and limb in pursuit of their goal. Whether searching for Atahualpa's treasure in the treacherous Llanganatis, Drake's silver off the Isla de la Plata, the Quiñara treasure at Vilcabamba, the guard ship Jesús María off Chanduy, the Inca gold-mines, El Dorado, or Atlantis: wonderful, courageous dreamers, each worth a hundred grey men. Men who lived many lives and countless hardships, abandoning the comforts of life at the first twinkle of a wandering star. What matters the cost? Who can price a dream? Are they really dreamers, or messengers send to remind us what the spark of life is all about. Huddled together like plotting pirates, boasting incredible memories, swopping stories of jungles, mountains and seas, each a knarled historian in his field, with real-life experiences to make James Bond and Indiana Jones wonder why life is so damned dull. Here and there a tremor in the voice indicates silent tears, or rejoicing, that they are seldom the failures the envious and scornful would have them believe. Failure at what? Because they live in tune with Nature's laws of discovery? Because without their dreams other men's dreams collapse? Rather are they free spirits, Knights of a Round Table tempered by Nature's love of trickery and deceit, tolerably comfortable disclosing their failures amid shrieks of

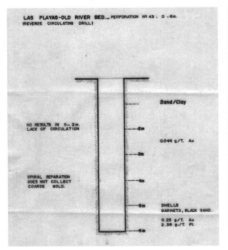 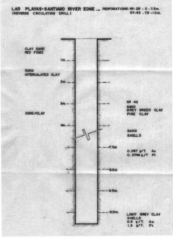

Ecuadorian coastal gold and platinum study

laughter from brother victims. Sensitive, warm-hearted, and full-blooded. These are the explorers - not seekers of treasures, but seekers of life!

Ah!... Life?... Truth? Was I trying to justify my own failures or did I really have a guiding star all these years? Content with knowing what life and truth are *not* - rather than what they are - is the closest we ever get? Why search for a home that is already in your heart?

I have been criticised by friends, scorned by others, enough for me to question my judgement. Painful though it is to recall criticisms, here are a few:

Juan Moricz. 'Don't press me for information! You will only make me angry and think you are another Erich von Daniken!'... and later: 'You have invaded my intellectual kingdom, taken advantage of my work!'

Andrés Fernández-Salvador Z.: 'You manipulate people!'

Stanley Wright (Guayaquil): 'You are a foreigner here, so you must expect to be screwed!'

Presley Norton (Archaeologist): 'Stanley is the first martyr to science fiction!'

The Shuar have a word: 'Imiárma', which means something similar to lines written by Scottish poet, Robert Burns:

Juan Moricz: Farewell to a legend

'O wid God the gift tae gie us, tae see oursels as ithers see us.'
How true!

§§§

I believe at this stage of the narrative I can claim to have faithfully and objectively presented the story of the Caves of the Tayos in a manner that serves the objectives of the British-Ecuadorian Scientific Expedition of 1976, and the separate, more protracted and private investigation of the Tayos treasure enigma. Regarding the latter we now return to the astonishing story left off with Don Andrés Fernandez-Salvador Z. in February 1979.

Petronio's Story: The Keystone

20

There is much I could say about Petronio – full name Lucio Petronio Jaramillo Abarca - whose seminal role in the *Treasure of Tayhuantinsuyu* was confided to me in detail, both written and verbal, during six years of friendship and collaboration, ample time for me to assess whether he was telling the truth, perpetuating a lie, or living a dream.

I have no doubt, after listening to Andrés *and* Petronio, that Juan Moricz's account originated from two meetings with Petronio after being advised by Andrés in 1964-5. Understandably, Petronio embellished his story to safeguard the location of the treasure. During my association with him we agreed that was best way to protect our families.

Location aside, Petronio never hesitated to give me details of his discovery.

'The Treasure consists of chambers filled with statues, two libraries, one of metal, the other of what I can only describe as crystal tablets; one library engraved, the other with channels housing encrustations.'

Born in 1929, his physical association with the treasure began in 1946, 18 years before Moricz arrived in Ecuador.

Here is my translation of the written testimony of Petronio concerning the events that occurred in the house of Alfredo Moebius.

'The first of my fatal interviewers to receive the most complete and detailed affirmation that the Cave of the Tayos did not correspond with the Cave of the TAYUS was Juan Moricz. I met Moricz in the house of Moebius in 1964. The only thing that Moricz came to know about the Metal Library and the Treasure of the TAYUS is what he heard from my lips. But he deformed the story by locating the treasure, 'to his entire satisfaction', in the province of Morona-Santiago. Every word I spoke, Moricz asked me to amplify and to give specific explanations. I gave them to him – statues and columns, capitals, vaults, stairs, labyrinths, instruments, tunnels, ramps, platforms, light, rooms and tables, figures and chairs, everything... dimensions, colours, heights, hardnesses, weights, etc. etc. He continued to question me. I repeated what I had said. Afterwards I questioned him and he repeated what I had said.

'The few times I met with Moricz (the last time being in April 1969) were sufficient for him to arrange his agreements with Erich von Daniken. I remember, after he had made his first journey to the Cave of the Tayos in 1965, he spoke with me, insisting I should lead him to the treasure, that he would be 'Chief of the Expedition', that he must be the first to 'tread on the rungs', like a conqueror on the high seas: sad dreams of an enigmatic adventurer.

'In 1969, the magazine Vision produced an account of a subterranean world found in Ecuador by Juan Moricz, mentioning that the discovery arose from an 'old tale' by one Captain Jaramillo. That Captain Jaramillo was me!'

'The claims by Moricz to property and treasure rights in the province of Morona Santiago always made me smile.' PJA

§§§

'The second person was Alfredo Moebius, a german gentleman in his sixties, green eyes, Caucasian countenance, a support platfom under his lacquered shoe presumably compensating for some disability in his leg. He used to walk by the office where I worked in the Avenue Colón in Quito, it being close to his flat in the Avenue Rabida. We became casually acquainted.

'One day, when we became more closely acquainted, he said, 'What a surprise ... to know Petronio Jaramillo Abarca. Are you *the* Petronio Jaramillo Abarca?'

'I imagined my popularity had to do with some publicity material which had been thrown from small planes over Quito, advertising some of the products I sold.

'Why?

'Moebius not only stared at me, but measured me. He walked to one side to look at me again. Then he measured me again, after which he greeted me effusively, as if I were and old friend, saying, 'Why are you so important to me?'

'Could Señor Moebius please explain why I am so important to him?'

'He waited a moment, then concluded, 'Tomorrow will be very important!'

'Some days passed, then Moebius communicated to me that he had been to the Oriente and had just returned from Puyo, the source of some of my products. For a moment, I thought he might be a shareholder in my supplier's company and that his purchases in Puyo were simply to check prices.

'Soon afterwards he invited me to his house. Heavy iron doors, big doberman dogs, a wooden leg, and a blond girl he presented as his daughter who spoke perfect Spanish. His Spanish was not good and on occasion she translated those parts he could not fully understand.

'I invited you so we could talk about the 'Cuava de los Tayos,' he prompted, as soon as we were seated.

'This time, it was I who looked, measured, then asked, 'Why? What has happened to the Cave of the Tayos?'

'You know exactly where the Cuava de los Tayos is located,' he replied.

'In the province of Morona Santiago, up the River Coangos. That is no secret since many people know about it!'

'I am not referring to the Cave of the Birds, but the Cave of the Treasure. Where is the treasure Cave?'

'In a faraway and secret place, far from the Tayos.'

There was a long silence, then he muttered, 'I don't believe it! I simply don't believe it!'

'That is you problem, Señor Moebius!'

He held his head firmly. Often he would interlink his fingers, loosen them, put one arm under his armpit, with the other grasping his elbow, then unfold them. He munched his teeth for a moment ... then, very suavely, asked, 'The treasure is not in the Cuava de los Tayos of the birds?'

'It is not in the Cave of the Tayos birds!'

'But it is very close? Is that true?'

'Faraway, very distant.'

'What is distant for you?'

'The same as for you.'

'Miles? Kilometres?'

'Yes ... Miles ... Kilometres.'

'Many miles?'

'Depends.'

'Depends on what?

'On the place from which you want to measure.'

'Oh! Yes! Of course! That's correct!'

We fell into to a long silence.

'The tradition of El Dorado was no more than the romanticising and poetic transmission of an ancient truth, jealously guarded, hidden and respected. Those tortured in Quito (by the Conquistadores) signalled only to the east and nothing more.' (PJA)

§§§

'It was also in the house of Moebius that I first met Pino Turolla. There were five of us present then - Juan Moricz, Turolla, Moebius, his daughter and myself. The object of the reunion? ... that PJA repeat his novel account regarding the Cave of the Tayos. So I did!

'Two days later Turolla met with me again in Quito and, over a map, managed to get me to point with my finger to the location of the Cave of the Tayos birds. Some days later he returned to say that he had found the place. 'I have come from there!' he told me.

'This time, however, Turolla was very clear and energetic. He insisted I lead him to the treasure cave. He asked that, when he recorded my words, I should not mention the difference in location between the two caves, nor their contents. He was now certain there were two specific caves – the Bird cave and the Treasure cave.

'He began to get violent when he could get no more out of me. He was not happy that I should telephone Miami to get somes references. Indeed, in that instant, he became extremely angry when I said I wanted to check out where he had first obtained information about me and my story. When I finally did call Miami to find out something about such a distinguished person I was told he was a 'profazador', which sent me scurrying to the dictionary for the meaning of such a singular profession.

'I never saw Turolla again except to hear that he had written a book called *Beyond the Andes* about his frustrating adventures in Ecuador, which included some reference to me and my story.

'I will never forgive him for his aggression towards me. All I remember of this gentleman is his nervous, middle-aged, convulsive energy, his hypocritical actions and his much-repeated phrase, 'Look at me! ... Look at me!'

'With all the data they proceeded in their own way. Moebius, Moricz, Turolla and Erich von Daniken did what they did, together or separately. The explanation I gave concerning the different geographical characteristics between the two sites was continually ignored. In the end they got angry with each other and everything fell apart, so truth found its justice.

'I adopted the same method with everyone who solicited information about the Cave of the Tayos, and equally with those who attempted to draw my tongue about the location of the treasure. My sincerity was interpreted as a charming perversity, forgivable, a trick to lead them along other paths, believing that further inside the Tayos bird cave they would find the treasure. Well! Let them believe! I alone protect it, with my silence! Ask Moebius, Moricz, Turolla - or Gastón Fernández Borrero, who visited me in Esmeraldas a few days before the arrival of Neil Armstrong to accompany Stanley Hall into the Cave of the Tayos in 1976.' (PJA)

§§§

Petronio would have been innocent of the background linking Turolla with the renowned yugoslav-born american Dr. Andrija Puharich, inventor, parapsychologist, master hypnotist, CIA intelligence adviser, groomer of Uri Geller, collaborator with movements like those of the elitist Schwaller de Lubicz, Dr. James J. Hurtak, L. Ron Hubbard and others of similar esoteric ilk. Puharich's experiments in remote viewing, psychic channeling of 'alien intelligences', and hallucinegenic shamanism, continues to influence psychic experimentation in the present millenium. It says much for the commitment of Petronio that, possibly a target of this group and despite being shaken, he sent the disconsolate Turolla and his agenda packing. Where Moebius and Moricz might have fitted into this elitist-synarchic global scenario can only be speculated upon. In 1995 a female regional representative of James Hurtak visited me 'urgently' in Quito to enquire of my interest in a reunion with him later that year. Subject?... the *Cave of the Tayos*! Thankfully, that was the last I heard of the proposal.

The information Petronio confided in the 1990s confirmed to me that it was definitely not the Cave of the 'Tayos', but the Cave of the

'Tayu', which contained the treasure; and, significantly, that it was positively *not located in the province of Morona Santiago as claimed by Moricz in his notarised document.*

My first contact with Petronio occurred six months after the death of Moricz, when intuitive impulses and a sense of obligation impelled me to evolve the metal library story through to its completion. I found him in self-imposed exile in the coastal city of Esmeraldas, re-married with a second family and employed as a professor of social sciences at the Universidad Luis Vargas.

Our first meeting, in September 1991, followed by a second in October, are again best described in his own words, which also best serves the reader to gain further insight into his character and personality.

§§§

FIRST MEETING WITH STANLEY HALL: 1991: by Petronio Jaramillo A.: (Translation by S. Hall):

'We are now a few months after the death of Juan Moricz, which occurred in Guayaquil in February 1991. My son Mario Petronio, then 14 years old and living with me in Esmeraldas received, when I was not at home, a telephone call from Stanley Hall Armstrong (Armstrong being his mother's maiden name), who asked for me. They spoke for only a few minutes.

'Some nine days later he called again and, this time, spoke with me direct. I joked, 'Your call is 16 years late, because you came to Ecuador in 1975, and now it is 1991!'

Stanley Hall was not entirely unknown to me. I had heard of him one way or another since 1976 when he had descended with Neil Armstrong into the Tayos Caves, earlier visited by Juan Moricz, Pino Turolla, and many native Shuar who over the years had never publicised the fact.

'Hall had known Moricz much longer than I had (and for sure had heard him speak of the TURUL, sacred bird of the Hungarian Magyars, whose progenitors were the Tayus, a belief (of Moricz) which Hall confirmed to me.) But, above all, he had brought Neil Armstrong to Ecuador.

'I thought Hall had organized his scientific expedition in search of the treasure that Moebius, Moricz and Turolla had heard about from me; so I remember him as having led men 'by the fierce amazon jungle', there to descend with Armstrong, two armies, and dozens of scientists, into the Cave of the Tayos. I recall he did not arrive at any agreement with Moricz, also that Moricz and Gastón Fernández had mutually ignored each other. Moebius, Moricz, and Turolla had similarly ignored *me* regarding the true location of the Cave of the TAYUS, and so, with the publication of Erich von Daniken's book, the world was fooled. Finally, I remembered how Turolla had tried to fix (with me) the exact location of the treasure.

'All this and much more came to mind when Stanley Hall identified himself on the other end of the telephone line. When I heard his voice all the images returned, including those of Moebius, Moricz, Turolla and von Daniken. They were not happy memories.

'He said he was coming to Esmeraldas for personal reasons and wanted to talk to me about the Cave of the Tayos. When he finally arrived I found him to be pleasant, cultured and practical. Nothing of greed, nothing of treasure!

'I related to him verbally as I had done with others the Legend of El Dorado and the Cave of the Tayos, just as I had written it in a novelised but nevertheless sincere form, emphasising, as I had done with others, its coded and inexact nature with respect to location and

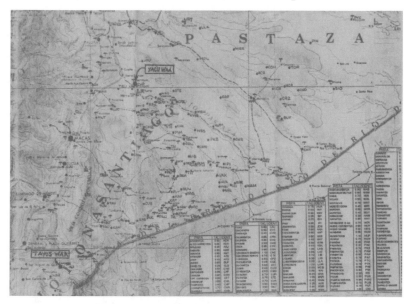

Shuar Map

route; also, that my words were formulated to mislead and divert profane eyes away from the treasure; in short, clarifying the difference between the Cave of the Tayos and the Treasure Cave of the Tayus.

'However, my strategy did not impress Stanley Hall. He was a Scottish engineer and all that interested him was the history of the Tayus and the anthropology of my brain. He, in turn, told me about his expedition of 1976, of which Neil Armstrong was Honorary President and participant.

'Neil Armstrong, I thought, the first man to walk on the Moon, descended a gigantic cave full of beautiful Tayos birds. Surely his presence must have been directed at superior objectives – possibly because the army of expeditionaries might emerge with the metal library? These were my thoughts!

'Listening to my detailed remarks, Hall refuted them from the understandable viewpoint that his expedition was eminently scientific; but my eyes detected disappointment at having caused, without wanting to, frustration for Armstrong.

'He suggested that, perhaps guided by myself, he could bring Neil Armstrong back to know the Treasure Cave of the Tayus. It could be planned for 3 months time, before the start of the rainy season.

§§§

SECOND MEETING: STANLEY HALL AND BRITISH AMBASSADOR

'A month later, I received a second visit from the Scotsman Stanley Hall, accompanied by an excellent English gentleman.

'My house is built on a small hill, without paved access, accommodated among trees, without any type of executive comforts. There, within the sitting room, in a formal atmosphere, we began a conversation. After the welcoming and introductions I felt moved to stand to attention. I was in the presence of none other than the British Ambassador to Ecuador, His Excellency Ambassador Frank Wheeler; about two metres tall, deep blue eyes, perhaps 50 years old, of athletic build. He had brought a book, in English, which he presented to me. I thanked him and we sat down.

To help soothe my nervousness the Ambassador stated his admiration for some paintings on the walls. This gave me time to pull myself together before I launched forth with a hurried and banal question.

'And how are you, Mr. Ambassador?'

'Well! Very well! He replied, smiling.

We had established the precise channel of communication that Stanley had planned in a calculated manner. There we were, those two on the offensive and I, an ex-military, small-calibre artillery officer, on the redoubt, firing on command at the 'expeditionaries' and answering questions against a British offensive that was ever more concrete, ever more pointed and penetrating.

Their questions reached deep down inside me. Was it possible they might access the secret I had guarded for 50 years? During the conversation, when my ammunition was finished, Hall looked me square in the eyes and said, *'Neil Armstrong is the person who could ensure that nobody*

Petronio Jaramillo and Stan Hall 1996

would leave you to one side. The whole world respects him!

This forced a tremendous dilemma upon me. I thought a bit, and was a long time silent. They had touched, for the first time, the basic chords of my symphony. The anthropology worked marvellously. The name of Neil Armstrong had introduced the security that I needed.

The Ambassador - without doubt the most valiant of Ambassadors - was assuming the risk of a story that might not be genuine, and the person responsible for this would be Stanley Hall - another brave man!

Inspired by Hall, who had written a manuscript of his 1976 expedition, I was satisfied to collaborate with him because he, free of avarice, manifested a singular predisposition to understand the risks of the situation, leaving aside the urgency related to the arrival of the rainy season and accepting that the occupation of the Treasure Cave needed to pass various stages, such as the divulgence of the culture of the Tayus, establishment of a World Institute of Epistemological Studies, careful selection of the occupation team, formation of a Tayus Association, and arrangements for the jurisdiction, security and administration of the territory and the deposit.

The story of Stanley Hall, which forms the first part of this project, constitutes the most honourable experience of his life, though frustrating both for him and for millions of people who expected more of his venture; all because he lacked the hidden steps veiled inside my story which, for the first time, I intend to place at the disposition of Humanity.'

From his early teens Petronio had been raised by someone he called uncle *Blanco Pelado* (sometimes Blanquito) presumably a reference to his baldness. There is no doubt in my mind, though Petronio never divulged it directly, that this uncle was the mysterious person - possibly Gilberto, a brother of his mother Doña Sarah Jaramillo Abarca who before he died passed on details about the Treasure Cave.

Armed with this information Petronio visited the Cave. Ten years later, in 1956, he noted down his experiences. Then, in 1964-5, Alfredo Moebius, Pino Turolla, Andrés Fernández-Salvador Z., and Juan Moricz, entered the story.

Here is Petronio's written summary of his first visit to the treasure cave.

'After my predecessor (Blanco Pelado) died I set out to follow the route he had indicated. It was 1946. I was 17 years old!

'The instructions were reliable. I walked over sand, stones, rocks and stairways, crawled on all fours through water, moved right, upwards … I arrived at the floor of the Cave, opened my eyes and, Oh!… It was true… It was the cave of the Treasure, the Cave of the Tayus!

'My predecessor had seen the treasure and given me instructions and explanations on how to observe and understand it; but when I stepped into that deposit it proved to be much bigger, and very disconcerting.

'The verbal description he had given was intended to match my youth but when I actually experienced it physically it was so different. The antecedents did not serve me at all. Between our two conceptions there was an age difference of 50 years in understanding and culture. Such was the impact it almost shocked me to death. What I had conceived in my mind as no great thing was in reality the greatest treasure on Earth as I have since confirmed and re-confirmed. For sure, it was short of nothing.

'I knew then that I had the serious responsibility of one day divulging its contents and organizing its occupation; but, at the same time, I foresaw the brutal looting and pillaging it could generate.

'When I visited the cave in 1956 I decided to recount it (to others) in the manner outlined to me by my predecessor, namely, an amalgam of facts and images, a mixture of truth and fiction that, anybody would note, did not contain a clear definition of the treasure. This was because I did not have any translation of the metal *or crystal* archives, and thus decided not to make the matter public yet.

'When the whirlpool in my mind began to clear and I understood more of what the discovery would mean I decided to proceed carefully with any plan for its divulgence.'

§§§

Petronio's description of the contents of the caves, which he gave to me in writing - and which I rigorously and repeatedly re-confirmed with him in discussions over a period of 6 years - is summarised as follows:

'First, I looked inside a small chamber and saw some golden toys and, amongst these, small balls of gold, marbles, of different sizes. Climbing to a second chamber, my astonishment increased. There were thousands of animal figures, some positioned normally, others on their side, others with their feet in the air, others seated; cattle and horses in abundance, not an elephant nor fly was missing. Beetles, sparrow hawks, mastodons, reptiles, so many it was like a Christmas store. In the centre were cats on pedestals, so finely made they seemed ready to miauw; crocodiles, bullocks, rams, shrews, ostriches, hippopotami, all on pedestals made of brilliant stones, of different colours, though I could not tell whether or not these were rubies, emeralds, diamonds, or sapphires, because I knew nothing about precious stones; but I could not rid my head of the possibility that that is what they were. They were large, marvellous crystals that caught the light and dispersed it in a thousand sparkling beams.

'I saw them all, touched them, admired their perfection. Some made me afraid, they seemed so alive, even menacing. I could not lift any of them; they were so heavy they seemed fixed to the ground on their mysterious pedestals.

'Even more intriguing, there was a human skeleton, with bones of gold, lying on its back, with its 208 bones perfectly joined, on a bed made of crystal, but a crystal purer than the purest water. I did not know which to admire more, the crystal coffer or the skeleton.

'Moving to a third chamber, imagine my surprise to discover fig-

Another doorway enigma

ures, half human, half animal, as if all the mythologies had united to display themselves in gold and precious stones, in postures characteristic of defence, attack, and in various capricious positions. There were bodies with heads of hawks, with horses' feet, with wings; birds with human arms and legs; hyenas with faces of princesses, of parrots, of insects; spiders with faces of women; donkeys with faces of men. A multitude of combinations of beast and human, all in expressive attitudes which, in that moment of wonder for me, I could not easily interpret; only that they seemed to come from the distant age of Osiris, Pthat, Thoth and Anubis.

'In a better-lit corner of the [third] chamber was an impressive, overwhelming, figure; half-human, seated in front of a cauldron in which it appeared he had been cooking children. I left with this scene of Molochian horror filling my mind and passed to the next [fourth] chamber.

'This [chamber] I wish that I had entered first. Here was a sense of harmony. Objects were set in arrangements more in sympathy with my mentality. There were few statues, but the picturesque scene began with a woman breast-feeding her baby, in perfect attitude and form, as if to accentuate the natural act, only her breast had the form of the Earth. Another, similar, female statue was seated with a child on her lap, putting something [breast?] in its mouth which was also shaped like the Earth. Another female statue was standing with one hand directing her child as if showing it how to walk. Another had her child half-hidden in her cloak, as if trying to conceal it from something, to protect it; here, a ball, or Earth, was under the feet of the child. The final statue showed a child sleeping on its mother's lap, whereas she, as is natural, watched over its dreams; there was no ball here.

'That chamber was so peaceful, filled with so many representations of global maternity that I slept for a while. When I awoke the chamber was dark. I was tired, mentally exhausted from seeing and thinking on such marvels. Continuing my reconnaissance I passed about ten more (chamber) entrances containing what I can only describe as other marvels.

'Then, I came upon the big one, the majestic one, where light shone like the Sun. It was not another cave but the continuation of the same nave. The floor was covered with pieces of crystal quartz and coloured stones, all reflecting the light. Some walls were crystal [in appearance], some covered in a vitreous material. Vaults joined together in various forms and heights. (There were) Doors on every side, sealed hermetically with a vitreous covering, each 25 to 40 centimetres wide. When I shone my flashlight on them, I was answered by thousands of little rainbow colours that surprised me in the way they seemed to hold the light. Other doors were red and seemed to be covered in myriads of rubies.

'There were crystal-like columns of various colours; cylindrical, squared, angular, half-moon, trapezoidal; all in the form of structural supports with some parts formed by crystals.

'Each moment, I found myself uttering words like - Marvellous! Incredible! Colossal! As I witnessed these wonders, I asked myself: 'How is it possible this world of wonders is not inhabited? How is it possible the owners have disappeared and left all this?

'Then, all of a sudden, an overwhelming sight appeared before me, unbelievable in my wildest imaginings. Entire libraries, full of heavy, voluminous books!

'Moving over to one of the books I glanced through one or two pages of opaque, yellow metal. They seemed to be written by a single person, in a near perfect script, similar to modern taquigraphy; in low-relief, the impression on the other side of the page confirming the script was stamped one side only. Also there were known symbols - crosses, circles, semi-circles, squares, triangles, stars.

'Turning more pages I saw what appeared to be mathematical formulae, illustrative designs; geometrical, zodiacal, ecliptic and spacial figures, in minute detail, but in signs and letters of a language unintelligible to me. Every moment I was astonished.

'There were thousands of volumes. Lifting one was like moving a hundred pounds weight. I put one onto a table of four legs covered in gold; then, I lifted down seven books, but could not replace them, due to the effort required. The bookshelves were covered in beaten gold. The furniture was the same. All the supports of gold, gold, gold! How much more was in the other chambers? What did the symbols mean?

'I had to go back again some day … It did not matter if I had to climb great ridges or descend dangerous chasms; that the larger part of the journey was swampland, unhealthy, infernal; that an army would be needed to transport equipment; or that metal bridges and ladders would be needed to fix enough lighting in the Caves.

'The tradition of El Dorado, the Treasure of Atahualpa and Ruminahui, was no more than the romanticising and poetic transmission of an ancient truth, jealously guarded, hidden and respected, some of which may have been used to pay the ransom of Atahualpa. El Dorado exists! The indigenous guardians never gave it away. Those who were tortured in Quito signalled only to the east and nothing more.

'There was a time when the Atlantic Ocean reached as far as the Andes and it was there that the great empires were formed. Between the ocean and the Andes were the spurs, or lower ridges, of the Eastern Cordilleras, where today are concealed the tombs of sunken ships and the refuges of ancient pirates. Here is where can be found the Cave of the Tayus! El Dorado! In the furthest eastern hills of Ecuador, in the fourth chain of the mountainous eastern Cordilleras where the Amazon region commences, lies the lost history of the world.'

§§§

Six years is a long time to assess a situation, and readers can be reassured that all the questions they would have wished to ask Petronio were asked, often repeatedly, during that time. The following are some examples:

Q. 'You must realise there are animals and insects in your treasure of artifacts that do not correspond with the orthodox view of evolutionary development on the American continent?'

A. 'Yes! Of course I realise that, but nevertheless they are there.'

Q. 'If only one page of writing from pre-colonial America could be found it would cause a global sensation, yet you claim to have found a metal library containing thousands of books?'

A. 'Yes!'

Q. 'What about the other library of transparent tablets you were unable to scratch with a knife?'

A. 'I cannot explain that either. These tablets were not stacked like the metal books, but with each tablet inclined backwards against others behind it, stacked on both sides of gold-leafed furniture fabricated like trestles.'

Q. 'How are the leaves of the metal books held together? By copper wire, perhaps?'

A. 'No! They are bound in a fashion similar to a hardback book.'

Q. 'What size are the metal sheets and how many do you estimate are in each book?'

A. 'Each metal sheet is about 40 x 20 centimetres, and there are about 50 leaves in each book, stamped to form a bas-relief on one side. There are tinges of green in the metal. The sizes of the books vary and, I estimate, from lifting some of them, that they average between 20 and 40 kilograms each. The seven books I took down from a shelf were each too heavy for me to lift back up again.'

Q. 'What did you make of the inscriptions and symbols?'

A. 'The script is similar to modern shorthand: like Sanskrit or Pali or

PETRONIO JARAMILLO ABARCA

Bloque 4, Dept. 14
(Sra. Sara Abarca)
Quito, Ecuador.
Telefono: 593-2-242233

FECHA: 19 de Marzo de 1997
DE: Petronio Jaramillo Abarca
A: Embajador Frank Wheeler: Santiago, Chile
REF:

1. Estamos muy contentos de conocer que usted pasará por Ecuador en el futuro proximo. Siempre estaremos agradecidos su comprensión para la creación de un Instituto Internacional de Patrimonio Cultural presidido por un Comité de Embajadores de Quito con fin de preservar los patrimonios ineditos.

2. Queremos continuar el proyecto: primero, edición de libro; segundo, selección de los ocupantes; tercero, conformación de una Institución Internacional dentro de UNESCO; cuatro, formación de una Sociedad Internacional que obtenga propiedad territorial, con los permisos, concesiones y licencias juridicas pertinentes; quinto, ocupación y administración.

3. Reiteramos a usted sentimientos de absoluta sinceridad, cordialidad y agradecimiento. Siempre seremos buenos amigos. Aspiramos su irreemplazable coordinación.

Esperamos conversar con usted.

Saludos,

Petronio Jaramillo Abarca

Petronio letter to Ambassador Frank Wheeler

Middle-Eastern as you have suggested. Some of the symbols, such as circles, squares, hexagons etc., were bisected by two parallel lines, some zigzagged, others S-shaped or L-shaped.'

Q. 'What size are the transparent tablets?'

A. 'Smaller than the metal leaves, maybe about 30 x 15 centimetres, smooth and hard. The thickness is about 5 or 6 millimetres, with rounded edges.'

Q. 'Are there any writings or other markings on the transparent tablets?'

A. 'Each is grooved with a series of channels about 5 millimetres wide by 3 millimetres deep. The channels are filled with small diamond-shaped encrustations, as if sculptured by some kind of engraving machine. There were also workshops of small, simple machines for making jewellery and metal adornments such as buttons, many of which were lying about on the floor.'

Q. 'Why did you not take photographs or bring out some pieces as evidence?'

A. 'First, it did not seem right to remove something that belonged to the civilization that placed them there. Second, access is underwater, below river level: it would have been physically impossible for me to remove books or artifacts: also, such action would have placed my life in immediate danger. Third, I did not have a camera: nor could I have taken photographs that could not easily be considered fakes.'

Q. 'When will the Cave of the Tayus be occupied?'

A. 'It will take place when the existence of the civilization of the TAYUS has first been announced, the occupation team has been selected, the administration of the deposit has been legitimized publicly and privately without risks and, especially, when the territorial jurisdiction and its international security have been duly guaranteed.

'At the time of occupation we (referring to me) would be pleased to have the collaboration of Neil Armstrong – not for sensationalism – but because there is no question of his scientific and technological abilities; also the certainty that, if he enters this other world, he will not think it necessary to appropriate it. I have no material interest in the treasure of the Tayus, in the same way that Armstrong does not own a single square metre of the lunar Sea of Tranquility in spite of leaving his footprints there.

'I have scratched the initials 'PJA' on each book that I moved, it being impossible to mark the crystal books. I have done the same on some of the gold-covered walls of the Cave, discreetly of course, since never did I think my initials signified right of property but rather a sentimental act. I also wrote three other names besides my own, each with a date.'

'I want to thank British Ambassador Frank Wheeler and Stanley Hall for the idea of forming a Committee of Ambassadors to oversee the international organization of the occupation project.' (PJA.)

Treasure Analysis and Location

21

Here is the sequence of events involved in the treasure trail:

1946: Petronio's first visit to the treasure cave.

1956: Petronio records his story to-date.

1964: Petronio is variously interviewed: by Alfredo Moebius, Andrés Fernández-Salvador Z., Pino Turolla and Juan Moricz.

1965: First visit by Moricz to the Cave of the Tayos in Morona-Santiago.

1968: Mormon expedition to the Cave of the Tayos region.

1969: 'Expedition Moricz' to the Cave of the Tayos. Media announcement.

1972: Moricz and Dr. Peña take Erich von Daniken on trip to Cuenca.

1974: Notarised document of Moricz's alleged discoveries (6th June).

1975: First meeting of Stan Hall and Moricz. 'Stones' expedition to Mendez.

1976: British-Ecuadorian Expedition: Tayos Caves of Morona-Santiago.

1978: Moricz introduces Hall to Don Andrés Fernández-Salvador Z.

1979: Important Hall/AFS meeting on Moricz, Dyott, and Jaramillo.

1982: Moricz invites Hall to bring Cumbaratza gold-mining projects to attention of international Mining Companies and come to Ecuador. Hall begins in-depth historical investigation of the Empire of Tayhuantinsuyu and Reino de los Kitus.

1991: Moricz dies suddenly in February. In September Hall meets Petronio
Jaramillo for the first time. Start of 6-Year collaboration.

1996: Petronio and Hall update their stories: formulate plan for expedition.

1998: Petronio is assassinated near his house in Esmeraldas.

1999: Hall makes reconnaissance trips to the Oriente.

2005: Hall publishes calculated location of the treasure. Informs Ecuadorian Embassy in the U.K. on January 17th.

Correlation of Clues

Flashbacks and memories from conversations with Petronio over our six years together years included his mention of: the predecessor... treasure not located in Morona Santiago ... first treasure visit when 17 years old, in 1946... treasure of the Tayu part of the same treasure as that of Atahualpa... where two great rivers join... escarpment region... two hills ten metres high at the edge of a river... white rock formation... cave entrance on a river bank... treasure entrance through underwater canal... treasure below river level... best entered in the dry season... located in territory of the Huamboyas, Canelos and Achuyanos (Achuar?)... two hours trek from the nearest road access... jaguar territory... antagonistic indigenous population... stream immediately inside the cave... roar of waterfall during storm.

Seldom did Petronio mention any two clues in the same conversation but collectively they pointed towards one specific area, where a cave entrance on the banks of a river can be found about two hours from the nearest road access. Other clues included the following:

1. The predecessor had to be his 'uncle', Blanquito, or Blanco Pelado, the now deceased military officer, in whose care Petronio remained for some years up to his 17th birthday.

2. The treasure is *not* located in the province of Morona-Santiago, nor is it in Zamora Chinchipe. Was it in *Pastaza*?

3. The nearest junction of two great rivers would be at the confluence of the Palora and the Pastaza, the latter flowing from the Sierra by way of Baños and Shell Mera, *also the simplest expedition route from the Sierra to the Pastaza region*. Impelled by the 1941-42 conflict with Peru, construction of the Baños-Shell Mera road was completed by the Ecuadorian army in 1946 and extended to Puyo in 1947, dates that coincide with the first time the 17-year-old Petronio could reasonably have accessed the Pastaza region.

4. What might be described as *escarpments*, cliffs of white stratified limestone ideal for cave formation, are visible where the Puyo - Macas bridge crosses the Pastaza river. The cliffs downriver rise from 10 – 20

metres above river level and there are two hills at *the only place downriver where water gouges out and enters the fossilised rock strata.* The sedimentary formations where cave systems exist in the Oriente is known to geologists as the Napo Formation, the name derived from the province of Napo.

5.   Petronio repeatedly stated:

a) The cave entered a cliff face directly from a river bank.

b) The access to the treasure chamber is by an underwater passage inside the cave, the top of which is visible during the dry season from October to March: and…

c) the treasure is located *below* the level of 'the river.'

6.   Two tribes mentioned by Petronio as lacking attention by historians are the *Canelos* and the *Huamboya.* During the Shuar uprising of 1599 they sided disastrously with the Spanish. Both were concentrated in the Pastaza region.

7.   The Achuyanos, a 'cover' name given to me by Petronio, are probably the Achuaris, or Achuar.

8.   The location is indicated by the increasing roar of a waterfall entering a pothole within 30 minutes of the start of a heavy rainstorm.

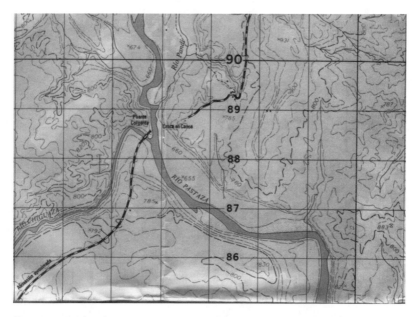

Pastaza map location

§§§

What does it mean if the eight clues coincide to focus on a particular location? Should the search, therefore, be concentrated in the Pastaza province south of the Canelos community some 25 kilometres south of Puyo in the territory as far as the Pastaza river? There is a cave system in jaguar country a day and a half's trek south-east of the village of Canelos, close to the confluence of the Bombonoza and Umupi. The region is peppered with caves containing Tayos birds. However, the principal entrance is on the banks of the Pastaza two hours walk downriver from the suspension bridge at Sharupe.

Reconnaissance
in Pastaza

22

In May 1999, I set off with Petronio's son Mario Petronio to where the River Oso joins the Copatasa (Shuar: Kupatas) in Pastaza province. We had driven past Baños and stayed overnight at the Hotel Amazonico in Puyo before taking the Macas road to Sharupe. There, a Shuar woman invited us to park the Trooper by her house, a short distance from her little store. Her husband, a surly and resentful mestizo from Quito, was occupied with some companions with whom he had, for three days, been drinking local 'fire-water' mixed with hallucigenic drugs. Adopting a mindless and aggressive attitude he attacked me with fists and feet flying. Two of his swaying companions tried to calm him but he broke away, still screaming abuse, and entered the house. I feared he might fetch a gun but instead he appeared with two large bottles of beer. With open chest and a mighty roar to the heavens he smashed them together to make jagged weapons for his second attack. As he lurched forward I had no option but to stand my ground, fists raised, eyes focussed on his jaw, knowing I had to knock him cold with a single blow, since hitting him twice would make *him* the victim. Again his drunken companions, to their credit, tried to restrain him but, after throwing away the bottle-necks, our warrior lifted up two half bricks, screaming he was going to 'destroy my gringo face' - at which moment I came to the intelligent conclusion we should get the hell out of there.

I signalled Mario and our Shuar guide, Bosco, coincidentally the aggressor's brother-in-law, equally an unknown quantity and himself recovering from the marathon drinking session, but, as it turned out, the best of the bunch. Also set to join us was his teenage nephew, José Antonio, at that moment valiantly trying to prevent the roaring demon from attacking me with the bricks. We scrambled into the Trooper and roared off like bats out of hell, stopping at a nearby schoolroom where the teacher and her husband offered to care for the vehicle.

At mid-day we finally set off on foot along the north bank of the Pastaza. Unfortunately, our hazy-headed Shuar guide became uncertain on how to reach the Jibaria of his aunt's family, where he intended we spend the night. We hoped to reach it in daylight but finished up in the dark walking by the river, the only light coming from a torch up front and cigarette lighters that burnt our fingers. By good fortune Bosco's coded calls into the night resulted in the sudden appearance of a kerosene lamp swaying back and forth some 50 metres through the trees. Thankfully we entered the Jibaria, kindly received by Bosco's elderly aunt, understandably wary since she was alone babysitting eight children whose parents were off on some visit. We slept fitfully that night. God knows what would have happened had the parents returned that night in the same state as those at Sharupe. It had been quite a day!

Early next morning we thanked our Shuar hostess, distributing token presents and sweets to the children before continuing on our way. At mid-day, brewing some noodle soup, we were caught by a thunderstorm. Amid much hilarity, sheltering under the forest canopy, huge raindrops soon penetrated through the foliage, splashing hot soup onto our hands and faces.

An hour later we came upon a Shuar community. At first we were welcomed and invited to sit beside the leaders, the wife of one breastfeeding her baby. However, as the conversation progressed, we were bombarded with questions. Between gulps of the inevitable chicha, it became clear some wanted to confiscate our equipment and send us back. I fronted my position as Honorary Brother and international representative of the Shuar Federation, quoting the names of five presidents known to me. This ruse plus a gift of some batteries for their disfunctional radio solved the problem.

By the end of the meeting, Bosco, still wobbly from his earlier drinking session, got drunk again and, by the time we reached the next Shuar community at Chiwintza, he was more interested in the local festive spirit to be followed by a good siesta. The latter he badly needed and, although his idea of distance and time was at times hilarious, at least he had kept us more or less on the right track. We left him and nephew Antonio behind to make our way to the next community of Kumai, hoping that before nightfall he would catch up and bring the equipment under his care.

We arrived just before dark. Bosco arrived an hour or so later, spouting a tearful 'how-could-I-have-forsaken-him' story about José Antonio who had decided the going was too tough and was on his way back alone, not an attractive prospect. I was almost 63 years of age and therefore not too impressed by his reason for returning but, yes, the going *was* tough. Mario, a strong youngster, had done everything physically possible to make my journey less arduous.

The Kumai community seemed friendlier, offering us accommodation in an empty hut. We had walked 40 kilometres in exhausting conditions. Our food was reduced to a few tins of tuna, some bread buns and packets of noodle soup, and we were down to the last gas container for the mini-cooker.

After the ritual of questions from community leaders our trusty guide left us to continue his unending fiesta with new-found companions. We passed the next few hours listening to their drunken yells, which, with customary bravery, I interpreted as arguments about who should dispose of us over the nearby cliffs. Frankly, I had been shaken by the hostile treatment at Sharupe and the previous community. Our welcome seemed to be deteriorating the further we moved into the interior. This fact, coupled with the food shortage and physical difficulties, compelled me to tell Mario we must go back the next day. After all, we were on a territorial reconnaissance – not yet an expedition.

There was never doubt in my mind about Mario's sincerity and determination to press on but, even if we arrived at our objective near Copatasa, it was clear there was nothing we could do without further resources, military protection and professional cavers and scientists. Mario, in good faith, had accomplished all he could in his attempt to take me to where he thought - based on the sparse information he had from his father - the treasure existed. I reminded him we had responsibilities to honour, especially to his father; that if something should happen to us on this trip the project would never take place. He reluctantly agreed.

To return by the same route we had come from Sharupe was too dangerous. Using the community radio I requested air assistance from the evangelical station at Shell Mera, called 'Alas de Socorro', to fly us out of Kumai. Next morning, after donating what we could to the community, we heard the sound of a small one-engined Cessna. The pilot circled around, indicating he preferred the Chiwintza airstrip. So, together with a Shuar messenger I had agreed could fly back with us, we said goodbye to the community before trudging off at a fast pace through the forest.

With the four of us plus luggage crammed into the aircraft we roared off over the edge of a high cliff, thankful to be airborne, the green expanse of the cloud-patched forest far below. A few days later I left for the U.K. holding doubts about the geological possibly of there being caves near the Oso - Copatasa union. I arranged for Mario, at the first break in the weather, to fly from Shell Mera and check his clues with a view to returning with cavers in October 1999. Although delayed for a week, he finally flew over the area and reported his satisfaction that we were homing in on the right location.

He believed this based on what his father had said, positively enough to justify a commitment to next time venture beyond Kumai, even in dangerous circumstances. His certainty was based on a rough map given him by his father that marked a location with a cross due north of Kumai, but nowhere near the Oso-Copatasa union. Here was a dilemma. Despite geological arguments to the contrary, there was little option but to show good faith, follow through Mario's interpretation to the end and see what happened.

Due to a current economic depression forcing large numbers of Ecuadorians to leave the country I arranged sponsorship for him to visit the U.K., which would offer safe and tranquil respite from the emotional pressures he had been under since his father died. Understandably, recalling our good times in Esmeraldas he - in his own words - saw me as a replacement father, a bond amply tested on the trip to Kumai. In Scotland, in June 1999, armed with a sponsored course in English and scuba-diving lessons, he rapidly recovered his amiability and confidence.

In October, I returned to Ecuador with two British cavers. At the last minute, Mario had some urgent priority that detained him in the U.K., but I had all the details required, so his absence was not a complication. On arrival I found the Ecuadorian Army was unable to assist me due to the eruptions of volcanoes Pichincha and Tungurahua. We flew south by helicopter from Quito, passing close to Cotopaxi and the fiery Tungurahua. Refuelling at Shell Mera we headed past Sharupe then down the river Pastaza before turning north to the confluence of the Copatasa and the Oso.

The area was pure flood plain with none of the Napo geological features that could produce caves, confirming advice from Dr. John Aspden of the British Geological Survey in Quito. Nevertheless, it was a necessary mission in the programme of eliminating negatives. We landed on a small island - the only place possible - in the middle of the Copatasa just below its confluence with the Oso. The pilot wisely kept the rotor running as we unloaded 150 kilos of tents and equipment, shouting above the noise he would await my satellite telephone contact for the return journey.

It was the beginning of the dry season. The rivers were low but the volumes of the flood debris piled high against earthen banks ominously highlighted previous flood levels. The storage tent was erected on a sand bank and the sleeping tent on a hill among trees.

Once camp was set up we crossed waist level through the gently flowing Copatasa to the east bank. The objective was to climb and cut our way with machetes to where, looking westward, we could see two hill peaks I sought. According to Mario's description these peaks would be from where it *should* be possible to jump 10 metres into the river to enter the treasure cave. The only peaks we saw were three kilometres distant in mountainous area, the same when looking east from Puyo. These mountains of the Napo Formation would certainly have caves but, from where we stood, they were too far away and inaccessible. I was by now leaning more to my own location model, based years of data and what I understood of Petronio's mindset.

Re-crossing the Copatasa above the Oso we walked on clay-sand beaches two kilometres upstream without encountering rock formations necessary for caves. The area was distinctly unpromising.

Early next morning, watching a snake crossing on the current, we crossed waist-high to the north bank of the Oso, heading for a dried-out oxbow lake. The cavers expertly used a compass and marked trees to make sure we could find the way back. The jungle growth became impassable. Failing a breakthrough to the west bank of the Copotasa, we followed a small stream the cavers rightly calculated was a better route back the mouth of the Oso.

I began to wilt and fell behind, at one point slithering down a gully and under overhanging tree roots into thick mud. My companions were now far ahead and had crossed the Oso by the time I arrived on the bank. There was no way I could complain at their frustration and disappointment at not finding caves. By the time I reached the riverbank the rain was rapidly swelling both rivers. The two cavers had crossed only a short time before. By the time I waded into the Oso with pack and machete the water had risen almost to shoulder-height and I was being lifted off my feet. Trying to stay cool and use the river junction currents to help me cross I had fearful visions of some opportunistic anaconda pulling me down. Thankfully reaching the shore of the island I followed the cavers up to the campsite as if nothing untoward had bothered me. The river had at least cleaned off the mud collected from my tumble in the gully.

The island may have been the only place to land the helicopter; but now we were dangerously positioned below the flooding union of two rivers. There were no native communities within half-a-day's walk. The island at night seemed infested with insects of a particularly carnivorous kind, their bloodsucking habits hardly assuaged by the knowledge many would be unknown to science. It was an unlikely place to find a treasure cave, not a place I could believe Petronio or sane person would visit under any circumstances. I assumed Mario had misread and/or misunderstood his father's instructions or deliberately misled me. The latter possibility I discarded as ridiculous considering our comradeship on the earlier trip to Kumai. It was a costly, but necessary, eliminatory exercise. I was disappointed even though mentally prepared for it.

Now I had to focus the eliminating process on two locations that fitted my own location model, based on the jigsaw of information I had inherited from Petronio and key factors apparently unknown to Mario. One more reconnaissance was necessary.

In May 2000, I returned to Sharupe accompanied by two excellent students specialising in bats and oilbirds, recommended by Drs. Giovanni Onore and Tjitte de Vries of the Catholic University in Quito. We headed along the north side of the Pastaza for two hours to a large cave entrance. Immediately inside at the bottom of a steep slope was a stream flowing parallel with the Pastaza, obviously entering the sedimentary structure upriver. We named the cave *Yacu Waa*, meaning 'River Cave' in the Shuar tongue. Another name suggested by our Shuar guide Bosco was *Anaconda Waa* from his earnest belief that every evening a giant anaconda slithered into the cave from the Pastaza.

We were eager to explore but after a short distance inside I slipped and cricked my back, making it impossible for me to continue further. All I could do was hand over my torch and resign to the opportunity of examining the area.

Bosco had explained that the rain normally fell late afternoon. My companions had entered at 11.55 a.m. and agreed to return by 3.00 p.m. so I had time to look around. Suddenly, I felt very much alone.

Always full of surprises, Nature released a torrential downpour that was clearly going to last past three o'clock. Given the possibility of a deluge coming over the cliff, blocking or entering the cave, I pressed flat against an adjacent rockface, soaked through but reasonably safe. Moments later there was a thunderous roar, increasing in volume, of water plummeting into a deep sump in the ground.

I yelled into the cave to warn my companions but got no reply, confirming they had gone in a surprisingly long distance – perhaps kilometres? Now they could be in the same kind of danger from flash flooding as occurred with a school group visiting caves in Morona-Santiago some years earlier. Should they not appear soon, I would be scampering back to Sharupe for assistance.

Standing there alone in the downpour, in the middle of nowhere, head drooping like a sorrowful horse, was truly an eerie experience. At any moment I expected floodwater over the cliff to wash me down the Pastaza. Slowly, I forced my mind to reassess the fundamental reason I was there.

I began to analyse the location critically, particularly the stratified, white, geological limestone formations. How did this cave site fit the demands of the jigsaw? Two hours trek from the nearest road… entrance from the bank of a river… a 10-metre drop from the entrance to a stream inside (same to the nearby Pastaza)… white rock escarpment formations… etc.

Since my companions didn't hear my calls, here was evidently an extensive cave system, most likely part of a much larger complex.

From an aerial photograph, an interesting geological and topographical feature indicated that between Sharupe and the mouth of the Copataza I was standing at the only place where the Pastaza visibly entered, pounded and gouged out the limestone cliffs. To reach the cave from Sharupe, it had been necessary to descend to a beach only vsible when the Pastaza was low, cross a small river, walk along stepped, fossilised, limestone ledges sculptured by the river, scramble over rectangular rocks fallen from overhanging limestone strata, then climb back up the riverbank to the cave. The water entering the limestone up river would be augmented by clifftop rainwater dropping through fissures. On the trip with Mario to Kumai I had seen evidence an underwater stream flowing out into the Pastaza from the base of a limestone cliff, a short distance downriver from this particular cave entrance.

To my relief, at 2.50 p.m. precisely, I heard the voices of my companions. They emerged, wet and dishevelled, smiling nervously, reporting how they had walked about two kilometres without reaching the end of the system. The return trip was accomplished in half the time but they had been surprised by heavy cascades of water coming from fissures above and around them, at one place raising the water in the cave to chest level. With the changed circumstances there had been, at one point, a difference of opinion on which was the correct route back but, fortunately, they had agreed on the right direction. Inside were colonies of oilbirds and bats similar to the Tayos Cave of the River Coangas, but the cameras had proved inadequate due to the heights of the cave ceilings. It was disappointing for the students, but they were delighted to have discovered nocturnal creatures in the cave and breezed with ideas of a return journey using better camera equipment, and the setting up of a pilot biosphere station.

Returning to the U.K., I analysed the information I had gathered at Yacu Waa. Would the physical characteristics of this cave match the treasure cave requirements?

Years before I developed a process of locking away an idea for my intuition to work on before applying logic and reason, a combination of intuitive distillation and functional relativity I call *empirical revelation*. By peering through a stack of information windows, improbable details are eliminated to produce data that relates to core data. The process might take seconds, hours, months, occasionally years, depending on facts, sequence, chance, the timing of flashbacks, incoming information, and application of empirical revelation processes proportional to applied intuition and reason. The ER process works for me in a way that neither haste nor urgency will improve. Some psychologists and inventors swear the digestion of a single idea can take up to 15 years.

Application of the ER process on this occasion was essential because of the variety of information from so many sources. Shifting data around might have produced better insights, but I doubt it.

What, I wondered, would emerge from Petronio's concoction of reality and fantasy? My brain continued stacking windows of data on prehistory, history, mythology, geography, chronology, geology, vulcanism, anthropology, archaeology, topography, infrastructure, and climatology (also including known periodic global catastrophies of recent millenia, these usually followed by droughts and inundations that would have determined decisions on where to take refuge or to hide treasure.)

When I had processed the data, the revelation produced by the ER Window model matched a specific location, namely the river cave, *Yacu Waa*, and, if not that specific cave, then somewhere close. Was Yacu Waa actually the river cave described by Petronio in his 'cover-up' narrative; or was it for real, or both? No other cave known to me passed the ER test. (Ref: www.goldlibrary.com)

Here was an enigma. I knew Petronio had been in or near Yacu Waa at least once. There would have been no reason for him to bother sending me down a false trail because, when he was alive, I had no idea that Yacu Waa existed. The ER window model pointed to the very cave location he believed nobody could decode.

Reassessment

23

There is something awesome about standing alone in a storm-lashed jungle, pondering angrily on distorted history and a vision of what might correct it. A jungle is not the primeval paradise many visualise. Something is always waiting to harm you, to consume you - not cannibals, but the forest itself! Exhaustion, fear, poisonous reptiles, insects and plants, many of unknown species, treacherous swamps, tree spines eager to pierce your skin, disease and sickening infection, fast-rising rivers ready to sweep you away if anacondas or jaguars do not get you first. As for sheltering in caves, sleep if you dare! Smoking volcanoes threatening to erupt, toxic gas clouds hanging triumphantly over ancient settlements that had the affrontery to locate on their alluring slopes. Menacing electrical storms, pierced by brilliant rays of sunshine, illuminating vast, green expanses that extract your salty sweat as mercilessly as the local vampires suck your blood. Explorers are never lost – they fall down exhausted and are eaten!

If there occurred a threshold in my investigations it was when I stood at the mouth of Yacu Waa, far from creature comforts and books, drenched by the storm, fearful of Nature's anger flashing and roaring around me. Maybe because death could have come so easily then, perhaps from lightning or flood, I thought on adventurous friends no longer alive who would be laughing at my sorry predicament. Bob Holt, the poetic ex-marine, veteran of the Korean campaigns, who risked life and limb in the Llanganatis and finally died there with last words, 'Get me out of this f****** war!' on his lips. Diego Arias, Llanganati veteran surely annoyed that he died in a stupid car crash and not amid his favourite mountains. Dick Mapleston, who always seemed to have been where others wanted to go; submarine electronics engineer, inventor of crab traps, designer-builder of racing cars and boats,

Llanganati and Spanish galleon explorer, diver, savant, and half a book more. Jack Kabatznik, intellectual and electronics wizard, whose pub cry of, 'Don't listen to Stan Hall! He'll drive you crazy!' haunts me still.

There I was, imagining and overlapping past histories and peoples that had inhabited this beautiful land. Emperor Huanya Capac, descendent of legendary founder Manco Capac, invading Quito only for his generals to be stunned by the similarities in language, dress and customs of Cuzcañeos and Quiteñians; Dominican Padre Juan de Velasco, an 18th Century 'Herodotus', founder of Ecuadorian prehistory; Padre Marcos de Niza who had entered Quito with Diego Benalcazar two centuries earlier and recorded the history of the Kitus and their conquest by the Shyri- Caras; visions of battles heaving back and forth across the Altiplano; cities razed by earthquakes and armies; hordes of warriors directed by fanatical priests, carrying sacred treasures and archives of millenia down Cordillera *senderos* marked by inscribed stones, depositing their precious cargo in secret caves with guardianship entrusted to a single dynasty under pain of death.

Nations like the Kitus, Caras, and Puruhaos of Juan de Velasco's 3-Volume *Historia del Reino de Quito*, together with others, like the Hunos, Intis, Capas, Apus, Amautas, Amurus and Arnauans to name a few, were linked to *Atl-Antis*, the Empire of the 'Old Andes', forerunner of the Empire of the 'Tayu' of Tayhuantinsuyu. These names first drew my attention to early indo-akkad-sumerian connections in South America, supporting the scytho-magyar-sumerian theories of Juan Moricz and Padre Gregorio García.

There existed so much interlocking evidence that I could now understand how Moricz might claim the writing on the metal library was Magyar without actually having seen it!

I had used the empirical revelation window process to analyse global history and distil akkad-sumerian and scytho-magyar influences in the Andes region and, at least to my own satisfaction, I had results sufficient for the libraries of Tayhuantinsuyu to be desired - but not indispensable – for this purpose.

For another manuscript, *Savage Genesis*, I developed a mytho-historical model to help me recognize entirely different origins for human civilization and the birth of the planets that form a plausible bridge into the 'impossible' libraries (Ref: www.goldlibrary.com). I am now convinced about the birth of Jupiter from a *proto*-Saturn within the last 80,000 years and of Earth as a former satellite of Saturn: also, that

Venus was 'born from the head' of Jupiter in the middle of the 2nd Millenia BC, wreaking havoc and the widespread migration of 'chosen' - consequently warring - peoples, identical records of which are detectable in the mytho-histories of all the nations.

I am also convinced Catastrophism is the missing link between Evolutionism and Creationism and rationally explains the interchange of power and divinity between priests and planets, angels and sky-gods, the developments of religions and the cause of wars. With my ER model it was simpler to understand historical enigmas, especially South America as *the missing page of prehistory* and *the true cradle of civilization*. Here is where historians, americanologists and the world media could re-discover Mankind's lost millenia.

In conclusion, I believe that spectacular libraries and treasures of the Empire of Tayhuantinsuyu are deposited in the Yacu Waa area of Pastaza. My only claim is to have placed signposts for those with better resources to finish the job. Those who fish only to throw the fish back into the water will understand this sentiment. Maybe the journey to the treasure is more important than presence at its discovery.

Petronio, Moricz, Erich von Daniken, Stanley Hall, and Dr.Gerardo Peña Matheus ('unsung hero' of the Moricz campaign) were not the first into this astounding story, but they were as essential for its devel-

Hall by his calculated treasure location

opment as the sequential birth of the planets was necessary for the realisation of the Solar System.

A word of caution! Anybody who takes the reins of the treasure project had better consider the possible ramifications carefully and honestly take stock of their ethical, moral and intellectual qualifications, motivations, and suitability. Dark factors *will* conspire against anyone ever bringing out the treasure safely. Not greed, not gold-fever, but the realization of a new historical dimension will be vital to a successful outcome.

For me, it was enough privilege to have gone to the edge, to finally accept the libraries and other treasures exist based on my assessment that Petronio had reported them faithfully and in detail. If criticisms are levelled at 'the two legitimates'- as Petronio liked to call us - on how we managed our project, let it be understood it was me who failed him and not vice-versa. Until the day he died, at no time did he hold back on our plan for the expedition of occupation.

The immeasurable challenge of the treasure of the Tayu - or, if you prefer, *Tayos* - has consumed a number of lives, as it almost did mine on more than one occasion. I have recognised wisdom as the mother of discovery. As I write, the treasure rests in huge chambers, silent and remote, ringing with the laughter of mysterious guardians ready to deal with those who would seek to possess it! Who knows? - maybe that is how it should remain!

The End

Epilogue

A metamorphosis in my thinking occurred during the drafting of the manuscript for this book. Never will I believe in Loch Ness Monsters or UFOs until someone drags one to my doorstep. I have always been the one to pump reality into wide-eyed adventurers referred by family, friends or local bar owners. Yet, in the end, I accepted the existence of the impossible gold and crystal archives, explained to me, not by Juan Moricz, whom, together with Magyar predecessors (ref: www.goldlibrary.com) I credit more with unearthing lost Magyar history - but by Petronio Jaramillo!

Statues and other treasures aside, no gold or – let us describe it thus - quartz-crystal library, of the size and content described, could be possible in a South America barren of ancient script unless compiled by an advanced civilization destroyed or dispersed by global cataclysms. My maxim that politics comes out of history which comes out of geography which comes out of geology had inexorably drawn me to Catastrophism as the missing link between evolutionism and creationism, which led me to invent a new model for the creation(s) of the Solar System (ref: www.goldlibrary.com) based on the mytho-historical record (see Appendix). This Solar model indicates the route I followed in an attempt to accommodate the impossible libraries of the Atl Andes. *I could be wrong*, but it will remain my model until someone comes up with a better one.

To some extent Juan and Petronio were two hemispheres welded together by my hand. Yet we three were only parts of an evolving story that included many essential elements; especially the infinite loyalty, patience and integrity of Dr. Gerardo Peña Matheus; the military, scientists and diplomatic officials involved in the expedition processes; those journalists and critics who faithfully followed and reported the story over the years; the indigenous Shuar; the silent voices of the ancient chroniclers; past explorers and historians who added spice and excitement to the labyrinth of knowledge and investigation; the sponsors who contributed along the way; the fickle, the scornful and the ill-informed, who had to be outwitted or tolerated. All of those voices call for recognition, but none more so than Juan and Petronio whose spirits watch over the unfolding of this amazing story.

Appendix: Mytho-Historical Theory of Creation and Human Origins

I had been studying the Solar System wearing a 'catastrophist' hat for occasional journeys into prehistory. Why? Maybe because I thought I had discovered something, or maybe because I dreaded one day being all dressed up with nowhere to go. If, as I have observed, politics comes out of history, history out of geography and geography out of geology, then, I needed to know - How were the planets formed? Not a silly question, since everything that pertains to Humanity depends on the answer.

It might sound presumptious to say I used Albert Einstein's method of supporting intuitive leaps with bricks of reason, or Dmitry Mendeleyev's exception principle used for predicting missing elements in his Periodic Table, yet these sparked my empirical distillation of mytho-history to determine the origins of the Solar System and Humanity!

In the secluded world of astrophysics, the 'tidal', 'accretion', 'disk-instability' and 'passing-crashing star' theories all lack something compact. With so many opinions, theories and 'rethinks' around, sprinkled with distinguished scientists taking up varied and sometimes opposing positions, there had to be room for my mytho-historical-model!

The mythological record conceals, but also reveals, a history of interplanetary cataclysms, curiously telling of a time when planets seemed closer and bigger – and they were evidently more important than the Sun and the Moon. Later, due to impacts on the collective human psyche caused by orbital planetary changes and cataclysms, the planets and their cometary offspring were opportunistically transformed by astrologer-priests into gods, goddesses, and angels, later to be immortalised in word and stone.

Since time immemorial, titles such as 'Sons (and daughters) of the Sun' and 'Born from the Sun' have identified kings, khans, incas, pharoahs and other rulers as earthly representatives of the Sun God. But, was there some prehistoric source that gave rise to this custom? And was it of a celestial nature? Egyptian records tell us that, in the beginning, only one brilliant globe circled the heavens - Ur-Atum! In our model, we identify this entity with the Grecian proto-Uranus, 'born' from its mother, Gaia, goddess of the Earth!

We have to introduce three assumptions to cover an immeasurable period of 'primordial chaos.' First, that the birth of Suns and planets occurs by absorption, agitation, and explosive discharge of electro-magnetically - or *galactically* - charged material from similarly charged interiors of larger bodies. Second, that the Sun erupted in this way from some Great Star, the inner part of its spiralling tail cannibalised by massive gravitational forces, the outer part forming faint rings, circling at a great distance around the Solar System, leaving scattered a vast ocean of dust and ash, variously called by ancient peoples the Apsu, Nun, etc. Third, that the Sun, similar to its own birth, ejected a spinning, gas globe and tail called (in our model) proto-Gaia.

Here, written mytho-history switches in to confirm p-Gaia as the mother of p-Uranus and the residual Gaia. In turn, p-Uranus, agitated by *galactricity* and the same internal nuclear and electro-magnetic disturbances as its predecessors, collides with its mother Gaia, giving birth to the Titans, the Cyclops, and Giants – in our model, huge gas moons! The residual Uranus is recognised by witnesses as ruler of the heavens, until it collides with, and is 'disembowelled' and 'dethroned' by, the youngest Titan-moon, identified in our model as p-Saturn. In the resulting chaos Gaia – now proto-Earth - is captured in an orbit around p-Saturn.

If there were ever a Golden Age of Saturn – or rather 'p-Saturn' - it would be at this time, ending when p-Saturn is similarly dethroned by its own violent offspring, Jupiter with its huge serpentine tail (Typhon/Tiamat/Ahriman etc). P-Saturn, during its birth-emission of Jupiter, also produces Neptune - which spins off the vastly more powerful Jupiter in an opposite axial rotation – together with a host of bright, crackling comets, among these, p-Mercury, p-Mars, and p-Moon. The latter p-planets become charged and pock-marked from collisions with the debris in Typhon's tail and the vast quantity of ejected comets, meteors, asteroids milling around in the Apsu, in addition to 'bolts from heaven' and 'swords of gods' unleashed by the gas giants, their moons and tails. The continual bombardment generates melting temperatures, remanent magnetism, and radioactivity within the surface strata. (Note: Lunar craters Tycho and Aristarchus each show striking evidence of a single massive interplanetary discharge, similar to the effects of lightning striking poles on golf-course putting greens.)

The mytho-histories of ancient Arcadian, Preselenian and Phrygian peoples of the Mediterranean area mention a period when the Earth had no Moon, and when the 'messenger of the gods', Mercury (Hermes/Thoth), with (smoking) rod and entwining serpents, endangered the Earth on three occasions.

Neptune, together with the diminished Saturn and Uranus, were cast out, like the Egyptian Osiris (Saturn), into the Taieous (Tayos?), or 'netherworld', cooling and forming rings of debris, irrefutable evidence of cataclysmic contacts. Today, Neptune and Uranus are recognised as too far distant from the Sun to have formed where they are now situated.

The last recorded 'galactrically' generated virgin birth is that of Venus 'springing from the head' of Jupiter, as Athena sprang from the head of Zeus and Horus the younger from Horus the Elder, its axis spinning, like Neptune, contrary to that of the other planets. Homer – like writers of many old nursery rhymes, including Hey Diddle Diddle and Cock Robin, Jack and Jill, etc. - mentions collisions between Athena-Venus, Ares-Mars, Hermes-Mercury and Aphrodite-Moon in his account of the Trojan Wars – incidentally, a good starting point for historians and astrophysicists to review the current orthodoxy. All the major mythologies of the world recount the same story only using different names for the planets; some, like the Egyptians, using different names for the same planet, depending with which quarter of the day it is identified. Today, the days of the week carry the names of the seven major solar globes – evidence of their impact on peoples before the Solar System became sufficiently stable for Time to be measured with confidence.

Beginning with p-Gaia's virgin birth of Ur-Atum, the above cataclysmic events reflect the creation sequence evidenced in the global mytho-historical record. In our model we have employed a type of 'reverse osmosis' to fabricate the pre-Ur-Atum period, a reasonable approach given the similar electromagnetic, physical and mechanical forces involved.

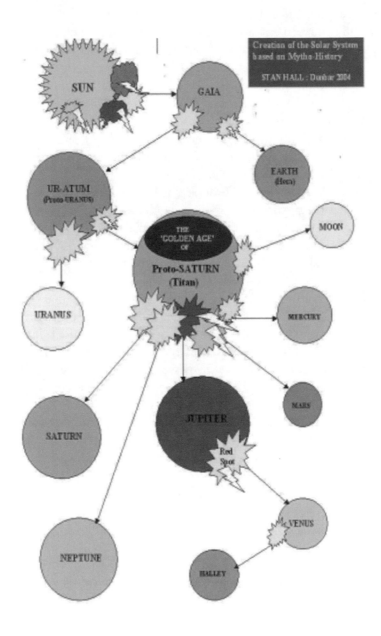

Hall Mytho-Historical Model of the Creation Process

Interim Observations

1. Planets may be classified as 'female' since they generate 'virgin' births. No 'male' planets exist, either for astronomical or mytho-historical purposes, the male characteristics having been introduced by adoring priesthoods and cults that were the the first to recognise the impact - physically, mentally and emotionally - that galactrically charged celestial bodies in close proximity had on themselves and other biological life around them. A virgin female planet is therefore like a daughter that originates inside her mother but lives outside her.

2. The explosive, spinning births of gas giants, and the tails and moons and new heavens and ages they created (including formation of the Asteroid Belt, the biblical 'hammered bracelet'), were recorded by literate peoples.

3. Our hypothesis requires and explains how interplanetary catastrophism is the missing link between evolutionism and creationism.

4. Here identified is the source of the covenanted exchange of power and divinity between priesthoods and planets, rooted in the cataclysms and wars of mytho-history.

5. Various gas and rock planets in their proto-stages were once close to the Earth, evidenced in the vastly more important role the planets play in the mytho-historical record when compared to the Sun and Moon. (Note: Uranus (1781) and Neptune (1846) were only rediscovered after the invention of the telescope.)

6. That the four gas giants and Venus since the early 1980s were found to be much hotter than expected supports the mytho-historical creation model. *How was it possible that we had to wait until recently to acknowledge the existence of the planets as clearly mentioned in mytho-historical records?* That the axial rotation of Neptune is contrary to the other gas giants makes sense if it spun out from p-Saturn at the same time as Jupiter. In our model, Uranus, which existed first, was correctly named in the 18th Century, as was Neptune later.

7. All ancient tales of serpents, dragons, celestial gods, avenging angels, extraterrestrial beings, lightning weapons, swords of god, pillars of smoke and fire, warlocks, hobgoblins and all, as well as thousands of other miraculous and enigmatic events, all find a logical place in our mytho-creational model.

Sky Born

The question of when - measured in billions, millions or thousands of years - each major virgin birth created a new heaven, and when and how human consciousness, spirituality, love, and distortions such as gigantism and mutations, might have evolved, remains an enigma. The problem arises because, in the mytho-historical record, p-Uranus emanates from the goddess Gaia, or proto-Earth. Gaia was identified as a goddess because, emerging as a brilliant gaseous globe from p-Uranus, she also appeared to be producing a brilliant new partner, Uranus. Somebody, before Time was measurable, and lost in the mists of the mythological ages, recorded the events. But *who?*

If our mytho-historical Creation model is to function, given the identical emanations known to have been recorded globally by different observers, Gaia must be - or be part of - the original giant globe, which gave birth to p-Uranus/Ur-Atum. In our model, Gaia was subsequently captured by p-Saturn before being forcibly rejected and deluged - with warm, saline water, as well as showers of 'alluvial' gold and platinum metals that must surely represent the legendary Golden

Newton Stone, Scotland. Unique prehistoric confirmation of 'virgin' planetary births.

228

Fleece - during the birth of Jupiter and its tail. It is precisely during the birth of Jupiter and, later, Venus that ancient peoples mention that showers of gold and platinum occurred. (Writer: also mercury, nickel, rubidium and other metals of the platinum family including the iridium of the currently erroneous dinosaur extinction theory.)

The creation-myth similarities between Mesopotamian, Egyptian, Indian, Scandinavian and American mythological records are astonishing, though the Asian and Amerindian mytho-histories lack detail. The records could not be so similar unless the same celestial events were witnessed globally.

Our model now begs consideration of a most extraordinary possibility relating to human origins and the 'impossible' libraries of the Andean Tayos legend.

Let us assume that survivors of major interplanetary cataclysms would be too traumatised to save and compile records. Let us also assume that Jupiter - the vacuum cleaner of many asteroids and comets that could have devastated the Earth as they did other planets and moons – did not appear until the end of the Golden Age of p-Saturn. Given these factors we would be required to either discard our Creation model or introduce a literate, extra-solar civilization, either before, or at the beginning of, the p-Saturn Golden Age. Such a civilization, and the cataclysmic events, new ages, and new heavens it dutifully recorded for posterity in what we call the mytho-histories, must have existed in comparatively recent times, when the mytho-history of early Humanity was evolving.

Somebody, somewhere, was there!

LOST CITIES

LOST CITIES OF ATLANTIS, ANCIENT EUROPE & THE MEDITERRANEAN
by David Hatcher Childress
Atlantis! The legendary lost continent comes under the close scrutiny of maverick archaeologist David Hatcher Childress in this sixth book i the internationally popular *Lost Cities* series. Childress takes the reader in search of sunken cities in the Mediterranean; across the Atl Mountains in search of Atlantean ruins; to remote islands in search of megalithic ruins; to meet living legends and secret societies. Fron Ireland to Turkey, Morocco to Eastern Europe, and around the remote islands of the Mediterranean and Atlantic, Childress takes the reade on an astonishing quest for mankind's past. Ancient technology, cataclysms, megalithic construction, lost civilizations and devastatin wars of the past are all explored in this book. Childress challenges the skeptics and proves that great civilizations not only existed in th past, but the modern world and its problems are reflections of the ancient world of Atlantis.
524 PAGES. 6x9 PAPERBACK. ILLUSTRATED. BIBLIOGRAPHY & INDEX. $16.95. CODE: MED

LOST CITIES OF CHINA, CENTRAL INDIA & ASIA
by David Hatcher Childress
Like a real life "Indiana Jones," maverick archaeologist David Childress takes the reader on an incredible adventure across some of the world's oldest and most remote countries in search of lost cities and ancient mysteries. Discover ancient cities in the Gobi Desert; hear fantastic tales of lost continents, vanished civilizations and secret societies bent on ruling the world; visit forgotten monasteries in forbidding snow-capped mountains with strange tunnels to mysterious subterranean cities! A unique combination of far-out exploration and practical travel advice, it will astound and delight the experienced traveler or the armchair voyager.
429 PAGES. 6x9 PAPERBACK. ILLUSTRATED. FOOTNOTES & BIBLIOGRAPHY. $14.95. CODE: CHI

LOST CITIES OF ANCIENT LEMURIA & THE PACIFIC
by David Hatcher Childress
Was there once a continent in the Pacific? Called Lemuria or Pacifica by geologists, Mu or Pan by the mystics, there is now ample mythological, geological and archaeological evidence to "prove" that an advanced and ancient civilization once lived in the central Pacific. Maverick archaeologist and explorer David Hatcher Childress combs the Indian Ocean, Australia and the Pacific in search of the surprising truth about mankind's past. Contains photos of the underwater city on Pohnpei; explanations on how the statues were levitated around Easter Island in a clockwise vortex movement; tales of disappearing islands; Egyptians in Australia; and more.
379 PAGES. 6x9 PAPERBACK. ILLUSTRATED. FOOTNOTES & BIBLIOGRAPHY. $14.95. CODE: LEM

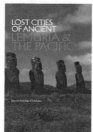

LOST CITIES OF NORTH & CENTRAL AMERICA
by David Hatcher Childress
Down the back roads from coast to coast, maverick archaeologist and adventurer David Hatcher Childress goes deep into unknow America. With this incredible book, you will search for lost Mayan cities and books of gold, discover an ancient canal systen in Arizona, climb gigantic pyramids in the Midwest, explore megalithic monuments in New England, and join the astonishin; quest for lost cities throughout North America. From the war-torn jungles of Guatemala, Nicaragua and Honduras to the deserts mountains and fields of Mexico, Canada, and the U.S.A., Childress takes the reader in search of sunken ruins, Viking forts, strange tunnel systems, living dinosaurs, early Chinese explorers, and fantastic lost treasure. Packed with both early and current maps, photos and illustrations.
590 PAGES. 6x9 PAPERBACK. ILLUSTRATED. FOOTNOTES. BIBLIOGRAPHY. INDEX. $16.95. CODE: NCA

LOST CITIES & ANCIENT MYSTERIES OF SOUTH AMERICA
by David Hatcher Childress
Rogue adventurer and maverick archaeologist David Hatcher Childress takes the reader on unforgettable journeys deep into deadly jungles, high up on windswept mountains and across scorching deserts in search of lost civilizations and ancient mysteries. Travel with David and explore stone cities high in mountain forests and hear fantastic tales of Inca treasure, living dinosaurs, and a mysterious tunnel system. Whether he is hopping freight trains, searching for secret cities, or just dealing with the daily problems of food, money, and romance, the author keeps the reader spellbound. Includes both early and current maps, photos, and illustrations, and plenty of advice for the explorer planning his or her own journey of discovery.
381 PAGES. 6x9 PAPERBACK. ILLUSTRATED. FOOTNOTES. BIBLIOGRAPHY. INDEX. $16.95. CODE: SAM

LOST CITIES & ANCIENT MYSTERIES OF AFRICA & ARABIA
by David Hatcher Childress
Across ancient deserts, dusty plains and steaming jungles, maverick archaeologist David Childress continues his world-wide ques for lost cities and ancient mysteries. Join him as he discovers forbidden cities in the Empty Quarter of Arabia; "Atlantean" ruin in Egypt and the Kalahari desert; a mysterious, ancient empire in the Sahara; and more. This is the tale of an extraordinary lif on the road: across war-torn countries, Childress searches for King Solomon's Mines, living dinosaurs, the Ark of the Covenan and the solutions to some of the fantastic mysteries of the past.
423 PAGES. 6x9 PAPERBACK. ILLUSTRATED. FOOTNOTES & BIBLIOGRAPHY. $14.95. CODE: AFA

24 hour credit card orders—call: 815-253-6390 fax: 815-253-6300
email: auphq@frontiernet.net   www.adventuresunlimitedpress.com   www.wexclub.com

LOST CITIES

TECHNOLOGY OF THE GODS
The Incredible Sciences of the Ancients
by David Hatcher Childress

Popular *Lost Cities* author David Hatcher Childress takes us into the amazing world of ancient technology, from computers in antiquit to the "flying machines of the gods." Childress looks at the technology that was allegedly used in Atlantis and the theory that the Grea Pyramid of Egypt was originally a gigantic power station. He examines tales of ancient flight and the technology that it involved; ho the ancients used electricity; megalithic building techniques; the use of crystal lenses and the fire from the gods; evidence of variou high tech weapons in the past, including atomic weapons; ancient metallurgy and heavy machinery; the role of ancient inventors suc as Nikola Tesla in bringing ancient technology back into modern use; impossible artifacts; and more.

356 PAGES. 6x9 PAPERBACK. ILLUSTRATED. BIBLIOGRAPHY. $16.95. CODE: TGOD

VIMANA AIRCRAFT OF ANCIENT INDIA & ATLANTIS
by David Hatcher Childress, introduction by Ivan T. Sanderson

Did the ancients have the technology of flight? In this incredible volume on ancient India, authentic Indian texts such as the *Ramayar* and the *Mahabharata* are used to prove that ancient aircraft were in use more than four thousand years ago. Included in this book the entire Fourth Century BC manuscript *Vimaanika Shastra* by the ancient author Maharishi Bharadwaaja, translated into English k the Mysore Sanskrit professor G.R. Josyer. Also included are chapters on Atlantean technology, the incredible Rama Empire of Ind and the devastating wars that destroyed it. Also an entire chapter on mercury vortex propulsion and mercury gyros, the power sourc described in the ancient Indian texts. Not to be missed by those interested in ancient civilizations or the UFO enigma.

334 PAGES. 6x9 PAPERBACK. RARE PHOTOGRAPHS, MAPS AND DRAWINGS. $15.95. CODE: VAA

LOST CONTINENTS & THE HOLLOW EARTH
I Remember Lemuria and the Shaver Mystery
by David Hatcher Childress & Richard Shaver

Lost Continents & the Hollow Earth is Childress' thorough examination of the early hollow earth stories of Richard Shaver and th fascination that fringe fantasy subjects such as lost continents and the hollow earth have had for the American public. Shaver's rar 1948 book *I Remember Lemuria* is reprinted in its entirety, and the book is packed with illustrations from Ray Palmer's *Amazin, Stories* magazine of the 1940s. Palmer and Shaver told of tunnels running through the earth—tunnels inhabited by the Deros and Teros humanoids from an ancient spacefaring race that had inhabited the earth, eventually going underground, hundreds of thousands of year ago. Childress discusses the famous hollow earth books and delves deep into whatever reality may be behind the stories of tunnels i the earth. Operation High Jump to Antarctica in 1947 and Admiral Byrd's bizarre statements, tunnel systems in South America an Tibet, the underground world of Agartha, the belief of UFOs coming from the South Pole, more.

344 PAGES. 6x9 PAPERBACK. ILLUSTRATED. $16.95. CODE: LCHE

A HITCHHIKER'S GUIDE TO ARMAGEDDON
by David Hatcher Childress

With wit and humor, popular Lost Cities author David Hatcher Childress takes us around the world and back in his trippy finalé to the Lost Citie series. He's off on an adventure in search of the apocalypse and end times. Childress hits the road from the fortress of Megiddo, the legendary citade in northern Israel where Armageddon is prophesied to start. Hitchhiking around the world, Childress takes us from one adventure to another, to ancien cities in the deserts and the legends of worlds before our own. Childress muses on the rise and fall of civilizations, and the forces that have shape mankind over the millennia, including wars, invasions and cataclysms. He discusses the ancient Armageddons of the past, and chronicles recent Middl East developments and their ominous undertones. In the meantime, he becomes a cargo cult god on a remote island off New Guinea, gets dragged int the Kennedy Assassination by one of the "conspirators," investigates a strange power operating out of the Altai Mountains of Mongolia, and discover how the Knights Templar and their off-shoots have driven the world toward an epic battle centered around Jerusalem and the Middle East.

320 PAGES. 6x9 PAPERBACK. ILLUSTRATED. BIBLIOGRAPHY. INDEX. $16.95. CODE: HGA

IN QUEST OF LOST WORLDS
Journey to Mysterious Algeria, Ethiopia & the Yucatan
by Count Byron Khun de Prorok

Finally, a reprint of Count Byron de Prorok's classic archeology/adventure book first published in 1936 by E.P. Dutton & Co. in New York. In this exciting and well illustrated book, de Prorok takes us into the deep Sahara of forbidden Algeria, to unknown Ethiopia, and to the many prehistoric ruins of the Yucatan. Includes: Tin Hinan, Legendary Queen of the Tuaregs; The mysterious A'Haggar Range of southern Algeria; Jupiter, Ammon and Tripolitania; The "Talking Dune"; The Land of the Garamantes; Mexico and the Poison Trail; Seeking Atlantis—Chichen Itza; Shadowed by the "Little People"—the Lacandon Pygmie Maya; Ancient Pyramids of the Usamasinta and Piedras Negras in Guatemala; In Search of King Solomon's Mines & the Land of Ophir; Ancient Emerald Mines of Ethiopia. Also included in this book are 24 pages of special illustrations of the famous—and strange—wall paintings of the Ahaggar from the rare book *The Search for the Tassili Frescoes* by Henri Lhote (1959). A visual treat of a remote area of the world that is even today forbidden to outsiders!

324 PAGES. 6x9 PAPERBACK. ILLUSTRATED. $16.95. CODE: IQLW

THE LAND OF OSIRIS
An Introduction to Khemitology
by Stephen S. Mehler

Was there an advanced prehistoric civilization in ancient Egypt? Were they the people who built the great pyramids and carved the Great Sphinx Did the pyramids serve as energy devices and not as tombs for kings? Mehler has uncovered an indigenous oral tradition that still exists in Egypt and has been fortunate to have studied with a living master of this tradition, Abd'El Hakim Awyan. Mehler has also been given permission t present these teachings to the Western world, teachings that unfold a whole new understanding of ancient Egypt and have only been presente heretofore in fragments by other researchers. Chapters include: Egyptology and Its Paradigms; Khemitology—New Paradigms; Asgat Nefer—Th Harmony of Water; Khemit and the Myth of Atlantis; The Extraterrestrial Question; more.

272 PAGES. 6x9 PAPERBACK. ILLUSTRATED. COLOR SECTION. BIBLIOGRAPHY. $18.95. CODE: LOOS

ANTI-GRAVITY

ANTI-GRAVITY

Leonard G. Cramp

THE A.T. FACTOR
PIECE FOR A JIGSAW III

A SCIENTIST'S ENCOUNTER WITH UFOs

THE A.T. FACTOR
A Scientists Encounter with UFOs: Piece For A Jigsaw Part 3
by Leonard Cramp

British aerospace engineer Cramp began much of the scientific anti-gravity and UFO propulsion analysis back in 1955 with his landmark book *Space Gravity & the Flying Saucer* (out-of-print and rare). His next books (available from Adventures Unlimited) *UFOs & Anti-Gravity: Piece for a Jig-Saw* and *The Cosmic Matrix: Piece for a Jig-Saw Part 2* began Cramp's in depth look into gravity control, free-energy, and the interlocking web of energy that pervades the universe. In this final book, Cramp brings to a close his detailed and controversial study of UFOs and Anti-Gravity.
324 PAGES. 6x9 PAPERBACK. ILLUSTRATED. BIBLIOGRAPHY. INDEX. $16.95. CODE: ATF

UFOS AND ANTI-GRAVITY:
PIECE FOR A JIG-SAW
by Leonard G. Cramp

COSMIC MATRIX
Piece for a Jig-Saw, Part Two
by Leonard G. Cramp

Cosmic Matrix is the long-awaited sequel to his 1966 book *UFOs & Anti-Gravity: Piece for a Jig-Saw*. Cramp has had a long history of examining UFO phenomena and has concluded that UFOs use the highest possible aeronautic science to move in the way they do. Cramp examines anti-gravity effects and theorizes that this super-science used by the craft—described in detail in the book—can lift mankind into a new level of technology, transportation and understanding of the universe. The book takes a close look at gravity control, time travel, and the interlocking web of energy between all planets in our solar system with Leonard's unique technical diagrams. A fantastic voyage into the present and future!
364 PAGES. 6x9 PAPERBACK. ILLUSTRATED. BIBLIOGRAPHY. $16.00. CODE: CMX

Leonard G. Cramp

UFOS AND ANTI-GRAVITY
Piece For A Jig-Saw
by Leonard G. Cramp

Leonard G. Cramp's 1966 classic book on flying saucer propulsion and suppressed technology is a highly technical look at the UFO phenomena by a trained scientist. Cramp first introduces the idea of 'anti-gravity' and introduces us to the various theories of gravitation. He then examines the technology necessary to build a flying saucer and examines in great detail the technical aspects of such a craft. Cramp's book is a wealth of material and diagrams on flying saucers, anti-gravity, suppressed technology, G-fields and UFOs. Chapters include Crossroads of Aerodynamics, Aerodynamic Saucers, Limitations of Rocketry, Gravitation and the Ether, Gravitational Spaceships, G-Field Lift Effects, The Bi-Field Theory, VTOL and Hovercraft, Analysis of UFO photos, more.
388 PAGES. 6x9 PAPERBACK. ILLUSTRATED. $16.95. CODE: UAG

THE ENERGY GRID
HARMONIC 695
THE PULSE OF THE UNIVERSE

BRUCE L. CATHIE

THE ENERGY GRID
Harmonic 695, The Pulse of the Universe
by Captain Bruce Cathie.

This is the breakthrough book that explores the incredible potential of the Energy Grid and the Earth's Unified Field all around us. Cathie's first book, *Harmonic 33*, was published in 1968 when he was a commercial pilot in New Zealand. Since then, Captain Bruce Cathie has been the premier investigator into the amazing potential of the infinite energy that surrounds our planet every microsecond. Cathie investigates the Harmonics of Light and how the Energy Grid is created. In this amazing book are chapters on UFO Propulsion, Nikola Tesla, Unified Equations, the Mysterious Aerials, Pythagoras & the Grid, Nuclear Detonation and the Grid, Maps of the Ancients, an Australian Stonehenge examined, more.
255 PAGES. 6x9 TRADEPAPER. ILLUSTRATED. $15.95. CODE: TEG

THE HARMONIC
CONQUEST OF SPACE
BRUCE CATHIE

THE BRIDGE TO INFINITY
Harmonic 371244
by Captain Bruce Cathie

Cathie has popularized the concept that the earth is crisscrossed by an electromagnetic grid system that can be used for anti-gravity, free energy, levitation and more. The book includes a new analysis of the harmonic nature of reality, acoustic levitation, pyramid power, harmonic receiver towers and UFO propulsion. It concludes that today's scientists have at their command a fantastic store of knowledge with which to advance the welfare of the human race.
204 PAGES. 6x9 TRADEPAPER. ILLUSTRATED. $14.95. CODE: BTF

THE BRIDGE
TO INFINITY
HARMONIC

THE HARMONIC CONQUEST OF SPACE
by Captain Bruce Cathie

Chapters include: Mathematics of the World Grid; the Harmonics of Hiroshima and Nagasaki; Harmonic Transmission and Receiving; the Link Between Human Brain Waves; the Cavity Resonance between the Earth; the Ionosphere and Gravity; Edgar Cayce—the Harmonic of the Subconscious; Stonehenge; the Harmonics of the Moon; the Pyramids of Mars; Nikola Tesla's Electric Car; the Robert Adams Pulsed Electric Motor Generator; Harmonic Clues to the Unified Field; and more. Also included are tables showing the harmonic relations between the earth's magnetic field, the speed of light, and anti-gravity/gravity acceleration at different points on the earth's surface. New chapters in this edition on the giant stone spheres of Costa Rica, Atomic Tests and Volcanic Activity, and a chapter on Ayers Rock analysed with Stone Mountain, Georgia.
248 PAGES. 6x9. PAPERBACK. ILLUSTRATED. BIBLIOGRAPHY. $16.95. CODE: HCS

Man-Made UFOs 1944-1994
50 Years of Suppression

MAN-MADE UFOS 1944—1994
Fifty Years of Suppression
by Renato Vesco & David Hatcher Childress

A comprehensive look at the early "flying saucer" technology of Nazi Germany and the genesis of man-made UFOs. This book takes us from the work of captured German scientists to escaped battalions of Germans, secret communities in South America and Antarctica to todays state-of-the-art "Dreamland" flying machines. Heavily illustrated, this astonishing book blows the lid off the "government" UFO conspiracy" and explains with technical diagrams the technology involved. Examined in detail are secret underground airfields and factories; German secret weapons; "suction" aircraft; the origin of NASA; gyroscopic stabilizers and engines; the secret Marconi aircraft factory in South America; and more. Introduction by W.A. Harbinson, author of the Dell novels *GENESIS* and *REVELATION*.
318 PAGES. 6x9 PAPERBACK. ILLUSTRATED. INDEX & FOOTNOTES. $18.95. CODE: MMU

FREE ENERGY SYSTEMS

HARNESSING THE WHEELWORK OF NATURE
Tesla's Science of Energy
by Thomas Valone, Ph.D., P.E.
A compilation of essays, papers and technical briefings on the emerging Tesla Technology and Zero Point Energy engineering that will soo change the entire way we live. Chapters include: Tesla: Scientific Superman who Launched the Westinghouse Industrial Firm by John Shatlan Nikola Tesla—Electricity's Hidden Genius, excerpt from The Search for Free Energy; Tesla's History at Niagara Falls; Non-Hertzian Wave: True Meaning of the Wireless Transmission of Power by Toby Grotz; On the Transmission of Electricity Without Wires by Nikola Tesla; Tesla Magnifying Transmitter by Andrija Puharich; Tesla's Self-Sustaining Electrical Generator and the Ether by Oliver Nichelson; Self-Sustainin Non-Hertzian Longitudinal Waves by Dr. Robert Bass; Modification of Maxwell's Equations in Free Space; Scalar Electromagnetic Wave: Disclosures Concerning Tesla's Operation of an ELF Oscillator; A Study of Tesla's Advanced Concepts & Glossary of Tesla Technology Term: Electric Weather Forces; Tesla's Vision by Charles Yost; The New Art of Projecting Concentrated Non-Dispersive Energy Through Natura Media; The Homopolar Generator: Tesla's Contribution by Thomas Valone; Tesla's Ionizer and Ozonator: Implications for Indoor Air Pollutio by Thomas Valone; How Cosmic Forces Shape Our Destiny by Nikola Tesla; Tesla's Death Ray plus Selected Tesla Patents; more.
288 PAGES. 6x9 PAPERBACK. ILLUSTRATED. $16.95. CODE: HWWN

THE ENERGY MACHINE OF T. HENRY MORAY
by Moray B. King
In the 1920s T. Henry Moray invented a "free energy" device that reportedly output 50 kilowatts of electricity. It could not be explained by standard scieno at that time. The electricity exhibited a strange "cold current" characteristic where thin wires could conduct appreciable power without heating. Mora suffered ruthless suppression, and in 1939 the device was destroyed. Frontier science lecturer and author Moray B. King explains the invention with today' science. Modern physics recognizes that the vacuum contains tremendous energy called the zero-point energy. A way to coherently activate it appear surprisingly simple: first create a glow plasma or corona, then abruptly pulse it. Other inventors have discovered this approach (sometimes unwittingly) t create novel energy devices, and they too were suppressed. The common pattern of their technologies clarified the fundamental operating principle. Kin hopes to inspire engineers and inventors so that a new energy source can become available to mankind.
192 PAGES. 6x8 PAPERBACK. ILLUSTRATED. REFERENCES. $14.95. CODE: EMHM

QUEST FOR ZERO-POINT ENERGY
Engineering Principles for "Free Energy"
by Moray B. King
King expands, with diagrams, on how free energy and anti-gravity are possible. The theories of zero point energy maintain there are tremendous fluctuations of electrical field energy embedded within the fabric of space. King explains the following topics: Tapping the Zero-Point Energy as an Energy Source; Fundamentals of a Zero-Point Energy Technology; Vacuum Energy Vortices; The Super Tube; Charge Clusters: The Basis of Zero-Point Energy Inventions; Vortex Filaments, Torsion Fields and the Zero-Point Energy; Transforming the Planet with a Zero-Point Energy Experiment; Dual Vortex Forms: The Key to a Large Zero-Point Energy Coherence. Packed with diagrams, patents and photos. With power shortages now a daily reality in many parts of the world, this book offers a fresh approach very rarely mentioned in the mainstream media.
224 PAGES. 6x9 PAPERBACK. ILLUSTRATED. $14.95. CODE: QZPE

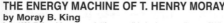

THE TIME TRAVEL HANDBOOK
A Manual of Practical Teleportation & Time Travel
edited by David Hatcher Childress
In the tradition of The Anti-Gravity Handbook and The Free-Energy Device Handbook, science and UFO author David Hatcher Childress takes us into th weird world of time travel and teleportation. Not just a whacked-out look at science fiction, this book is an authoritative chronicling of real-life time trave experiments, teleportation devices and more. The Time Travel Handbook takes the reader beyond the government experiments and deep into the uncharte territory of early time travellers such as Nikola Tesla and Guglielmo Marconi and their alleged time travel experiments, as well as the Wilson Brothers o EMI and their connection to the Philadelphia Experiment—the U.S. Navy's forays into invisibility, time travel, and teleportation. Childress looks into th claims of time travelling individuals, and investigates the unusual claim that the pyramids on Mars were built in the future and sent back in time. A highl visual, large format book, with patents, photos and schematics. Be the first on your block to build your own time travel device!
316 PAGES. 7x10 PAPERBACK. ILLUSTRATED. $16.95. CODE: TTH

THE TESLA PAPERS
Nikola Tesla on Free Energy & Wireless Transmission of Power
by Nikola Tesla, edited by David Hatcher Childress
David Hatcher Childress takes us into the incredible world of Nikola Tesla and his amazing inventions. Tesla's rare article "The Problem of Increasing Huma Energy With Special Reference to the Harnessing of the Sun's Energy" is included. This lengthy article was originally published in the June 1900 issue of Th Century Illustrated Monthly Magazine and it was the outline for Tesla's master blueprint for the world. Tesla's fantastic vision of the future, including wireles power, anti-gravity, free energy and highly advanced solar power. Also included are some of the papers, patents and material collected on Tesla at the Colorad Springs Tesla Symposiums, including papers on: •The Secret History of Wireless Transmission •Tesla and the Magnifying Transmitter •Design and Constructio of a Half-Wave Tesla Coil •Electrostatics: A Key to Free Energy •Progress in Zero-Point Energy Research •Electromagnetic Energy from Antennas to Atom •Tesla's Particle Beam Technology •Fundamental Excitatory Modes of the Earth-Ionosphere Cavity
325 PAGES. 8x10 PAPERBACK. ILLUSTRATED. $16.95. CODE: TTP

THE FANTASTIC INVENTIONS OF NIKOLA TESLA
by Nikola Tesla with additional material by David Hatcher Childress
This book is a readable compendium of patents, diagrams, photos and explanations of the many incredible inventions of the originator of the modern era o electrification. In Tesla's own words are such topics as wireless transmission of power, death rays, and radio-controlled airships. In addition, rare materia on German bases in Antarctica and South America, and a secret city built at a remote jungle site in South America by one of Tesla's students, Guglielmc Marconi. Marconi's secret group claims to have built flying saucers in the 1940s and to have gone to Mars in the early 1950s! Incredible photos of thes Tesla craft are included. The Ancient Atlantean system of broadcasting energy through a grid system of obelisks and pyramids is discussed. •His plan tc transmit free electricity into the atmosphere. •How electrical devices would work using only small antennas. •Why unlimited power could be utilizec anywhere on earth. •How radio and radar technology can be used as death-ray weapons in Star Wars.
342 PAGES. 6x9 PAPERBACK. ILLUSTRATED. APPENDIX. $16.95. CODE: FINT

24 hour credit card orders—call: 815-253-6390 fax: 815-253-6300
email: auphq@frontiernet.net   www.adventuresunlimitedpress.com   www.wexclub.com

REICH OF THE BLACK SUN
Nazi Secret Weapons and the Cold War Allied Legend
by Joseph P. Farrell

Why were the Allies worried about an atom bomb attack by the Germans in 1944? Why did the Soviets threaten to use poison gas against the Germans? Why did Hitler in 1945 insist that holding Prague could win the war for the Third Reich? Why did US General George Patton's Third Army race for the Skoda works at Pilsen in Czechoslavakia instead of Berlin? Why did the US Army not test the uranium atom bomb it dropped on Hiroshima? Why did the Luftwaffe fly a non-stop round trip mission to within twenty miles of New York City in 1944? *Reich of the Black Sun* takes the reader on a scientific-historical journey in order to answer these questions. Arguing that Nazi Germany actually won the race for the atom bomb in late 1944, *Reich of the Black Sun* then goes on to explore the even more secretive research the Nazis were conducting into the occult, alternative physics and new energy sources. The book concludes with a fresh look at the "Nazi Legend" of the UFO mystery by examining the Roswell Majestic-12 documents and the Kecksburg crash in the light of parallels with some of the super-secret black projects being run by the SS. *Reich of the Black Sun* is must-reading for the researcher interested in alternative history, science, or UFOs!
352 PAGES. 6x9 PAPERBACK. ILLUSTRATED. BIBLIOGRAPHY. $16.95. CODE: ROBS

HITLER'S FLYING SAUCERS
A Guide to German Flying Discs of the Second World War
by Henry Stevens
Learn why the Schriever-Habermohl project was actually two projects and read the written statement of a German test pilot who actually flew one of these saucers; about the Leduc engine, the key to Dr. Miethe's saucer designs; how U.S. government officials kept the truth about foo fighters hidden for almost sixty years and how they were finally forced to "come clean" about the foo fighter's German origin. Learn of the Peenemuende saucer project and how it was slated to "go atomic." Read the testimony of a German eyewitness who saw "magnetic discs." Read the U.S. government's own reports on German field propulsion saucers. Read how the post-war German KM-2 field propulsion "rocket" worked. Learn details of the work of Karl Schappeller and Viktor Schauberger. Learn how their ideas figure in the quest to build field propulsion flying discs. Find out what happened to this technology after the war. Find out how the Canadians got saucer technology directly from the SS. Find out about the surviving "Third Power" of former Nazis. Learn of the U.S. government's methods of UFO deception and how they used the German "Sonderbueroll" as the model for Project Blue Book.
388 PAGES. 6x9 PAPERBACK. ILLUSTRATED. INDEX. $18.95. CODE: HFS

LEY LINE & EARTH ENERGIES
An Extraordinary Journey into the Earth's Natural Energy System
by David Cowan & Chris Arnold

The mysterious standing stones, burial grounds and stone circles that lace Europe, the British Isles and other areas have intrigued scientists, writers, artists and travellers through the centuries. They pose so many questions: Why do some places feel special? How do ley lines work? How did our ancestors use Earth energy to map their sacred sites and burial grounds? How do ghosts and poltergeists interact with Earth energy? How can Earth spirals and black spots affect our health? This exploration shows how natural forces affect our behavior, how they can be used to enhance our health and well being, and ultimately, how they bring us closer to penetrating one of the deepest mysteries being explored. A fascinating and visual book about subtle Earth energies and how they affect us and the world around them.
368 PAGES. 6x9 PAPERBACK. ILLUSTRATED. BIBLIOGRAPHY. INDEX. $18.95. CODE: LLEE

MIND CONTROL AND UFOS
Casebook on Alternative 3
by Jim Keith
Drawing on his diverse research and a wide variety of sources, Jim Keith delves into the bizarre story behind *Alternative 3*, including mind control programs, underground bases not only on the Earth but also on the Moon and Mars, the real origin of the UFO problem, the mysterious deaths of Marconi Electronics employees in Britain during the 1980s, top scientists around the world kidnapped to work at the secret government space bases, the Russian-American superpower arms race of the 50s, 60s and 70s as a massive hoax, and other startling arenas.
248 PAGES. 6x9 PAPERBACK. ILLUSTRATED. $14.95. CODE: MCUF

UFOS, PSI AND SPIRITUAL EVOLUTION
A Journey through the Evolution of Interstellar Travel
by Christopher Humphries, Ph.D.

The modern era of UFOs began in May, 1947, one year and eight months after Hiroshima. This is no coincidence, and suggests there are beings in the universe with the ability to jump hundreds of light years in an instant. That is teleportation, a power of the mind. UFOs sometimes float along close to the ground, in complete silence. That is levitation, another power of the mind. If it weren't for levitation and teleportation, star travel would not be possible at all, since physics rules out star travel by technology. So if we want to go to the stars, it is the mind and spirit we must study, not technology. The mind must be a dark matter object, since it is invisible and intangible and can freely pass through solid objects. A disembodied mind can see the de Broglie vibrations (the basis of quantum mechanics) radiated by both dark and ordinary matter during near death or out-of-body experiences. Levitation requires warping the geodesics of space-time. The latest theory in physics is String Theory, which requires six extra spatial dimensions. The mind warps those higher geodesics to produce teleportation.
274 PAGES. 6x9 PAPERBACK. ILLUSTRATED. REFERENCES. $16.95. CODE: UPSE

SAUCERS OF THE ILLUMINATI
by Jim Keith, Foreword by Kenn Thomas
Seeking the truth behind stories of alien invasion, secret underground bases, and the secret plans of the New World Order, *Saucers of the Illuminati* offers ground breaking research, uncovering clues to the nature of UFOs and to forces even more sinister: the secret cabal behind planetary control! Includes mind control, saucer abductions, the MJ-12 documents, cattle mutilations, government anti-gravity testing, the Sirius Connection, science fiction author Philip K. Dick and his efforts to expose the Illuminati, plus more from veteran conspiracy and UFO author Keith. Conspiracy expert Keith's final book on UFOs and the highly secret group that manufactures them and uses them for their own purposes: the control and manipulation of the population of planet Earth.
148 PAGES. 6x9 PAPERBACK. ILLUSTRATED. $12.95. CODE: SOIL

ANCIENT SCIENCE

THE GIZA DEATH STAR
The Paleophysics of the Great Pyramid & the Military Complex at Giza
by Joseph P. Farrell

Physicist Joseph Farrell's amazing book on the secrets of Great Pyramid of Giza. *The Giza Death Star* starts where British engineer Christophe Dunn leaves off in his 1998 book, *The Giza Power Plant*. Was the Giza complex part of a military installation over 10,000 years ago? Chapter include: An Archaeology of Mass Destruction, Thoth and Theories; The Machine Hypothesis; Pythagoras, Plato, Planck, and the Pyramid; The Weapon Hypothesis, Encoded Harmonics of the Planck Units in the Great Pyramid; High Freguency Direct Current "Impulse" Technology The Grand Gallery and its Crystals: Gravito-acoustic Resonators; The Other Two Large Pyramids; the "Causeways," and the "Temples"; A Phase Conjugate Howitzer; Evidence of the Use of Weapons of Mass Destruction in Ancient Times; more.
290 PAGES. 6x9 PAPERBACK. ILLUSTRATED. $16.95. CODE: GDS

THE GIZA DEATH STAR DEPLOYED
The Physics & Engineering of the Great Pyramid
by Joseph P. Farrell

Physicist Joseph Farrell's amazing sequel to *The Giza Death Star* which takes us from the Great Pyramid to the asteroid belt and the so-calle Pyramids of Mars. Farrell expands on his thesis that the Great Pyramid was a chemical maser, designed as a weapon and eventually deployed – with disastrous results to the solar system. Includes: Exploding Planets: The Movie, the Mirror, and the Model; Dating the Catastrophe and the Compound; A Brief History of the Exoteric and Esoteric Investigations of the Great Pyramid; No Machines, Please!; The Stargate Conspiracy The Scalar Weapons; Message or Machine?; A Tesla Analysis of the Putative Physics and Engineering of the Giza Death Star; Cohering th Zero Point, Vacuum Energy, Flux: Synopsis of Scalar Physics and Paleophysics; Configuring the Scalar Pulse Wave; Inferred Applications i the Great Pyramid; Quantum Numerology, Feedback Loops and Tetrahedral Physics; and more.
290 PAGES. 6x9 PAPERBACK. ILLUSTRATED. BIBLIOGRAPHY. INDEX. $16.95. CODE: GDSD

PIRATES & THE LOST TEMPLAR FLEET
The Secret Naval War Between the Templars & the Vatican
by David Hatcher Childress

The lost Templar fleet was originally based at La Rochelle in southern France, but fled to the deep fiords of Scotland upon the dissolution of the Order by King Phillip. This banned fleet of ships was later commanded by the St. Clair family of Rosslyn Chapel (birthplace of Free Masonry). St. Clair and his Templars made a voyage to Canada in the year 1398 AD, nearly 100 years before Columbus! Chapters include: 10,000 Years of Seafaring; The Knights Templar & the Crusades; The Templars and the Assassins; The Lost Templar Fleet and the Jolly Roger; Maps of the Ancient Sea Kings; Pirates, Templars and the New World; Christopher Columbus—Secret Templar Pirate?; Later Day Pirates and the War with the Vatican; Pirate Utopias and the New Jerusalem; more.
320 PAGES. 6x9 PAPERBACK. ILLUSTRATED. BIBLIOGRAPHY. $16.95. CODE: PLTF

CLOAK OF THE ILLUMINATI
Secrets, Transformations, Crossing the Star Gate
by William Henry

Thousands of years ago the stargate technology of the gods was lost. Mayan Prophecy says it will return by 2012, along with our alignment with the center of our galaxy. In this book: Find examples of stargates and wormholes in the ancient world; Examine myths and scripture wit hidden references to a stargate cloak worn by the Illuminati, including Mari, Nimrod, Elijah, and Jesus; See rare images of gods and goddesses wearing th Cloak of the illuminati; Learn about Saddam Hussein and the secret missing library of Jesus; Uncover the secret Roman-era eugenics experiments at th Temple of Hathor in Denderah, Egypt; Explore the duplicate of the Stargate Pillar of the Gods in the Illuminists' secret garden in Nashville, TN; Discover th secrets of manna, the food of the angels; Share the lost Peace Prayer posture of Osiris, Jesus and the Illuminati; more. Chapters include: Seven Stars Unde Three Stars; The Long Walk; Squaring the Circle; The Mill of the Host; The Miracle Garment; The Fig; Nimrod: The Mighty Man; Nebuchadnezzar's Gate The New Mighty Man; more.
238 PAGES. 6x9 PAPERBACK. ILLUSTRATED. BIBLIOGRAPHY. INDEX. $16.95. CODE: COIL

EXTRATERRESTRIAL ARCHAEOLOGY NEW EDITION!
by David Hatcher Childress

Using official NASA and Soviet photos, as well as other photos taken via telescope, this book seeks to prove that many of the planets (and moons) of our solar system are in som way inhabited by intelligent life. The book includes many blow-ups of NASA photos and detailed diagrams of structures—particularly on the Moon.
•NASA PHOTOS OF PYRAMIDS AND DOMED CITIES ON THE MOON. •PYRAMIDS AND GIANT STATUES ON MARS. •HOLLOW MOONS OF MARS AND OTHER PLANETS. •ROBOT MININ VEHICLES THAT MOVE ABOUT THE MOON PROCESSING VALUABLE METALS. •NASA & RUSSIAN PHOTOS OF SPACE-BASES ON MARS AND ITS MOONS. •A BRITISH SCIENTIST WH DISCOVERED A TUNNEL ON THE MOON, AND OTHER "BOTTOMLESS CRATERS." •EARLY CLAIMS OF TRIPS TO THE MOON AND MARS. •STRUCTURAL ANOMALIES ON VENUS, SATURN JUPITER, MERCURY, URANUS & NEPTUNE. •NASA, THE MOON AND ANTI-GRAVITY. PLUS MORE. HIGHLY ILLUSTRATED WITH PHOTOS, DIAGRAMS AND MAPS!
320 PAGES. 8x11 PAPERBACK. BIBLIOGRAPHY & APPENDIX. $19.95. CODE: ETA

THE ORION PROPHECY
Egyptian and Mayan Prophecies on the Cataclysm of 2012
by Patrick Geryl and Gino Ratinckx

In the year 2012 the Earth awaits a super catastrophe: its magnetic field will reverse in one go. Phenomenal earthquakes and tidal waves will completel destroy our civilization. Europe and North America will shift thousands of kilometers northwards into polar climes. Nearly everyone will perish in the apoca lyptic happenings. These dire predictions stem from the Mayans and Egyptians—descendants of the legendary Atlantis. The Atlanteans had highly evolve astronomical knowledge and were able to exactly predict the previous world-wide flood in 9792 BC. They built tens of thousands of boats and escaped t South America and Egypt. In the year 2012 Venus, Orion and several others stars will take the same 'code-positions' as in 9792 BC! For thousands of year historical sources have told of a forgotten time capsule of ancient wisdom located in a labyrinth of secret chambers filled with artifacts and documents from the previous flood. We desperately need this information now—and this book gives one possible location.
324 PAGES. 6x9 PAPERBACK. ILLUSTRATED. BIBLIOGRAPHY. $16.95. CODE: ORP

MYSTIC TRAVELLER SERIES

THE MYSTERY OF EASTER ISLAND
by Katherine Routledge
The reprint of Katherine Routledge's classic archaeology book which was first published in London in 1919. The book details her journey by yacht from England to South America, around Patagonia to Chile and on to Easter Island. Routledge explored the amazing island and produced one of the first-ever accounts of the life, history and legends of this strange and remote place. Routledge discusses the statues, pyramid-platforms, Rongo Rongo script, the Bird Cult, the war between the Short Ears and the Long Ears, the secret caves, ancient roads on the island, and more. This rare book serves as a sourcebook on the early discoveries and theories on Easter Island.
432 PAGES. 6x9 PAPERBACK. ILLUSTRATED. $16.95. CODE: MEI

MYSTERY CITIES OF THE MAYA
Exploration and Adventure in Lubaantun & Belize
by Thomas Gann
First published in 1925, *Mystery Cities of the Maya* is a classic in Central American archaeology-adventure. Gann was close friends with Mike Mitchell-Hedges, the British adventurer who discovered the famous crystal skull with his adopted daughter Sammy and Lady Richmond Brown, their benefactress. Gann battles pirates along Belize's coast and goes upriver with Mitchell-Hedges to the site of Lubaantun where they excavate a strange lost city where the crystal skull was discovered. Lubaantun is a unique city in the Mayan world as it is built out of precisely carved blocks of stone without the usual plaster-cement facing. Lubaantun contained several large pyramids partially destroyed by earthquakes and a large amount of artifacts. Gann shared Mitchell-Hedges belief in Atlantis and lost civilizations (pre-Mayan) in Central America and the Caribbean. Lots of good photos, maps and diagrams.
252 PAGES. 6x9 PAPERBACK. ILLUSTRATED. $16.95. Code: MCOM

IN SECRET TIBET
by Theodore Illion
Reprint of a rare 30s adventure travel book. Illion was a German wayfarer who not only spoke fluent Tibetan, but travelled in disguise as a native through forbidden Tibet when it was off-limits to all outsiders. His incredible adventures make this one of the most exciting travel books ever published. Includes illustrations of Tibetan monks levitating stones by acoustics.
210 PAGES. 5x9 PAPERBACK. ILLUSTRATED. $15.95. Code: IST

DARKNESS OVER TIBET
by Theodore Illion
In this second reprint of Illion's rare books, the German traveller continues his journey through Tibet and is given directions to a strange underground city. As the original publisher's remarks said, "this is a rare account of an underground city in Tibet by the only Westerner ever to enter it and escape alive! "
210 PAGES. 5x9 PAPERBACK. ILLUSTRATED. $15.95. Code: DOT

DANGER MY ALLY
The Amazing Life Story of the Discoverer of the Crystal Skull
by "Mike" Mitchell-Hedges
The incredible life story of "Mike" Mitchell-Hedges, the British adventurer who discovered the Crystal Skull in the lost Mayan city of Lubaantun in Belize. Mitchell-Hedges has lived an exciting life: gambling everything on a trip to the Americas as a young man, riding with Pancho Villa, questing for Atlantis, fighting bandits in the Caribbean and discovering the famous Crystal Skull.
374 PAGES. 6x9 PAPERBACK. ILLUSTRATED. BIBLIOGRAPHY & INDEX. $16.95. Code: DMA

IN SECRET MONGOLIA
by Henning Haslund
First published by Kegan Paul of London in 1934, Haslund takes us into the barely known world of Mongolia of 1921, a land of god-kings, bandits, vast mountain wilderness and a Russian army running amok. Starting in Peking, Haslund journeys to Mongolia as part of the Krebs Expedition—a mission to establish a Danish butter farm in a remote corner of northern Mongolia. Along the way he smuggles guns and nitroglycerin, is thrown into a prison by the new Communist regime, battles the Robber Princess and more. With Haslund we meet the "Mad Baron" Ungern-Sternberg and his renegade Russian army, the many characters of Urga's fledgling foreign community, and the last god-king of Mongolia, Seng Chen Gegen, the fifth reincarnation of the Tiger god and the "ruler of all Torguts." Aside from the esoteric and mystical material, there is plenty of just plain adventure: Haslund encounters a Mongolian werewolf; is ambushed along the trail; escapes from prison and fights terrifying blizzards; more.
374 PAGES. 6x9 PAPERBACK. ILLUSTRATED. BIBLIOGRAPHY & INDEX. $16.95. Code: ISM

MEN & GODS IN MONGOLIA
by Henning Haslund
First published in 1935 by Kegan Paul of London, Haslund takes us to the lost city of Karakota in the Gobi desert. We meet the Bodgo Gegen, a god-king in Mongolia similar to the Dalai Lama of Tibet. We meet Dambin Jansang, the dreaded warlord of the "Black Gobi." There is even material in this incredible book on the Hi-mori, an "airhorse" that flies through the sky (similar to a Vimana) and carries with it the sacred stone of Chintamani. Aside from the esoteric and mystical material, there is plenty of just plain adventure: Haslund and companions journey across the Gobi desert by camel caravan; are kidnapped and held for ransom; witness initiation into Shamanic societies; meet reincarnated warlords; and experience the violent birth of "modern" Mongolia.
358 PAGES. 6x9 PAPERBACK. ILLUSTRATED. BIBLIOGRAPHY & INDEX. $16.95. Code: MGM

24 hour credit card orders—call: 815-253-6390 fax: 815-253-6300
email: auphq@frontiernet.net   www.adventuresunlimitedpress.com   www.wexclub.com

ATLANTIS REPRINT SERIES

ATLANTIS: MOTHER OF EMPIRES
Atlantis Reprint Series
by Robert Stacy-Judd
Robert Stacy-Judd's classic 1939 book on Atlantis is back in print in this large-format paperback edition. Stacy-Judd was a California architect and an expert on the Mayas and their relationship to Atlantis. He was an excellent artist and his work is lavishly illustrated. The eighteen comprehensive chapters in the book are: The Mayas and the Lost Atlantis; Conjectures and Opinions; The Atlantean Theory; Cro-Magnon Man; East is West; And West is East; The Mormons and the Mayas; Astrology in Two Hemispheres; The Language of Architecture; The American Indian; Pre-Panamanians and Pre-Incas; Columns and City Planning; Comparisons and Mayan Art; The Iberian Link; The Maya Tongue; Quetzalcoatl; Summing Up the Evidence; The Mayas in Yucatan.
340 PAGES. 8x11 PAPERBACK. ILLUSTRATED. INDEX. $19.95. CODE: AMOE

MYSTERIES OF ANCIENT SOUTH AMERICA
Atlantis Reprint Series
by Harold T. Wilkins
The reprint of Wilkins' classic book on the megaliths and mysteries of South America. This book predates Wilkin's book *Secret Cities of Old South America* published in 1952. *Mysteries of Ancient South America* was first published in 1947 and is considered a classic book of its kind. With diagrams, photos and maps, Wilkins digs into old manuscripts and books to bring us some truly amazing stories of South America: a bizarre subterranean tunnel system; lost cities in the remote border jungles of Brazil; legends of Atlantis in South America; cataclysmic changes that shaped South America; and other strange stories from one of the world's great researchers. Chapters include: Our Earth's Greatest Disaster, Dead Cities of Ancient Brazil, The Jungle Light that Shines by Itself, The Missionary Men in Black: Forerunners of the Great Catastrophe, The Sign of the Sun: The World's Oldest Alphabet, Sign-Posts to the Shadow of Atlantis, The Atlanean "Subterraneans" of the Incas, Tiahuanacu and the Giants, more.
236 PAGES. 6x9 PAPERBACK. ILLUSTRATED. INDEX. $14.95. CODE: MASA

SECRET CITIES OF OLD SOUTH AMERICA
Atlantis Reprint Series
by Harold T. Wilkins
The reprint of Wilkins' classic book, first published in 1952, claiming that South America was Atlantis. Chapters include Mysteries of a Lost World; Atlantis Unveiled; Red Riddles on the Rocks; South America's Amazons Existed!; The Mystery of El Dorado and Gran Payatiti—The Final Refuge of the Incas; Monstrous Beasts of the Unexplored Swamps & Wilds; Weird Denizens of Antediluvian Forests; New Light on Atlantis from the World's Oldest Book; The Mystery of Old Man Noah and the Arks; and more.
438 PAGES. 6x9 PAPERBACK. ILLUSTRATED. BIBLIOGRAPHY & INDEX. $16.95. CODE: SCOS

THE SHADOW OF ATLANTIS
The Echoes of Atlantean Civilization Tracked through Space & Time
by Colonel Alexander Braghine
First published in 1940, *The Shadow of Atlantis* is one of the great classics of Atlantis research. The book amasses a great deal of archaeological, anthropological, historical and scientific evidence in support of a lost continent in the Atlantic Ocean. Braghine covers such diverse topics as Egyptians in Central America, the myth of Quetzalcoatl, the Basque language and its connection with Atlantis, the connections with the ancient pyramids of Mexico, Egypt and Atlantis, the sudden demise of mammoths, legends of giants and much more. Braghine was a linguist and spends part of the book tracing ancient languages to Atlantis and studying little-known inscriptions in Brazil, deluge myths and the connections between ancient languages. Braghine takes us on a fascinating journey through space and time in search of the lost continent.
288 PAGES. 6x9 PAPERBACK. ILLUSTRATED. $16.95. CODE: SOA

ATLANTIS IN SPAIN
A Study of the Ancient Sun Kingdoms of Spain
by E.M. Whishaw
First published by Rider & Co. of London in 1928, this classic book is a study of the megaliths of Spain, ancient writing, cyclopean walls, sun worshipping empires, hydraulic engineering, and sunken cities. An extremely rare book, it was out of print for 60 years. Learn about the Biblical Tartessus; an Atlantean city at Niebla; the Temple of Hercules and the Sun Temple of Seville; Libyans and the Copper Age; more. Profusely illustrated with photos, maps and drawings.
284 PAGES. 6x9 PAPERBACK. ILLUSTRATED. TABLES OF ANCIENT SCRIPTS. $15.95. CODE: AIS

THE HISTORY OF ATLANTIS
by Lewis Spence
Lewis Spence's classic book on Atlantis is now back in print! Spence was a Scottish historian (1874-1955) who is best known for his volumes on world mythology and his five Atlantis books. *The History of Atlantis* (1926) is considered his finest. Spence does his scholarly best in chapters on the Sources of Atlantean History, the Geography of Atlantis, the Races of Atlantis, the Kings of Atlantis, the Religion of Atlantis, the Colonies of Atlantis, more. Sixteen chapters in all.
240 PAGES. 6x9 PAPERBACK. ILLUSTRATED WITH MAPS, PHOTOS & DIAGRAMS. $16.95. CODE: HOA

RIDDLE OF THE PACIFIC
by John Macmillan Brown
Oxford scholar Brown's classic work on lost civilizations of the Pacific is now back in print! John Macmillan Brown was an historian and New Zealand's premier scientist when he wrote about the origins of the Maoris. After many years of travel thoughout the Pacific studying the people and customs of the south seas islands, he wrote *Riddle of the Pacific* in 1924. The book is packed with rare turn-of-the-century illustrations. Don't miss Brown's classic study of Easter Island, ancient scripts, megalithic roads and cities, more. Brown was an early believer in a lost continent in the Pacific.
460 PAGES. 6x9 PAPERBACK. ILLUSTRATED. $16.95. CODE: SOA

24 hour credit card orders—call: 815-253-6390 fax: 815-253-6300
email: auphq@frontiernet.net   www.adventuresunlimitedpress.com   www.wexclub.com

One Adventure Place
P.O. Box 74
Kempton, Illinois 60946
United States of America
Tel.: 815-253-6390 • Fax: 815-253-6300
Email: auphq@frontiernet.net
http://www.adventuresunlimitedpress.com
or www.adventuresunlimited.nl

ORDERING INSTRUCTIONS

✓ Remit by USD$ Check, Money Order or Credit Card

✓ Visa, Master Card, Discover & AmEx Accepted

✓ Prices May Change Without Notice

✓ 10% Discount for 3 or more Items

SHIPPING CHARGES

United States

✓ Postal Book Rate { $3.00 First Item / 50¢ Each Additional Item

✓ Priority Mail { $4.50 First Item / $2.00 Each Additional Item

✓ UPS { $5.00 First Item / $1.50 Each Additional Item
NOTE: UPS Delivery Available to Mainland USA Only

Canada

✓ Postal Book Rate { $6.00 First Item / $2.00 Each Additional Item

✓ Postal Air Mail { $8.00 First Item / $2.50 Each Additional Item

✓ Personal Checks or Bank Drafts MUST BE USD$ and Drawn on a US Bank

✓ Canadian Postal Money Orders OK

✓ Payment MUST BE USD$

All Other Countries

✓ Surface Delivery { $10.00 First Item / $4.00 Each Additional Item

✓ Postal Air Mail { $14.00 First Item / $5.00 Each Additional Item

✓ Payment MUST BE USD$

✓ Checks and Money Orders MUST BE USD$ and Drawn on a US Bank or branch.

✓ Add $5.00 for Air Mail Subscription to Future *Adventures Unlimited* Catalogs

SPECIAL NOTES

✓ RETAILERS: Standard Discounts Available

✓ BACKORDERS: We Backorder all Out-of-Stock Items Unless Otherwise Requested

✓ PRO FORMA INVOICES: Available on Request

Please check: ✓

| ☐ This is my first order | ☐ I have ordered before |

Name

Address

City

| State/Province | Postal Code |

Country

| Phone day | Evening |

Fax

Item Code	Item Description	Qty	Total

Please check: ✓ | Subtotal ▶ |
| Less Discount-10% for 3 or more items ▶ |

☐ Postal-Surface	Balance ▶
☐ Postal-Air Mail (Priority in USA)	Illinois Residents 6.25% Sales Tax ▶
	Previous Credit ▶
☐ UPS (Mainland USA only)	Shipping ▶
	Total (check/MO in USD$ only) ▶

| ☐ Visa/MasterCard/Discover/Amex |

Card Number

Expiration Date

10% Discount When You Order 3 or More Items!